FOUR THOUSAND BOWLS
OF RICE

for Ed Spasek
with best wishes,
Linda Goetz Holmes
June 17, 1999

Four Thousand Bowls of Rice

A prisoner of war comes home

Linda Goetz Holmes

ALLEN & UNWIN

First published 1993
Allen & Unwin Pty Ltd
9 Atchison Street, St Leonards, NSW 2065 Australia

National Library of Australia
Cataloguing-in-Publication entry:

Holmes, Linda Goetz.
Four thousand bowls of rice.

Bibliography.
Includes index.
ISBN 1 86373 579 8.

1. Dickson, Cecil.   2. Australia. Army. Pioneer Battalion, 2/2.
3. Burma-Siam Railroad.   4. World War, 1939–1945—Personal
narratives, Australian.   5. World War, 1939–1945—Prisoners and
prisons, Japanese.   6. Prisoners of war—Japan.   7. Prisoners of war—
Australia.   I. Title.

940.547252092

Set in 11/13 pt Bembo by Graphicraft Typesetters, Hong Kong
Printed by Kim Hup Lee Printing, Singapore

2   4   6   8   10   9   7   5   3

To All the Members of

the 2/2 Australian Pioneer Battalion

Wherever they Draw the Sweet Breath of Freedom

or

Wherever they Lie at Rest

Who Taught us all What Brotherhood Really Means

and

to Margaret

Who Loved her Gallant Lad With all her Heart

This Book is Respectfully Dedicated

Colonel J.M. Williams, OBE, ED, Commanding Officer, 2/2 Australian Pioneer Battalion. This photo was taken in 1941, when Williams was Second-in-command, 2/17 Australian Infantry Battalion.

(COURTESY OF J.M. WILLIAMS)

Foreword

Colonel J.M. Williams, OBE, ED
Commanding Officer, 2/2 Australian
Pioneer Battalion, 1941–45

Linda Holmes has written very vividly about her friend Cecil Dickson who was a Staff Sergeant in the 2/2 Pioneer Battalion and of his experiences as a prisoner of war of the Japanese, captured in Java and taken to Burma to work on the Burma Railway.

She has gone to a considerable amount of trouble to tell why the Japanese acted as they did during the building of the Burma Railway, and to explain the treatment they meted out to the prisoners of war in Japan.

There is another period in Sergeant Dickson's army experience which is yet unexplained, and which needs to be told about the action he and his unit took part in, and the part they played in changing the planned Japanese action.

After serving with distinction in the Syrian Campaign, the 2/2 Pnr Bn returned to Palestine and was brought up to strength and refitted and together with 2/3 MG Bn, 2/6 Fld Coy, 105 Gen. Tpt Coy, it set sail in the HMT *Orcades* on 1 February 1942 for an undisclosed destination.

After a false landing at Oosthaven, the *Orcades* arrived in Java on 16 February 1942. An exchange of cables with Australia resulted in the troops on the *Orcades* being ordered to land and join the American, British and Dutch troops on Java, under the command of Field Marshal Lord Wavell, and to guard five airfields with these troops.

When the Japanese landed on Java they were stopped by Black Force (Brig. A.S. Blackburn) at Llewiliang River, with the 2/2 Pnr Bn defending the bridge. At this stage, orders were received from the Dutch Command to withdraw to the capital and capitulate. We became prisoners of war of the Japanese on 5 March 1942.

During my interrogation by the Japanese Staff in Java, they pressed me for information regarding the whereabouts of the 6th and 7th Australian Divisions. They had assumed that these divisions had already landed in Java and had held up the initial advance of the Japanese. Now the 6th and 7th Divisions had disappeared!

We now know that both the 6th and 7th Divisions were diverted to Columbo, then sent unescorted, via the Indian Ocean, to Australia. These were the troops who stopped the Japanese advance on New Guinea.

The Japanese Task Force that landed in Java via the Sunda Straits, sinking the HMAS *Perth* and the USS *Houston* was at sea heading for Darwin when it heard that the 6th and 7th Divisions had landed in Java. It changed course and eventually landed in Java. The Japanese from this Task Force were trying to exchange their invasion money—Australian pound notes made in Japan—with the Australian prisoners of war for Dutch coins.

Did the landing of the troops from the *Orcades* in Java cause the Task Force heading for Australia to change course?

Over the years since World War II there have been many books telling of the experiences and hardships of those who were prisoners of war of the Japanese, but Linda Holmes has managed to produce an interesting book written from a totally different aspect.

I know something of the time spent by Les Hall in writing, checking and re-checking details for his oft quoted *Blue Haze*. I can only start to imagine the time, effort and patience it has taken Linda Holmes to produce *Four Thousand Bowls of Rice*. She should be well satisfied.

J.M. Williams
February 1993

Contents

Illustrations

Acknowledgements

Permission to quote from the work of the following is gratefully acknowledged: A.H. Bishop for permission to use excerpts from his unpublished manuscript, A Voyage With the Jap in South East Asia; the late Sir Edward Dunlop for permission to quote from the preface to his *War Diaries*; Benjamin Dunn for permission to use excerpts from his book, *The Bamboo Express*; The Rev. Dr Ernest Gordon for permission to use passages from his book, *Miracle on the River Kwai*; Leslie G. Hall to quote portions of his book, *The Blue Haze*, and his unpublished manuscript, The Queen of Hearts; Takashi Nagase for permission to use excerpts from his book, *Crosses and Tigers*; and H. Shigeru Yagake for permission to use portions of his essay which appeared in an edition of the newspaper *Rafu Shimpo*.

In addition, the author is grateful to artist Ronald Searle for permission to use portions of text from his book *To The Kwai—And Back*, and to the Australian War Memorial for Permission to reproduce the photographs, newspaper clipping and war diary from their archives, as well as the drawings from their exhibit, 'Prisoners of War', which appear in this book.

So many people, in several parts of the globe, helped this book to happen; it is daunting to wonder if I can name them all.

In Australia, special heartfelt thanks go to Margaret Dickson, whose willingness to share her precious mementos made this work possible; and to members of the Dickson and Dodgshun families—to Cecil's brother, John Dickson, who, though bedridden, provided biographical data and located a special photograph; to Celeste Dickson, Jeanette Malone, Barbara and Brian Clements and Maryan Reynolds, for sharing their memories.

To E.H. 'Ted' Hansen, President of the 2/2 Pioneer Battalion Association in Melbourne, for his hospitality; to George Murphy, Secretary of the Association, for endlessly and patiently supplying addresses of Pioneers, and offering so much friendship and technical assistance in other ways; to Lionel 'Snowy' Anderson for photo-copying Walter Summons' book and the entire Battalion History for me; to Pioneers Bob Adolphson, Harry Bishop, George Carroll, Leo Cornelius, Jack D'Argaville, Gordon Hamilton, Bill Mayne, Kevin Nolan, Tom O'Brien and Ron Winning for sharing recollections with such precision and detail; and to Harry Whelan, for his colourful insights about daily camp life among the Pioneers: I owe you so much. And I thank the many who dug out personal photographs and sent them halfway around the world for me to copy. I am in awe of Jack Hocking, whose carefully crafted and detailed newsletters are a tribute to the brotherhood which so clearly marks this Battalion.

I appreciate the reminiscences of Eileen Mitchell, for sharing what it was like to wait all those years.

Just about in a class by himself is Cal Mitchell, whose early and continued correspondence has been invaluable, who, by sharing the captivity photographs, has made this book special already, and whose interest, encouragement and friendship are so deeply appreciated.

To the Battalion Commanding Officer, Colonel J.M. Williams, who has taken the time to help me achieve an accuracy which would not otherwise have been possible, and who was gracious enough to write the Foreword for this book, my heartfelt thanks.

The kind interest and clarifications rendered by that busy legend, the late Sir Edward 'Weary' Dunlop, will long be remembered. Responding to my query about the incident described in Chapter 4, Sir Edward wrote in April 1992: 'I have a great respect for Cecil Dickson and your proposed book should be moving and interesting'. Thus began a year-long correspondence which I shall always treasure.

I appreciate the assistance rendered by W.H. Schmitt, Federal President, Ex-POW Association of Australia; and to Gordon Jamieson of that organisation. Public Lending Rights which accrue to the author will be donated to that organisation.

To playwright Jill Shearer for her resources and insights, I am much indebted.

Dr Michael McKernan, Director of the Australian War Memorial, found time to help me despite my choosing the day of their 50th Anniversary for my visit. I appreciate the kindness and accommodation shown to me by AWM staff, especially Pam Ray, Curator of Photographs, Marie Wood, Assistant Curator, Brendan O'Keefe and Janet Reed.

Don Richards, Libraries Manager at the Melbourne *Herald and Weekly Times*, and his staff have rendered the kind of assistance a researcher only dreams about: my thanks for their professionalism.

To Tom Gillespie, of the War Veterans Village in Narrabeen,

New South Wales, for the many ways he found to help me in my research and work, I am grateful.

It is not enough to thank POW author Les Hall for permission to quote from his works; his interest, encouragement and friendship are a most cherished result of this endeavour.

And it is difficult to find adequate words to thank Bruce Merchant, Senior Vice President, Bozell Jeffress Advertising in New York. A chance conversation at the Australian Consulate in New York has resulted in a steady stream of ideas and enthusiasm, from circulating my manuscript to lists of contacts to finding the best airline passage. The generosity of Bruce and his wife, Liz, in loaning me the use of their home in Fairlight still dumbfounds me.

However, the Australian who has truly made this book possible is publisher Mark Tredinnick, whose early interest and perception about my concept, and willingness to take it on, have meant everything to me.

Special thanks must go to my editor, Lynne Frolich, for guiding this work along its way to publication.

In Japan, I am indebted to my Wellesley College classmate, Michiko Hosomi Asano, for sharing her views, and to author Takashi Nagase for understanding the nature of my queries, and for taking the time to answer them so thoughtfully.

In the United States, I owe thanks to members of the Japanese-American community for their perspectives, resources and assistance; to my neighbour, Reiko Uyeshima for finding and translating the essay by Henry Shigeru Yagake, and for putting me in touch with Michi Nishiura Weglyn; and to Michi, whose resources and perceptions have provided my work with such valuable dimension; to The Rev. Yuri Ando, for sharing much insight and history; and to Meredith Judy of the Youth Fellowship at Hitchcock Memorial Church in Scarsdale, NY, for her sharp recollections and assistance in helping me contact Pastor Ando and others; to Yasuko and Ryushi Hara, for their friendship and the continuity which their remembrances allowed me to glean; to Reiko Sassa, Librarian at the Japan Society; and to Judith Harper at the Society as well. My special thanks go to Henry Shigeru Yagake, who added further thoughts for inclusion in my work.

Otto Schwarz, founder of the *USS Houston* Survivors Association, is a walking resource library, for which I am very grateful. Crayton 'Quaty' Gordon of the Lost Battalion Association has been most generous in sharing memories and resources as well, along with author Ben Dunn.

The Rev. Dr Ernest Gordon has given me several hours of his time and perspective, for which I am especially grateful.

Margaret Dickson's daughter, Susan Gross, and her husband, Ralph, have provided recollections, resources and travel tips over several years, capped by carrying two manuscripts to Australia; their friendship and guidance have meant much.

Edith Stark's recollections have been an unexpected treasure, and perhaps no one has illuminated Cecil Dickson's life more than The Rev. Peter D. MacLean, sometimes in ways he did not imagine.

I am indebted to Mary Allen, Librarian at Columbia Grammar School in New York, for her computer wizardry in tracking down source material; to Jean Lindsay, for her knowledge of the archives at the US Library of Congress; and to Andrew Malone, Librarian at the Australian Consulate in New York, for being such a constant resource.

Helen Fisher at the Australian Overseas Information Service has offered continued assistance from the beginning of this project. And Australian expatriate Joffré Burger has been a constant source of ideas and encouragement.

Perhaps no one has provided more consistent valuable advice than my friend and neighbour, literary agent Perlette Abecassis. And I owe much to another special friend and neighbour, publisher Ken Giniger, whose skills and contacts have been so encouraging. I am very grateful for his worldwide knowledge of the business. The expertise of retired publishing executives Strome Lamon (Simon and Schuster) and Robert Scudellari (Random House) has been very much appreciated as well.

Finally, and with a certain pride, I want to thank my sons: Ted for his steadfast encouragement, and Philip for his technical assistance, resources and sense of history.

Photo reproductions by Kate's One Hour Studio, Greenport, New York.

Introduction

Sometimes we learn about courage and bravery in the oddest ways. A light remark at the dinner table, thrown out with humour which belies the speaker's thoughts, can encapsulate unforgettable horror. Such a remark was made by my Australian friend Cecil Dickson one evening in 1979 at the dinner table in his stepdaughter's home on Shelter Island, off New York's peninsula which we call Long Island. Cecil began to chuckle as he passed along the serving dish of rice: 'Do you know, heh heh, I once had over 3800 consecutive meals of rice, and do you know [more laughter] *I still enjoy rice!*'

It was easy to share Dickson's obvious mirth—unless one happened to know that those '3800 consecutive meals' were a steadily diminishing starvation diet, grudgingly provided by Japanese captors—often for a demanded fee—as they brutally forced Dickson and thousands of other Prisoners of War to build the infamous Burma–Thailand Railway during World War II.

Dickson just happened to be the first ex-POW I met who had actually worked on the 'Railway of Death', as it is commonly called by those who saw 70 men die for each mile of track laid; and he also happened to be a member of No. 1 Mobile Force, the unit which toiled the hardest of all on that project.

Despite growing up in the home of a newspaper editor with international connections, like many Americans I first learned about 'The Bridge Over the River Kwai' by seeing the classic film based on Pierre Boulle's 1954 book. For many of us, that film provided our first awareness that such horrible brutality really occurred—and even then, the facts were skewed to make a good story. For example, the pride those POWs took in sabotaging the many bridges they were forced to build was lost in the image of glorious engineering achievement projected by the film.

But one thing the movie may have accomplished was to prompt the publication of several genuine accounts of what *really* happened in the jungles of Burma and Thailand: Ernest Gordon's *Miracle on the River Kwai* (1963); Leslie G. Hall's *The Blue Haze* (1985); Sir Edward 'Weary' Dunlop's *War Diaries* (1986); and, more recently, Peter N. Davies' *The Man Behind The Bridge: Colonel Toosey and the River Kwai* (1991), to name just a few.

According to Leslie Hall, himself a toiler on the Railway, 'Of all the forces on the Burma side of the death railway, no one suffered more than the No. 1 Mobile Force.' This force consisted primarily of two Australian units: one commanded by Lieutenant Colonel C.G.W. Anderson; and the second, which had as its core nearly an entire Australian unit, the 2/2 Pioneer Battalion, commanded by Lieutenant Colonel J.M. Williams. My friend Cecil Dickson was a Staff Sergeant and Company Quartermaster in the 2/2 Pioneers.

Dickson was one of the last Australian POWs to be shipped home. He arrived in Melbourne on 3 November 1945 aboard the *Circassia*, which carried the final group of ambulatory POWs to Australia— nearly three months after Emperor Hirohito signed the terms of surrender. While restlessly awaiting repatriation, Dickson, a journalist by profession, took the opportunity to write quite a few letters to his loved ones, describing his thoughts and hopes as he looked for news from Australia. Dickson's fifteen letters to his wife, written during this interval, are the basis for this book. Through them, and the reminiscences they provoke, we can even catch glimpses of occasional acts of kindness by the Japanese, contrasted with the daily kindness the prisoners showed toward one another, often at considerable personal risk and sacrifice.

Dickson's letters are augmented by the recollections of his Pioneer friends, as well as writings and anecdotes, some published and some printed here for the first time, of fellow Australian, American and British ex-POWs who shared the Railway experience—and even a couple of Japanese who had contact with the prisoners in Burma and Thailand.

In the concluding chapter, we will learn how some of Dickson's comrades feel, looking back on their experience from a lifetime's perspective. And we will reflect on how, even after a half-century, many Japanese still have not learned the truth about their nation's wartime behaviour.

The absence of bitterness and strength of will displayed in Dickson's remarkable letters draws us to examine more closely the life and spirit of one gallant Australian, who survived and overcame so very much.

Thomas Cecil Dickson was born on 6 October 1902 in Geelong,

Victoria, one of six children. His father, a pharmacist, was also Commodore of the Geelong Yacht Club, and the four boys, Everard, Stan, Cecil and John, and two girls, Blanche and Marie, became accomplished sailors under his guidance. Cecil was educated at Geelong Grammar School and Longerenong Agricultural College. As a young man, he tried life as a boundary rider for a cattle ranch in Logan Downs, Queensland, but found that his tastes had become too urbane for ranch life. However, his stint at jackarooing was not a total waste of time: through friendship with a local soldier-settler, Dickson became attracted to the fellow's sister, Winifred (known to her family and friends as Freda) Dodshun, whom he married in 1926.

Dickson's bride persuaded him to try life in her home town, Melbourne, where he found employment as a proofreader on the Melbourne *Argus*. Being the new man on staff, Dickson was assigned to the 'lobster' shift, named for the colour change observed in the eyes of those who toiled late at night in newspaper rooms. But he had the city to himself, so to speak, in the wee hours; and as a bicycle provided his transportation in those days, he took the liberty of riding it through the park to get home. Eventually, Dickson was able to put his land knowledge to use, rising to the position of Mining Editor on the *Argus*.

In 1940, when the 2nd Pioneer Battalion was being re-formed locally to meet the call of war, it became designated the 2/2 (for 2nd World War) Pioneers, and Dickson, along with his younger brother John, joined the Battalion on 6 June of that year. The unit underwent rigorous training at Puckapunyal for what was expected to be desert warfare in the Middle East, but the survival techniques honed at 'Pucka' turned out to be invaluable during the ordeals of jungle life in Burma and Thailand. The Battalion was sent to Syria, and distinguished itself in combat against the Vichy French.

In January 1942, the combat-seasoned unit was rushed, aboard the *Orcades*, back to the Pacific to defend Australia. Instead, in a decision which remains controversial to this day, the Battalion was put ashore at Java and placed under Dutch command. When the Dutch capitulated, nearly all of the Pioneer Battalion was forced to surrender to the Japanese as well. Only a few members of the unit remained aboard the transport ships; shortly after they reached Australia, the battalion was completely re-formed under the command of Lieutenant Colonel J.T. Lang, and saw combat in New Guinea, Tarakan and Balikpapan.

When Dickson finally got home in November 1945, he spent an idyllic vacation in Queenscliff with his wife, and then returned to

T. Cecil and John B. Dickson, Christmas 1940. This photo was taken just before the Battalion departed for combat in the Middle East.
(COURTESY OF JOHN B. DICKSON)

the *Argus*. He moved to the Melbourne *Age* briefly, before starting his own publication, the *Australian Industrial and Mining Standard*, in the late 1940s. During 1946–48 he also served as press liaison officer to the Duke of Gloucester, when the Duke was appointed as His Majesty's Governor-General of Australia.

Subsequently, Dickson was persuaded to join the international financial investment firm J.B. Were & Company, in its Melbourne office. But when a new manager fired a fellow Pioneer, Walter Summons, for whom Dickson had secured employment, Dickson became so incensed that he asked to be transferred to the firm's London office, where he remained for several years during the 1960s.

Freda Dickson's health began to fail, and the couple decided to return to Melbourne, where Freda died in 1968. Dickson travelled about for several years, visiting friends in England, the United States and other global spots of interest.

One object of frequent visitations for Dickson was Margaret Blair Eaton, whom he and Freda had met while posted in London with the Were firm. In 1976 he married Margaret, and brought her home to the Returned Services League War Veterans Village in Narrabeen, New South Wales, where Dickson's older brother, Stan, had already settled. They lived next door to one another for twelve years, until Cecil's death in August 1988, at the age of 85. His remains are interred in the family plot in Geelong.

After Cecil died, Margaret Dickson, sorting through her husband's belongings, came upon the packet of letters he had written home to his first wife between August and October 1945. They were neatly tied together, and stashed in the back of a drawer. She had never seen them during the dozen years of her marriage to Cecil. At Christmas 1988, Margaret brought the letters along on a visit to Shelter Island.

'Don't these sound just like Cec? I thought you'd like to see them,' Margaret said as she handed me the packet. 'I can hardly make out his handwriting in some places, though.'

I offered to type them for her, and as I transcribed each line, I marvelled at the same humour—and absence of bitterness—that Cecil had displayed nearly 40 years later at the dinner table. And then, there it was, in his second letter home: 'After all, more than 3800 consecutive meals of rice is a bit too much of a good thing!'

Barely two weeks after learning that the nightmare was over, and still confined to the camp where he had endured such torment, this man could already look back and joke about rice! It struck me that my own mother seemed to display more residual anger about the

Margaret and Cecil Dickson in front of the author's home, Shelter Island,
New York, May 1979.

Japanese, just because her favourite nephew, my cousin Bill Richardson, was scarred by his combat experiences on Guadalcanal, New
Caledonia and Okinawa. He lived, but she never again knowingly
bought anything made in Japan, and neither did Bill, for that matter.
So what kind of special breed were these men? The answer to my
question has been offered, in many shadings, by Cecil's comrades.
This is their story, and it is they who have made it come alive.

Many ex-POWs have kept their memories and mementos private
for a lifetime; some have been not even been shared with family
members until now. Published here for the first time, for example,
are the vivid recollections of Pioneer George Carroll, who was
shipped to Japan to work as a labourer in factories and shipyards.
Carroll's narrative is augmented by Pioneer Bill Mayne, who was
torpedoed along with Carroll while travelling to Japan, and who
worked with him in the same factory and shipyard locations.

Also published here for the first time are several photographs,
taken in captivity, which were given to the author by Pioneer Cal

Mitchell. To this day, secrecy has been maintained as to who actually took the photos, and how the camera(s) and film were hidden for over three years from the constant probing of Japanese bayonets, along with continual relocations. Until Mitchell shared these remarkable photos with the author, most of his fellow Pioneers had not seen them. When the snapshots were circulated, at a Pioneer Association barbecue in Jell's Park, outside Melbourne, in October 1991, all believed the photos were taken just after liberation, while everyone was still in the camps and undernourished. As Pioneer Harry Bishop commented in a letter to the author the following month, 'That is quite an achievement, as it means carrying a camera on many long marches, and there is a constant risk of bashing if it is found.'

In addition, the Battalion Commanding Officer, Lieutenant Colonel Williams, took several photos with his own camera while in captivity; the best surviving print, in Chapter 2, shows the Australian officers' quarters in Java. Colonel Williams' description of how his film was preserved and returned to Australia also appears in Chapter 2.

As a result of the preparation of this book, both Mr Mitchell and Colonel Williams have donated the captivity photographs shown here to the Australian War Memorial in Canberra.

Just as these photographs allow the reader a glimpse of the desperate daily life in the prison camps of Java, Burma and Thailand, so Dickson's letters provide a series of windows through which we glimpse an Australian citizen-soldier looking homeward as he remembers the most brutal days experienced by any troops, anywhere, during World War II.

1

A Sunday Lament

Sunday, 7 August 1988, 2.45 p.m.: Cecil Dickson sets off with a jaunty air to join neighbours for a walk up the hill to the 3.00 p.m. service at the Chapel in the War Veterans Village in Narrabeen, New South Wales. Margaret Dickson admires how natty her husband looks in his Harris tweed jacket, and how high his spirits are.

Tom Gillespie, Chairman of the Chapel Committee, greets Dickson at the entrance to the Chapel, but watches in puzzlement as Dickson peers intently inside, then looks upward. 'What does he see?' Gillespie wonders. An instant later, Dickson, 6'4" tall, topples forward on to Gillespie—a 'wee Scot' by some descriptions—and the two crash to the polished stone floor of the Chapel vestibule.

Margaret is summoned, along with Cecil's older brother, Stan, who lives next door. Together they sit, numbed, in the little room across from the Chapel, as the service goes on, draws to an end, and stunned worshippers begin quietly to leave the building. Two hours pass before a physician appears to make the sad pronunciation, and to sign the necessary form. Then Margaret, supported by Stan, stumbles back down the hill into the door of her home, and sinks into the little chair by the phone. With trembling fingers, she dials the overseas number to reach her daughter Susan, halfway around the globe on Shelter Island New York.

Sunday, 7 August 1988, 9.50 a.m.: The Reverend Peter D. MacLean is vesting in the sacristy at St Mary's Episcopal Church for the 10.00 a.m. service. He has looked forward to this day for weeks, because the liturgy will be highlighted by a young visitor, James Lawrence Hamilton Carruthers, who has brought his bagpipes to play at the service.

Jamie is preparing to lead the procession in the front door of the church and up the aisle, playing 'Going Home'. But the air is unbelievably heavy after a violent early morning thunderstorm, and out in the Parish Hall he struggles, perspiring in his starched Oxford

Piper James L.H. Carruthers, playing 'The Flowers of the Forest' outside St Mary's Episcopal Church, Shelter Island New York, 7 August 1988.

shirt, woollen kilt and knee-high socks, to keep each pipe drone in its proper pitch.

As Peter starts to leave the sacristy, Susan Gross hurries into the side door of the Parish Hall and moves toward him. He pauses as she pokes her head into the small room and says, 'Ma called from Narrabeen at seven this morning. Cecil died today, on his way into the Chapel service.' She turns away quickly and joins her husband, Ralph, to take their accustomed spot in the back pew.

Peter ponders a moment, then decides: this service will be a special send-off for Cec—what a stroke of luck that Jamie is here! He whispers a few words to Jamie, who nods in understanding, then starts his measured steps. 'Going home, going home, I am going home . . .' Peter's vision blurs as he thinks of Cecil, entering another sanctuary just a few hours earlier, and discovering he was already home.

As he climbs the chancel steps and turns toward the congregation, Peter's face contorts in a futile effort to control his tears as he recalls how Cecil was one of the few men with whom a priest could share feelings about serving as a Marine Corps chaplain in Vietnam, about watching comrades die, and about how you minister to young men whose lives are being snatched away by strangers without reason. Suddenly sensing how his face must look right now, Peter says only: 'Bagpipes always make me cry.'

Later in the service, he descends the chancel steps to make what everyone expects will be the customary announcements of parish family business. Instead, with a husky voice and his eyes fixed on the carpet, Peter finds words to tell the sad news from Australia. Then he looks up and says, with all the authority that he, a Bishop's son, can claim: 'Cecil Dickson taught us more about forgiveness than any clergyman—or any Bishop—has ever done.'

Peter takes his seat and bows his head, listening as Jamie, standing on a hillock in the churchyard, begins to pipe the classic Scottish lament, 'The Flowers of the Forest'.

The odyssey of Cecil Dickson through Burma and Thailand,
October 1942 to October 1945.

2

It's Good Being Free

30 AUGUST 1945: Barely two weeks after learning of the Japanese surrender, Staff Sergeant Cecil Dickson anxiously awaited word of how and when he would be sent home. He was in the enlisted men's camp near Nakom Nayok, in northern Thailand; a second camp for non-commissioned officers was nearby, and a third camp, where POW officers had been gathered, was several miles down the road.

Some Americans were being flown out immediately, and had offered to take mail along. Dickson got hold of a small, scarce piece of paper, and in a dozen abbreviated sentences this seasoned journalist encapsulated the last three and a half years—telling his wife that he and his brother were OK, and hoping she would contact the *Argus* publisher to say that Dickson was alive, and available for eyewitness reporting.

2/2 Australian Pioneer Battalion
Nakom Nayok POW Camp
Thailand
August 30, 1945

Darling Old Binkie,

It's pretty good being free but the great day will be when I see the old Missus again. Hope you are as fit as I am. Rumour says we are flying to India. This globetrotting is all very well, but give me the shortest & quickest way home! John is here and in good fettle. I had charge of the 54 Pioneers in this camp, but am now looking after pay for the Australia wing. Been here 2 months (60 miles N.E. of Bangkok). Previous 6 months near Petburi (150 mi. S.W. of Bangkok). Till going there was 14 months at Tamarkan, near KAMBURI, near Thailand end of the famous railway line, construction of which cost the lives of so many prisoners. After leaving Java in October 42 were 14 and a half months on the Burma section of the line. Year 1943 was a bad one for everybody, but after coming to Tamarkan I picked up gradually & was lucky

5

*not to return to the jungle. Remembrances family, friends, Mr Knox
and staff. Longer letter next time perhaps.*

   Tons of love,

   Pop

It had been a very tense month for all the prisoners: apprehension,
exhilaration and caution had formed a tumble of emotions within
each exhausted man's heart, and all with good reason. Since February,
Dickson had been the highest-ranking Pioneer in his camp, because
the Japanese moved officers and non-commissioned officers to different camps in early 1945. They planned to execute all POWs,
beginning with officers, as soon as British General Lord Louis
Mountbatten launched his expected invasion of Burma. By 30
August, the wariness among prisoners still had not eased very much
(see Chapter 5).

Excitement at the news of surrender, received on 17 August by
Dickson and his camp-mates, and a day earlier in other locations,
was tempered by the caution that, although in many instances the
Japanese and Koreans had quietly slipped away from the camps,
they were still armed and were likely to remain so until they heard
that Emperor Hirohito had signed the treaty of surrender. And it
was an open question as to how long it might take for word of this
formality to reach each Japanese, or what his individual reaction
might be.

So tension in the camps crackled like static in the wireless sets
which still had working batteries, or for which operators were able,
with considerable relish, to commandeer fresh batteries from suddenly
compliant Japanese. To compound the tension for the Australians,
British and Dutch, just the previous week—on 23 August—the OSS
(Office of Strategic Services) colonel in charge of operations in
Thailand notified POW officers that all Americans were to be flown
out of Thailand almost immediately, and American officers visited
camps to tell their lucky compatriots the good news.

Resorting to humour to break the taut atmosphere, someone then
formulated the following orders: 'The Australians are to report to
the nearest seaport; the Dutch are to go to the nearest railway station; the Americans are to report to the nearest airport; and the
English are to be issued a new pair of shoes.'[1] This witticism was to
prove fairly accurate: most Americans had been home for a couple
of months before many Australians, Dutch and English set foot on
their beloved home shores.

So the best Dickson and his comrades could do on 30 August was to give a smile and a handclasp to their departing American friends—and if they were lucky enough, to hand over a scribbled note as well.

Dickson had no way of knowing, as he wrote his first letter home as a free man, that Freda did in fact receive all six cards he was allowed to send during his long captivity. And it would be another two weeks before he learned that close friends from his battalion were rescued at sea the previous September, returned to Australia, and reported in detail his whereabouts and living conditions.

'After leaving Java in October '42 . . .' These six words encompassed the few days of valiant battle, the heartbreak of forced surrender, the loss of hope for escape, and the horror of a ship voyage to Burma under what Dickson would later term 'unspeakable conditions' without bothering to elaborate. As he wrote these words, Dickson no doubt assumed his wife had been notified that his battalion was forced to surrender on Java and that he was a Prisoner of War. But little did he know that Freda waited over a year before receiving official confirmation of his status, or that since November of last year she had been all too aware of conditions in the camps, and increasingly worried for his safety.

The Dicksons' niece, Barbara Clements, recalled that: 'When the newspapers began to print stories about the mistreatment of POWs, the situation at home grew even worse. It was a time of great strain for the family.'[2]

Dickson's last letter as a free man had been written on board the troopship *Orcades* in early 1942, and until now he had no way of knowing whether any subsequent mail he was allowed to write in captivity ever did reach home.

The *Orcades* was the last ship in a hastily assembled convoy rushing the Pioneers, now seasoned combat troops, from the Middle East towards home; most assumed they were being sent to defend Australia against a feared Japanese invasion. To their everlasting regret, the Pioneers were loaded aboard wearing winter clothes, with only backpacks and one blanket each—all baggage was put on another ship, which was sent on to Australia, with just a few members of the battalion on board. No one could foresee that the clothes on his back would be all he would have for the next three and a half years. In his memoirs, the legendary ex-POW physician, Sir Edward 'Weary' Dunlop, recalled how he became separated, in a truly bureaucratic bungle, from nearly all his painstakingly assembled medical supplies and field hospital equipment when he, too, boarded the *Orcades*.[3]

As the *Orcades* sailed from Suez, about 60 Japanese troop transports were already in the South China Sea. Apparently as a token of support to the Dutch, whose homeland was already under Nazi occupation, and whose airfields in Java were vital—and also to divert those Japanese troopships away from Australia—the British High Command decided that the *Orcades* should land its troops on Java, to join the token Australian forces already there. This was done over the vigorous protests of Australian Prime Minister Curtin, among others. But as military historian D.M. Horner points out in his book, *High Command*, 'The Americans recognised that Australia was a sovereign country; many British still tended to look upon Australia as a colony. British commanders often viewed Australian forces as an integral part of an imperial army (or navy or airforce) and they expected Australians to conform, without question, to British strategic direction.'[4]

Horner records in detail the political wrangling surrounding the deployment of Australian troops in Java; for the bewildered Pioneers aboard the *Orcades*, this meant disembarking, being ordered to return to the ship, and disembarking the second time, at Batavia.

Half a century later, the controversy surrounding the Allied decision to leave Australian troops on Java still has not subsided, because that move caused nearly 3000 Australian military personnel to be captured by the Japanese. In February 1992, the dispute erupted anew when Queen Elizabeth visited Australia, and the recently elected Prime Minister, Paul Keating, took the occasion to remind Britons that their government had 'decided not to defend the Malaysian Peninsula, not to worry about Singapore, and not to give us our troops back [from Java] to keep ourselves from Japanese dominion'.[5]

In retaliation, members of parliament in London taunted Mr Keating as presiding 'over a country of ex-convicts'. The continued use of this epithet keeps alive a smouldering resentment of the British by many Australians, who in turn regularly refer to the English as 'Pommies', a corruption of the word for a well-known local fruit. Pomegranates were what the red-cheeked newcomers, bundled up in their woollens as they arrived from England on government grants, looked like to Australian children earlier in this century. So the neighbourhood taunts began: 'immy-grant, jimmy-grant, pommy-grant!'[6]

Pioneer Captain Harry Bishop, in a 1992 letter to the author, reflected that when the Pioneers joined British Field Marshal Montgomery's forces to repel Rommel in the Middle Eastern desert, the British troops called the Australians 'descendants of convicts' which, Bishop noted, 'we did not appreciate'. This type of name-calling was remembered with special acrimony by several other Australians as well, because they were volunteers who had offered their services to the Crown in wartime.

With 924 of their Battalion put ashore on Java, the Pioneers joined with the 2/3 Machinegun Battalion, under the command of Brigadier A.S. Blackburn, and the resulting brigade, designated as Black Force, was placed under Dutch command. The Pioneers fought fiercely against the Japanese, despite being issued with outdated weapons and, on some occasions, using Biblical combat methods. Sergeant Harry Whelan, a member of the 2/3 MG Bn, remembered filling cloth bags with gravel from the ditches around their positions, and swinging the homemade missiles in hand-to-hand combat, in preference to using the Canadian Springfield rifles they had been issued with, which lacked bayonets. 'We actually did this—yes—a sort of David and Goliath manoeuvre', he recalled in a 1991 interview. In addition, as Cal Mitchell noted, the Springfield rifles had a .30 bore, so the Australians had to load their .303 rounds of ammunition by hand.

Almost as outdated as the weapons issued to the Pioneers was the intelligence they received from the Dutch about Japanese strength on Java. On one occasion, Dickson's friend Lieutenant Walter Summons, the unit's Intelligence Officer, asked Dutch Headquarters for information regarding Japanese deployment. The response: no update was available, because that morning's newspaper had not yet been delivered!

On 2 March, the Dutch area commander told Colonel Williams that, as far as he knew, there were no Japanese on the island. The next day, around noontime, a Dutch army intelligence report confirmed to Black Force Headquarters that there had been no Japanese landings on Java. Within minutes, five Japanese tanks approached the bridge which the Pioneers had been preparing to hold at Llewiliang.

Some American members of the 131st Field Artillery, Texas National Guard, who were not allowed to engage in combat, watched the Pioneers' awesome fighting skills from a nearby hill. 'I was proud to have been a POW with such brave soldiers,' said Otto Schwarz, a survivor of the sinking of the USS *Houston*, after listening to the Texans tell about some of the Pioneer exploits. Another American ex-POW, Benjamin Dunn, comments in his book, *The Bamboo Express*, '. . . The Dutch officials insisted they had the invasion under control. They even permitted the Australian infantry to attack at night against overwhelming odds and without any help from the Dutch and Javanese infantry.'[7]

This display of tenacity not only impressed the Japanese, it apparently made them believe they were dealing with two whole Australian divisions. Consequently, the Japanese invasion force headed for Australia was re-routed to Java.

It is estimated that the Pioneer unit killed at least 500 Japanese before being forced to surrender. According to the Battalion History, on 8 March the Dutch decided to capitulate, and the Australians, being under Dutch command, had no choice but to surrender as well. In fact, Lieutenant Colonel Williams and other top officers considered that in effect they became prisoners on 5 March, after meeting then and concluding that all hope of victory—or escape— had vanished. On 9 March the Battalion was ordered to withdraw, and to destroy or disable all weapons and vehicles. Pioneer Lieutenant Walter Summons described the desperation of a 'last mad rush to the south coast, hoping for ships . . .' which, of course, never materialised.[8]

Cecil Dickson wrote the chapter on Prisoners of War for the official *Story of the 2/2 Australian Pioneer Battalion*, and he graphically details how equipment was destroyed: 'Much material found its way into fast-running mountain rivers, and . . . Pioneers saw to it that many dozens of motor-vehicles and Bren-carriers were wrecked by running them down steep ravines.'[9] It was a wrenching decision for many members of the unit to discard their personal weapons.

However, 'A' Company of the Battalion did not receive the order to withdraw, and became cut off from the main force. Captain Ron Winning still recalled that time in precise detail half a century later:

> Our Commanding Officer, Lieut. Col. J.M. Williams, sent for me and gave me orders to move 'C' Company [Dickson's unit] out to a defensive position on the river, on our right flank.
> He expected we would be in action by nightfall. 'B' and 'D' Companies set an ambush on the main road, 'A' Company in reserve. I posted my guns and platoons, but for some reason the enemy attacked our left flank after losing heavily in the ambush. 'A' Company was sent out to the left and we never saw them again. They ran into the main Jap force and were decimated.
> We retreated and eventually ran out of land, and were captured.

The remnants of 'A' Company held out as guerrillas on Java for six months, until the only surviving officer, Lieutenant. R.W. Allen, was captured, along with Privates V.L.J. McCrae and S.A. Baade, and brought to the gaol at Batavia.

Perhaps the most poignant footnote to the Pioneers' combat experience in Java is this final communiqué, dated 3 March 1942 and

PLACE	DATE	SUMMARY OF EVENTS Routine training details and information given in Casualty Returns are NOT required	REFERENCES TO APPENDICES	C.O's. REPORT AND COMMENTS ON MONTH (On Operations, Equipment, Movement, Health, Administration, etc.)
	24 Feb. **Lt-Col.**Williams at Force HQ. conference on evacuation plans. 2 raids, one raid on TJILITAN dropped bombs and machine-gunned troops,4 casualties N.E.Hangar and posts hit. Other raid lot of bombs dropped on D Coy area. After having been in COCHIN a further 3 days the Shillong and Niger Stroom leave in same convoy as before.		The position on the island unknown. The only Casualty list received from Bn being that of 3/4 March by Cable. Earlier casualties known not being notified. Bn strength on 28th Feb was over 1000 men of whom were numerous missing after the 9th. I trust in the absence of definite information. All German officers except Capt Guild will later reported by Batavia Radio to be prisoners of war.
	25 Feb. Sophocles and Methura leave COCHIN without convoy. A Coy. further preparing defences. D Coy practising A,B,& C plans for counter attack. HQ.Coy.co-operating with Brens. 2 Alarms.Big raid on TANJOENG PRINK,BATAVIA,and KEMAJORN.Smoke of fires rising very high.		
	26 Feb. Orders received by convoy ex COCHIN to break up and proceed on own course to FREMANTLE,AUSTRALIA. JAVA Force:- Patrols now getting excellent knowledge of bush. A and HQ Coys. digging alternative positions. D Coy. again practising No report from B and C Coy. very heavy rain.Hot and sultry.No raids.New troops morale improving.		
	27 Feb. Raids on all dromes,and very heavy raid on harbour. Casualties not known. S.S. MU SUEH sailed for COLOMBO with Major Joss aboard,being evacuated sick.		
	28 Feb.-2 Mar. No information main body.		
	3 Mar. Capt. Guild and Lieutenants Stewart,Lang,and Allen reported missing by cable and othercasualties as per Part II orders.This is the last advice from Bn.All communication with outside world cut off.Force now isolated.		
	9 Mar. S.S."SOPHOCLES" arrives FREMANTLE.		

A150 Mob Print Sec AIF–2M–4/41–6.

Signature _____ J.H.Jas Major

Last entries in official pages of the War Diary for 2/2 Australian Pioneer Battalion before the unit was captured on Java.
Handwritten notations on right side of page were made by Major H.M. Joss, who was evacuated to Australia when he became ill.

(AUSTRALIAN WAR MEMORIAL, AWM 52 ITEM 8/6/2)

preserved as received, typed on a portable typewriter, on yellow copy
paper in the archives of the Australian War Memorial at Canberra:
'Capt. Guild and Lieuts. Stewart, Lang & Allen reported missing by
cable and all other casualties as per Part II orders. This is the last
advice from Bn. All communication with outside world cut off.
Force now isolated.'[10] One can only guess as to the spirits of the
Pioneer who sent that last, cryptic message.

For many Australians, contempt for the Dutch would linger
throughout their years of captivity together, surfacing in many ways.
As Harry Whelan phrased it: 'We were put ashore on Java as a
political gesture to the Dutch . . . to help [them] defend Java; and the
next thing we knew, the Dutch had surrendered . . . I've read every
account I could find on this, because three years and seven months
of the best years of my life were wasted, and I've always wanted to
know why.'

But Brigadier Blackburn, for one, did not feel the Australian effort
on Java was wasted. In a foreword to Walter Summons' book,
compiled in 1946, the Brigadier wrote:

> To many of the men who took part in the campaign in Java
> and to many people in Australia, it seemed at the time that the
> landing of Australian troops in that island was a needless waste
> of men . . . I can say however, without hesitation, that the
> resistance put up by that small force of Australians against a
> crack Japanese Division was not wasted. At that critical time,
> March 1942, every day, perhaps every hour, during which the
> Japanese advance on Australia was delayed, meant a big gain to
> this country . . . it contributed in no small measure to the fact
> that Australia was saved from invasion.[11]

Harry Bishop, thinking back to that time, shared this thought in
April of 1992:

> On Java we heard that one whole Jap convoy had no where to
> go. The rumour . . . was that [British General] Wavell set up
> . . . a propaganda campaign, with the cooperation of Americans,
> British and Dutch, to convince the Japs to land on Java. At this
> time, [the Japanese] could have landed anywhere on Western or
> Northern Australia.
> I believe that [Field Marshal Sir Thomas] Blamey's
> stubbornness allowed [American General Douglas] MacArthur
> to leave the Australians [ground forces] out of the Philippine
> campaign. This was a pity, as the Australian divisions which
> returned from the Middle East inflicted the first defeat on the

Japanese at Milne Bay, about the same time as the Coral Sea battle.

In retrospect, other Pioneer officers understood MacArthur's personal involvement with the Philippines, and were not surprised that he wanted to use his own troops for that invasion.

Bishop continued: 'I was impressed with [Lieutenant General Sir Edmund] Herring's handling of Blamey. There were two sides to [Herring's] character, but he had a clear idea of what needed to be done, and the need to do it quickly. But on the other side he often left a poor impression. As an example, there was the staff meeting at which he went to sleep after being out late the night before.'[12]

Author Benjamin Dunn wrote about how the American military contributed to the deception by allowing their vehicles to drive back and forth over the same roadways, in order to give the appearance of new equipment constantly arriving. But the scheme worked so well that it caused a handful of Allied officers to pay a very high price for this illusion, a few weeks later.

Recording those first few months of captivity for the Battalion History, Dickson wrote:

> It was difficult at this stage for members to realise that they were prisoners of war. Preoccupied with the task of taking over an island the size of Java, with its 42 million inhabitants, the Japanese allowed a maximum of freedom. Preconceived ideas of barbed-wire fences and armed guards had not yet eventuated, and the troops were free to visit shops and coffee-houses in the village, and even to hire a horse-drawn gharry to visit a neighbouring village, where other . . . Australians were quartered, and where a swimming pool provided facilities for many hours of enjoyment and sport. It was, from the point of view of the prisoners of war, an almost idyllic existence . . . Church parades were held regularly and were well attended [in stark contrast to later days of captivity: see Chapter 15].
>
> During the stay at Leles the Japanese invited their prisoners to write letters home, with no limit as to length nor restrictions of subject. As these letters never reached home, it might be supposed that they were sought by the Japanese merely with the object of gleaning as much information as possible, and that after close scrutiny by their intelligence service, they were destroyed . . .
>
> Japanese troops in Leles area were apparently unsuspecting types who did not think to check up on whether wireless sets were being used by their prisoners, so the C.O. was able with

his radio to receive B.B.C. and A.B.C. news daily. What he heard and relayed to the Battalion made it plain that Java had been so effectively isolated by enemy action that all thoughts of escape must be abandoned . . .[13]

Moreover, as Sergeant Crayton Gordon, a member of the Texas 131st Field Battalion, remembers: 'Those waters were full of sharks—man, no way did I want to jump in and swim!'

Dickson also notes, somewhat wistfully, a rare act of Japanese kindness he witnessed:

There must also, by the way, have been a human streak among the Japanese whose duty it was to keep a casual eye on the Pioneers. One night one of them, wandering through the market-place occupied by the Battalion, stooped down to pull the blanket over one of the slumbering men who had come uncovered during his restless sleep. Time was to show that not all of his fellow-countrymen were capable of such an act of simple humanity.

He tells how one Pioneer hit upon a way to help his comrades dispel their sense of foreboding as they settled down to sleep:

'Slim' Maher, a well-known character of C company, enhanced his reputation for native humour . . . with an act that he repeated many times as the Battalion settled down to sleep. After 'lights-out', which was a misnomer as there were no lights to extinguish, he would recite in his penetrating voice, with appropriate emphasis, a broadcast advertisement for a popular brand of cough remedy that had become familiar to radio listeners at home. Drowsy men almost shivered as the voice of 'Slim' quavered over 'icy blasts' and advised his listeners what to take for the protection of their chests.[14]

In mid-May, the prisoners were moved to a new location on Java, called the Bicycle Camp, and here their daily life took a decided turn for the worse. Dickson records what happened initially to jolt the prisoners:

In charge of the camp was Lieutenant Suzuki. He was not one of the vicious type of Japanese, but his sincerity was doubted, and if he ever did weep for the prisoners under his charge, the tears he shed were crocodile tears. It was while the camp was under his charge, and doubtless at his command, that the guards launched a campaign of vicious assaults on the prisoners of war—unprovoked bashings against which the victims had no redress. To Brig. Blackburn's protests against this harsh treatment, Suzuki would silkily reply that perhaps the prisoners were not saluting the guards properly (Japanese style) or standing properly to attention (Japanese style), and he would proceed to demonstrate the correct manner of carrying out these formalities. But the bashings continued.

Most POWs probably had no way of knowing that such treatment was a routine part of Japanese military training, and that Lieutenant Suzuki apparently decided, without explicitly announcing so, that the prisoners under his charge should be re-trained, 'Japanese style'. As Ruth Benedict points out in her landmark study of Japanese culture, *The Chrysanthemum and the Sword: Patterns of Japanese Culture*, correct forms of respect to superiors were insisted upon rigorously within the military ranks, and recruits who failed to observe standards exactly came to expect a sudden blow to the face or body. Even a smile or casual gesture was considered disrespectful, and punishment was routinely swift and brutal—out of all proportion, by Western standards, to the perceived offence.[15] Benedict's study was written to be used as a handbook for American occupation troops in 1945; but for the hapless prisoners on Java in 1942, there were no handbooks issued, so the treatment they encountered was baffling. To their horror, it became a nerve-racking part of their daily lives for the next three years.

In a 1992 conversation, Crayton Gordon summed up the prisoners' initial contact with the Japanese in this way: 'There were three things about the Japanese way of life that made it so very, very hard on us: religion, discipline and their standard of living. We didn't know much of anything about the Japanese culture when we were forced to surrender to them, but we sure learned pretty fast.'[16]

Religion for the Japanese includes a code of conduct and honour, intertwined with cultural heritage to create a deep sense of self. The belief that a *kamikaze*, or 'divine wind', spared their people from invasion by Genghis Khan in the thirteenth century, thus preserving their pure culture, reinforces the sense of oneness which is deeply embedded in the Japanese psyche.

This sense is arrived at through lifelong training which, if completed well, allows the will to be supreme over 'the almost infinitely teachable body', as Benedict phrased it. Ultimately, Benedict found, the purpose of such training is to free the Spirit to fulfil the Higher Law, which is duty to the Emperor. There is no such thing as standing up for what is right; the highest virtue for a Japanese is to fulfil whatever has been set forth as one's duty, at all costs, in order to maintain one's self-respect and, even more importantly, one's sense of honour.[17]

Just as firmly interwined in the Western cultural heritage is the Judeo-Christian tradition of human dignity, repentance and forgiveness. (The concept of 'forgiveness' appears several times in these pages; it is used not to convey pardon, but in the spiritual sense of abandoning the desire to 'get even', as exemplified in the Biblical story of Joseph forgiving his brothers.)[18]

But where East does not meet West is in the attitude towards human life, and this is what Crayton Gordon meant when he said the Japanese religion made it 'very, very hard on us'. While the Christian tradition teaches that every life has dignity and value, and that redemption is possible, the Japanese culture holds that if one dishonours oneself, such as surrendering to the enemy, one's life has lost its value permanently, and one has stained the family name for many, many future generations. There is no redemption: the only honourable act left is to end one's life.

Discipline, and more especially self-discipline, is also part of lifetime training for Japanese in all walks of life. The tenets of the Zen religion were adopted in particular ways to the Japanese military code. By gaining control over his mind, a soldier is taught to believe that he can meet any situation, so that eventually there is no break between a man's will and his act. This single-mindedness and utter concentration in fulfilling one's task confounded the prisoners, who observed it time and time again, and it reminded 'Weary' Dunlop of 'Some of the defects of an insect society'.[19] Yet former French Prime Minister Edith Cresson was roundly criticised in 1992 for describing the Japanese as 'ants'.[20]

As for the standard of living referred to by Crayton Gordon, this could perhaps be summarised as an assumption on the part of the Japanese that, for those contemptible Western soldiers who had allowed themselves to be taken prisoner, low living standards were to be expected.

During the month of May 1942, as the regimen being imposed upon them became more rigid and incomprehensible, the prisoners took every opportunity to calm their nerves with a touch of humour. Dickson recalls one such incident during those jittery days:

> The orderly-room corporal, Kitamura, was a fantastic little creature who wore high-heeled shoes. It was alleged that in Japan he was Suzuki's superior in a Government department, and it was even suggested that he had far more influence on camp policy than might have been expected from one of his rank. To demonstrate what a really good fellow he was, he once offered a prize of cigarettes for a literary competition among the

prisoners. The choice of subjects included: 'Your Home', 'Your Life in Batavia', 'A True Love Story', and last on the list, but by no means the least, 'Mr Kitamura'! Some of the entries written around the last-named title were not submitted for judging.[21]

But towards the end of May, a monumental event occurred which was to shake each prisoner to his core: their highest-ranking officers were taken away for questioning, and were not seen again for a month. During that time, they were subjected to the most brutal and constant torture. Dickson describes some of the treatment inflicted upon the Pioneers' commanding officer, Colonel Williams, who is acknowledged in several accounts to have received the worst treatment by the Japanese of any POW:

> The C.O. in particular came in for a very rough handling, but even the threat to shoot him failed to extract from him any information that would have helped the enemy. After having refused to answer questions put to him by a Japanese Colonel, he was placed in a cell with 16 native prisoners. He had no mosquito net, and there was not enough room to lie down. With little variation, the food ration per day was a plate of rice with a fish head, eaten with the fingers. During the period of questioning, the C.O. was not permitted to shave, and he was allowed only an occasional wash. Persistent refusal to capitulate to the Japanese inquisitors was met by a variation of the 'water treatment'—beer was forced into the C.O.'s lungs in an effort to make him talk. On one occasion he was taken out before a firing squad. Instead of the volley he expected, he received the praise of the Japanese officer for his bravery, and was returned to his cell.

Author Leslie Hall adds even more excruciating details about the procedures to which Colonel Williams was subjected:

> Lt. Col. Williams had been tied to a chair and his whole body bashed so badly, even his tormentors believed he was dying. When he did regain consciousness, dry rice was forced down his throat and a hose thrust into his mouth, allowing water to surge into his body. When the rice began to swell, his stomach was so swollen [it caused] intense agony . . . For once [the Japanese] did not jump on and off his swelling abdomen, [and] nature came to his aid . . . Many died from the rice and water punishment.[22]

Dickson's account continues: 'Capt. [S.J.] Handasyde's refusal to answer Japanese questions earned a different type of torture. Small pieces of bamboo were placed between his fingers, which were twitched together while the bamboos were twisted.'[23]

Pioneer Captains Ron Winning and A.H.J. Ross were given similar torment, and once again Leslie Hall supplies additional details:

> These officers . . . were strapped to chairs and bashed unmercifully with any weapon, be it wood or metal, the interrogating staff had to hand. Hour after hour the treatment went on and on and on. At times, a merciful fate intervened; they became oblivious to everything, unaware of darkness, light, days, hours or even meal times. The latter, few and far between.
>
> There was hardly any let up, even after cigarette lighter flames burned and blistered their swollen hands. The pain suffered then was maddening, but not enough to exact any information from the determined officers.[24]

Ron Winning remembered: 'I was alert enough to tell the Japs that I was not at the ambush where they lost so heavily. I told them I was stationed at the airport, and finally they believed me.'[25]

Dickson ends his account of this episode with typical understatement: 'When the C.O. and his officers were returned to the Bicycle Camp, the Japanese were none the wiser militarily, though no doubt they had been enlightened by the conduct of their prisoners.'[26]

Many years later, Benjamin Dunn, researching United States military files for his own book, found corroboration for the major reason the Australian Officers were subjected to such agony for so long: Japanese interrogators simply did not believe that there were only 500 American and less than 3000 Australian troops on Java, because Japanese businessmen and intelligence agents had said that 70 000 Americans and 40 000 Australians were on the way. The interrogators therefore demanded to know where all these troops were, and when they were arriving. It was only as the month of June drew to a close, and their own sources brought different information, that the interrogators allowed the officers to return to their units.[27]

Ron Winning also recalled how the Japanese tormented POWs with their invasion plans—up to a point: 'The Japs knew to a man how many Americans and Australians were on Java; their spies were on the wharf when we disembarked. However, they thought that reinforcements were on the way, which was quite incorrect. The battle which saved Australia from invasion was the Coral Sea battle, when the Japs lost heavily to the US Naval Force. POW work forces were employed by the Japs loading their ships—the Jap soldiers took great delight in telling us what they were going to do in Australia.

However, they didn't crow very much after the Coral Sea battle, and the ships that were loading supplies were finally used for their landing in New Guinea.'[28]

Recently, Colonel Williams confirmed the reasons for the treatment to which he was subjected, and his efforts to keep a record of it: 'I took a number of photos . . . of Officers returning from one month's interrogation and torture when the Japanese were trying to find the location of the 6th, 7th and 9th [Australian] Divisions who were supposed to land in Java. Only a small number of negatives were suitable for enlargement. Three and a half years is a long time to keep undeveloped films . . .'[29]

The Battalion Commander had buried his film, hoping to preserve it as evidence in War Crimes trials. When he was shipped to Burma, his adjutant, Captain Edward Campbell, dug up the film and kept it with him all the way through a sea voyage to Japan (under deplorable conditions), and many months of constant relocation as a factory labourer there—all the while risking severe beating or death if the film were discovered. Remarkably, Campbell was able to personally hand deliver the film to Colonel Williams at war's end but, as the Colonel mentioned, most of the negatives were badly deteriorated. In a letter to the author, he described how he got the films back to Australia on a priority basis, along with the list of Australian prisoners who were still alive:

> On 15 August 1945 Williams Force, composed mostly of 2/2 Pioneers, were in transit and had arrived at the Go-downs in Bangkok within days of the Japanese delivering peace in Thailand. No sooner had the official announcement been made when a small force of RAPWI (the Recovery of Prisoners of War and Internees) officers reported to our HQ to tell us they would supervise the return to Australia of all Prisoners of War. We then handed over a copy of our nominal roll.
>
> We also had a nominal roll of approximately 4000 names of Australian soldiers still alive at this date ready for dispatch to Australia, and I was selected by the senior officers in Bangkok to get this list to Australia by the quickest means. The only aircraft available was due to take off for Calcutta in one hour and I was available. I arrived at Calcutta that night. I also found another aircraft due for Columbo next morning, arriving there late afternoon. There was no cable office in Columbo, nor were any aircraft available. Eventually I caught a non-stop aircraft to Perth and landed in Melbourne on 11 September 1945 . . . I was tied up in Melbourne making sure every Pioneer was accounted for, especially in regards to medical history as a POW. I was one of

OFFICER BRINGS LIST OF 4,000 NAMES OF POW's IN SIAM

THERE was a dramatic moment at Essendon aerodrome last night, when Lieut-Colonel J. M. Williams, prisoner of war from Bangkok, Siam, stepped off a plane with a list of names of more than 4,000 Australian prisoners who were known to be alive in Siam at the end of August. He handed over the list to Major L. S. Walsh, of 2nd Echelon Records, who immediately rushed them to the city for transcription by a staff who were waiting to begin the long task of checking. They will remain on the job until it is completed.

Lieut-Colonel Williams, who comes from Sefton, NSW, was CO of the 2/2 Pioneer Battalion, a Victorian unit with a distinguished record in the Middle East. He suffered considerable ill-treatment and torture when captured by the Japanese.

The records which formed the list brought out by Lieut-Colonel Williams were kept by Australian prisoners themselves in Bangkok. The Japanese called in these lists, saying that they would preserve them, but once they got the lists they burnt them. Lieut-Colonel Williams, however, had kept a copy of the lists buried in the camp. He dug it up after the surrender and supplemented it with other names of men who came to the camp from outlying districts. The list gives the names of most of the 4,900 Australians who were in prison camps in Siam. Of these, 3,900 were described by Lieut-Colonel Williams as being recently fit. One thousand were receiving treatment in hospital. Most of these had dysentery, malaria, ulcers, or were suffering the effects of malnutrition.

HAS LIST OF CRIMINALS

Lieut-Colonel Williams said that he had a list of about 10 Japanese war crimin... worst bein...

veloped at once, and may give a pictorial record of some of the aspects of prison camp life. The pictures had to be taken surreptitiously.

NAMES OF POW's AT SINGAPORE

LIEUT-COLONEL J. M. WILLIAMS (left), of Sydney, first POW to return from Thailand and the second from any Japanese camp, arriving in Melbourne by plane from Perth last night. He is handing over to Major L. J. Walsh lists of about 4,000 names of Army personnel reported to have been alive in Thailand at the end of August. The names were collected by pilots who flew supplies to the camps.

Excerpts from Melbourne Argus, *pages 1 and 3, 12 September 1945 edition, describing Colonel J.M. Williams as the first recovered POW to arrive in Australia, carrying a list of names and his film, hidden during captivity.* (COPIED FROM ORIGINALS AT RESEARCH CENTRE, AUSTRALIAN WAR MEMORIAL)

the first ex-POW[s] to return to Melbourne, but I didn't see my wife or family in Sydney until I received my first three days leave on 25 December 1945.[30]

The news account of Colonel Williams arriving in Melbourne, published in the 12 September 1945 edition of the *Argus*, together with a photo showing him handing a briefcase containing the names of recovered Australian POWs—and his rolls of film—to a waiting officer, appears above.

One of the few surviving photos taken secretly in captivity by Colonel Williams in April 1942, at the Australian POW officers' quarters, Bicycle Camp, Java. Plot in right foreground is where vegetables were grown by the prisoners, though later confiscated by the Japanese. This film was buried, taken by sea to Japan and back, and spent nearly three years in various hiding places, before being brought to Australia for development by Colonel Williams. (COURTESY OF J.M. WILLIAMS)

One of the few photos which survived shows the Australian officers' quarters in the Bicycle Camp. Colonel Williams said the officers planted a vegetable garden on the lawn, but the Japanese confiscated the harvest for their own use. 'Once caught by the Japs we didn't try growing vegetables again', he commented.[31]

It was in the Bicycle Camp that POWs came to admire the Dutch women for their bravery. Staff Sergeant Tom O'Brien could recollect, even after half a century, vivid images of blonde-haired women and children appearing each day to sell sandwiches, cigarettes and candy to the prisoners. The Japanese would bash them with rifle butts, kick them and scatter their baskets of food. 'But they didn't care— they were right back the next day,' he said, shaking his head in wonder.

Lieutenant Cal Mitchell added his own indelible image: 'After we were captured, we were marching along a road, and this young Dutch girl with long blond hair sent her little girl running toward us from the side of the road—she had long blond hair too—to hand us sandwiches. The Jap guard bashed the little girl in the head with his rifle butt, and she fell down. The mother picked her up and carried her off. I don't know what happened to her, but I'll never forget that sight.'[32]

And the contempt was still there in Tom O'Brien's voice as he muttered: 'If the Dutch men had been half as brave as the women, the Japs never would have invaded Java.' Several others around him nodded in agreement.[33]

As the weeks wore on in Java, the harsh realities of life under the Japanese became more apparent. Because most of their equipment had been left on board the transport ship, the Australians had no utensils with which to cook food, even before their captivity; and it took the resourcefulness of Harry Whelan, a pilot, to visit the Dutch Air Force hangars and scrounge some tin cans for that purpose. By June, rations had become increasingly poor, consisting only of rice and a small quantity of green vegetables in a stew, just barely flavoured with pork. In growing numbers, the men fell ill with dengue fever, dysentery and severe eye infections, and tinea became rife throughout the camp.

Pioneers tried to keep up their spirits with work, regular exercises and games of volleyball, newly learned from the Americans. On 17 June, they observed the anniversary of the unit's first battle in Syria, now adding to their remembrance with the missing men from 'A' Company. As Dickson noted, 'The Pioneers recaptured for a brief quarter-hour something of the old "Pucka" [Puckapunyal training camp] spirit—the spirit that had carried the unit successfully through its training days and earned for it a proud reputation on the field of battle.'[34]

But the organised activities and diversions were abruptly ended in early July, when all POWs were forced to sign an oath of non-escape. Ironically for the Americans, Brigadier A.S. Blackburn, after initially holding out, authorised all men to sign the oath on the Fourth of July—American Independence Day.

On 8 October, 1200 POWs were packed aboard the *Kinkon Maru*, embarking at the same wharf where they had tied up aboard the *Orcades* just eight months earlier. They were taken to Changi Prison in Singapore, from which they departed a week later. This time, 1500 prisoners were squeezed aboard the *Maebisi Maru*. Before leaving, each POW was given a card to write home. Not only were these pieces of mail actually delivered to Australia, but the Japanese presented Colonel Williams with a bill for the postage! However, they broadcast some of the postcard messages over Singapore Radio; those few messages were picked up and relayed to the servicemen's families.

Under the command of Colonel Williams, the 1500 would become known as Williams Force, and would be taken to Moulmein, Burma, to begin constructing the railway from that end. Meanwhile, a second transport of approximately 1500 men, under Lieutenant Colonel 'Weary' Dunlop, would be designated Dunlop Force, and would start work on the railway from the Thailand end.

Dickson merely refers to the voyage as being taken under 'unspeakable conditions', but Harry Bishop graphically describes the hazards encountered by the men during that trip:

> The worst part was to climb down the hold every night at dusk, find the small space where one's gear had been placed, and then find space for everyone. In mid-afternoon on the fifth day we suddenly became aware that there were three Liberator [bombers] above us in close formation at about 10,000 feet . . . the target was the other transport . . . they scored a hit amidships . . . the ship was sinking . . . there was no sign that lifeboats had been launched . . . the bombers turned and circled for their second run . . . I found a spot below the poop deck, and lay down. There was a noise like an express train, and then I felt a blow on the head . . . I had been hit by an electric iron which had been hanging behind the door. The whole ship had vibrated like a dog coming out of the water . . . A Japanese sailor fell backwards on the deck almost at my feet [dead] . . . several POW were hit by shrapnel . . . the USS *Houston* survivors . . . told me that the [Japanese] Captain had a seaman lying on his back on the deck of the bridge, right alongside the wheel. His duty was to signal when he saw the bombs leave the plane. This gave the Captain a chance to shift his ship from the targeted line while the bombs fell. The Americans were very impressed by the Jap Captain's navigational skill![35] Nevertheless, about 12 POWs were killed during that raid. They were buried at the St Patrick's Mission in Moulmein.

At Moulmein, the group was divided into two units: Williams Force still included most of the Pioneers, although Ron Winning was detached to act as adjutant of the second unit, named Black Force after Lieutenant Colonel C. Black of the 2/3rd Motor Transport Company. Survivors of the HMAS *Perth* were attached to Williams Force. By the time the war ended, 2/2 Pioneers were recovered in seven different locations: Thailand, Java, Singapore, Indo-China (Vietnam), Sumatra, Borneo and Japan.

Of the 867 members of the Battalion who became prisoners of the Japanese, slightly more than half were in Williams Force in Burma. One hundred and eighteen 'A' Company personnel were missing in action; most later left Java and worked on the Thailand end of the railway. Fourteen Pioneers under Captain Harry Bishop became part of No. 5 Branch, and worked on the Burma section of the line; 68 remained in Java. (Dickson was Quartermaster of 'C' Company, in Williams Force.)

Until the railway was completed at the end of 1943, Williams Force was under the command of Lieutenant Colonel Nagatomo (later executed at the Tokyo War Crimes Trials, at which Colonel Williams was a major witness). Several accounts have appeared in various publications of Colonel Nagatomo's initial address to the troops of Williams Force, but it took Dickson to note that the Japanese commander chose to deliver his remarks in French, from which they were translated into English by a Dutchman. Dickson's summary follows:

> The gist of his remarks was that the men before him were but a rabble—the skeleton of a broken army. By the infinite grace of His Imperial Majesty the Emperor, their lives had been spared. They were now expected in effect to enter with unbounded enthusiasm into the task of assisting Japan in her high-minded endeavour of bringing civilisation and happiness to the world, most especially to South-East Asia. He was good enough to warn any potential slackers that idleness would be looked upon with grave disfavour. A muffled sound from the men on parade greeted his masterly oration. If Nagatomo's ears were keen and his powers of interpretation good, he would have recognised in it a rather prolonged and ill-suppressed demonstration of mirth. Nevertheless, despite an outward show of nonchalance, deep down in the hearts of prisoners there were growing misgivings as to the future.[36]

The misgivings of the prisoners were not lessened by Nagatomo's assurance that, even though Japan had not ratified the Geneva Conventions with reference to treatment of Prisoners of War (signed by most other nations on 27 July 1929), his government intended to act as if it had done so. Ironically, a memorandum delivered by the Japanese government to the United States Department of State via the Spanish Embassy in Washington, DC on 24 February 1942 also gave assurances that the treaty stipulations signed at Geneva would be applied to 'civil, as well as military prisoners who find themselves under Japanese jurisdiction'.[37]

With each passing day of their captivity, the POWs were reminded anew of how empty these assurances would be.

3

Too Much of a Good Thing

30 AUGUST 1945: Having been lucky enough to find two pieces of paper in one day, Dickson began a second letter to his wife, but he quickly ran out of space, and it would be another six days before he resumed writing it.

Dickson deliberately rephrased several points from the note he rushed to send off earlier that day, just in case this one reached Melbourne first.

From: VX 19618
S/Sgt. T.C. Dickson
2/2 Aust. Pioneer Bn.
Nakom Nai POW Camp
Thailand
August 30, 1945

My old Darling,

Of all the exciting events of the last week or two, this is by no means the least—to be able once again to communicate with you in a more or less normal manner. Next to seeing you again—which looks like being a reality very soon, the thing I look forward to is hearing from you and knowing you are fit. Of the latter I feel quite confident, but to hear direct from you, that you are well, will be a great joy. In all the long time we have been apart I have always felt that we have been close in spirit. What a magnificent day it will be when we are really together again. I know you will be anxious to know how I am. You will be glad to hear that you are not getting a physical wreck back on your hands. I am really quite fit, and have been for more than a year. My bad period was late 1943 and early 1944, as it was with many others. Very bad food and jungle conditions generally were responsible for that. After coming to

25

Thailand early in '44 was fortunate enough not to return to the
jungle, and have gradually picked up ever since. Apart from the
fact that I can do with some glasses, I am practically as good as
pre-POW days, and will be fully so on a good course of normal
food. After all, more than 3800 consecutive meals of rice is a bit too
much of a good thing! John also, who is in this camp, is in good
form, although at present suffering from a broken collarbone—not
serious. In mid-'43 he had a bad time but made a really good
recovery. Now that should be enough about the family health!

This is not a bad place—paddy fields with mountains close
at hand. Until two months ago we had been for six months near
PETBURI, 100 miles or so south-west of Bangkok. (This place
is about 60 miles north-east of Bangkok.) Today's report is that we
are to be flown to India, to recuperate at Bangalore, a hill station
inland from Madras. Time will prove whether that is correct or not.
As soon as the war ended officers were sent to take command, they
having been separated from the other ranks at the beginning of this
year. [This is where Dickson ran out of paper.]

How easily a string of well-chosen words can minimise endless
days of horror! 'My bad period was late 1943 and early 1944, as it
was with many others', Dickson wrote matter-of-factly. But all
available accounts and diaries recorded daily conditions during this
time which were so unbelievable that the reader sometimes needs to
scan sentences a second time before absorbing them fully.

As Leslie Hall pointed out, Dickson's unit, Williams Force, had the
toughest job on the railway. No doubt the Japanese couldn't believe
their luck at capturing a whole battalion of rugged Australians—and
an engineering battalion at that! So it is not surprising that Williams
Force became the core of 'No. 1 Mobile Force'—and mobile it was:
on the move constantly, under worsening weather, supply and jungle conditions. The heavy monsoon rains became incessant, as did
the screams of the guards. 'Speedo! Speedo!' They would shout
in broken English, all the time pelting the POWs with rocks, as the
prisoners tried to complete their impossible quotas of work with
primitive or worn tools.

Although the British had considered building a railway in this
location some years earlier, the idea was abandoned after a field survey
clearly showed that supplying construction crews—and keeping them
healthy in jungles infested with malaria-carrying mosquitos—would
be impossible. What an irony that so many POWs from the British
Empire would die a few years later proving this point to the determined servants of the Japanese Empire!

Crew of prisoners working by firelight at night, driving piles for Railway trestle, 1943. On one occasion, a crew released the pile suddenly, hoping to strike the Japanese engineer standing below. The plot failed by inches.
(MURRAY GRIFFIN: *BRIDGE WORK, THAILAND RAILWAY*, PEN AND BRUSH AND BROWN INK OVER PENCIL, HEIGHTENED WITH WHITE, 51.4 × 35.6CM. AUSTRALIAN WAR MEMORIAL, AWM 25107)

Of course, the British saw the railway as a possible convenience, whereas its construction was undertaken by the Japanese as a desperate necessity, after American submarines and British bombers so successfully disrupted Japan's cargo shipping routes through the China Sea.

Sergeant Kevin Nolan recalls how the POWs managed to slow— and sabotage—construction as much as possible, in spite of the rantings, rock peltings and beatings of their captors:

At different times I worked on all phases of the railway line. The first task allotted to us was clearing the route of the proposed embankment. This entailed some very hard work clearing thick stands of bamboo. The hollowed out bamboo provided some very welcome water containers, and also served as vats for fermenting rice, fruit and vegetable peelings, etc. Cal Mitchell was one distiller, and I well remember him regaling myself and 'Twin' Lew Whitfeld with a dram on a couple of occasions at the 35 Kilo camp. [Whitfeld was later nearly kicked to death by a guard.]

Trees large and small were felled, and the arrival of elephants which removed the large trunks was most welcome.

The next variation was to be required to dig and transport on 'tungahs' (two oat sacks suspended on bamboo rods) an amount of earth which could be comfortably shifted in half a day; however, it took all but two gangs a full day. The two in question would not listen to reason, being keen to get back to camp and play volleyball. We were still pretty fit then. Nippon became suspicious and progressively increased the requirements until it did take all day to accomplish.

Then came a stint in a bridge building gang, [beginning by] felling poles and lashing them into a scaffold 20 feet high. Sometimes I was on the end of one of 60 or so ropes pulled to the accompaniment of a chant. A better job was being one of four up the scaffold, controlling ropes that kept the pile directly under the 'monkey', a heavy weight that slid up and down a steel pointed shaft six centimetres thick and three metres long.

On one occasion we plotted what would now be labelled 'attempted murder'. As the monkey rose, the shaft left the guide hole in the top of the pile fractionally, whereupon on this occasion, we jerked the pile aside so that on the down stroke the shaft speared into the ground, narrowly missing its target, the Jap engineer officer who was measuring the effectiveness of each thump. We managed to convince him that it had been a most regrettable accident. Had it been fatal, I wonder what the consequences would have been?

The technique employed in the construction was so inept that we hoped we would never be required to traverse these structures [but some were, and their careful sabotage made the journey nerve-racking indeed].

Later we went back to the final stage of the embankment. The meeting of the two converging ends (of the Railway, one end begun in Thailand, and the other in Burma) was set for the deadline of March 28, 1943. That night, as in many others, we worked under oil flares. However, despite much screaming and ranting by the Japanese, the meeting was not achieved until the early hours of the morning. No doubt the fact that in some cases the labourers were having tungahs filled from pits on one side, carrying them over to the other side, tipping them and reloading with the same dirt and returning it to whence it originally came—had some bearing on this delay. In the gloom, there appeared to be much activity, but there wasn't much progress.

Next came the laying of wooden sleepers, followed by positioning of the heavy iron rails. By this time our physical condition was beginning to deteriorate and we found these tasks somewhat exhausting. The sleepers had to be bored, mostly by hand, and then the rails spiked onto them. I then discovered that I could hit a dog spike with about as much consistency as I hit a golf ball. Nippon was not amused.

A bit of comic relief came into life then when I, with seven others, [was] formed into a rail straightening gang. We would set out in the morning and with huge crowbars straighten the snake-like line of rails and sleepers which had warped so badly in the heat of the day. By the time we had covered a mile or so the sun was at it again and our straightened section was twisted again. The Jap sergeant in charge of us was a reasonable and intelligent man, and realising the utter futility of the operation, he used to get us well out of sight and repair into the bush, where he would conduct miniature sports meetings. Then towards evening we would straighten out the track on the way back to camp. Unfortunately that job didn't last very long. The section was ballasted, with the result that our labours with the bars really ground us down.[1]

Leslie Hall adds a poignant note about the elephants mentioned by Nolan:

The Nipponese, accepting the advice of the Australians, decided to corduroy (the mud-filled roadway) . . . trees had to be felled and carried . . . it was at this point the massive and wonderful elephants came to the aid of the POW. Even though they, too,

were ill-fed, they seemed to sense the need of the prisoners
. . . and without even a mahout [keeper], wrapped their trunks
around heavy logs, found the balance point, and carried them to
the lay-down area.[2]

But the assistance of the elephants was short-lived. According to
Colonel Williams, the Japanese decided that a few Australians could
do more work than an elephant.

And POW author Ernest Gordon's blue eyes still sparkled as he
recollected how the prisoners sabotaged each step as much as they
could, whenever a guard's back was turned: 'Shearing a bolt, splitting
wood—even planting termite's nests in structures, whenever one
was found along the way. The wooden bridge was so well sabotaged
it was unusable,' he said with pride.[3]

No wonder the ex-POWs were so incensed when Pierre Boulle's
portrayal became immortalised in the movie based on his book,
depicting the prisoners as being inspired by their leadership to show
the Japanese what a good job they could do! POW artist Ronald
Searle summarised the feelings of many: 'As for *The Bridge [Over]
the River Kwai*, it crossed the river only in the imagination of its
author; his idea of British behaviour under the Japanese was equally
bizarre.'[4]

Dickson always made fun of Boulle's title; since 'kwai' means
'river', he used to refer to the movie as 'The Bridge Over the River
River'. And Ernest Gordon added: 'It made a nice story, but most
of it never happened.'

It is difficult for most Westerners to imagine accomplishing anything in a climate where annual rainfall is the highest in the world,
averaging 10 000 millimetres (400 inches) per year in some parts of
Burma; and where roadways, campsites and everything else becomes
mired in knee-deep mud during the long monsoon season. Yet the
POWs were forced to work every day—and often long into the
night—during the awful year of 1943, until the converging parts
were finally joined at the 153-kilo peg, near Nieke, Thailand on 17
October 1943.

For this occasion, the Japanese command staged a ridiculous propaganda film, to be shown back home—and the 'stars' weren't even
in the show! The emaciated prisoners were kept out of sight, while
water was thrown on the bodies of well-fed Japanese 'workers' to
simulate sweat. Spikes were painted gold for the joining ceremony;
dignitaries stood by proudly as a brass band played in honour of the
hard-toiling Japanese nationals who had singlehandedly created this
important supply link for the Imperial Army.

Perhaps one reason the prisoners were not shown is that Article 31 of the 1929 Geneva Conventions reads: 'Work which a prisoner is called upon to perform shall have no direct connection with the operations of the War.'

Yet just a day before the film was made, Colonel Williams secretly recorded in his diary:

> The sick boys, who worked 18 hours, were not allowed to eat the meal taken out to them . . . the night shift returned to camp at 1330 hours after completing 31 hours straight. The day workers are still out and no one has any idea when they will be back. No instructions to send a meal, or meals, out to them. We can just wait . . . Capt. Handasyde was badly beaten today . . . the guard didn't like the look on his face . . . two more . . . succumbed to the ravages of the diseases which plagued them, and their bodies were laid to rest in the one peaceful area of this encampment . . . (just before dawn) the railway from Singapore to Moulmein, Burma became a fact. But at what a price! The lives of many thousands of prisoners of war and Burmese civilians![5]

The most consistent figures put the death toll—just for the construction of the railway—at 12 568 POWs, and between 50 000 and 80 000 civilian labourers.[6] The toll would keep mounting steadily, reaching over 15 000 by August 1945 and beyond.

So the creation of the Japanese propaganda film was all the more grating for the POWs to watch, capping as it did their previous weeks at the worst campsites yet endured. Since January 1943, the Japanese had been recording the weight, height and chest measurement of each prisoner, every month. One of the most chilling entries in Colonel Williams' diary is this one: 'Based on recent experiences at hospital camps, once the combined weight of prisoners decreases, so do rations, accordingly.'[7]

This policy was applied, on orders from Tokyo, to military and civilian prisoners in other locations, including women and children, who had the misfortune of being interned by the Japanese.[8]

Conditions and rations worsened steadily through the year, as work became harder and the hours longer. Weakening bodies invited disease, and there were plenty of insects to transport it. By early August, Colonel Williams noted desperately:

> Three days into August and our living conditions are worsening by the minute. The non-stop rain has made a mockery of the huts' roof structure, and the centre walkway is almost knee deep in mud. Water is pouring from top and sides. However, the

men are so wearied and done in, they just flop down on their bedspaces and seek solace in sleep . . . Informed we have to reduce our rice intake from 350 grammes per man per day to 250. If it was starvation previously, what now! Kitchen fires hard to keep alight with green wet wood . . . no matter . . . the Japanese demand hot water be provided for their daily baths . . . is it any wonder so many men are fading away.[9]

As usual, Colonel Williams protested conditions vigorously, and finally got permission to slaughter a yak cow. He noted bitterly: 'The Nipponese confiscated the greater portion of the beast and gave the prisoners the ribs (can't eat bones), one shoulder, and half of one leg . . . impossible to feed hundreds of men on such a meagre issue, but at least the sick will appreciate what broth can be made from it . . .'

On 28 September, Williams Force had arrived at 130 Kilo camp, which by all accounts—even that of a Japanese soldier—was the worst yet seen: two roofless huts, barely able to accommodate 600 men, became home to 900; there was no kitchen, so therefore no food could be prepared. It rained all night, and not one POW slept. For two days, the Japanese took all the POW tools to build a hut and kitchen for themselves, making it impossible for the prisoners to cut wood. With no fires, there could be no cooking, even in the open.

Takashi Nagase, then an interpreter for the dreaded *kempe tai* (military police), saw the 130 Kilo camp. Nearly half a century later, he still remembered it in detail:

> A funeral procession of prisoners was coming up. Comrades were carrying a body on a stretcher which was covered with a faded Union Jack, followed by a Japanese soldier with a gun. At the rear of the procession, four or five vultures followed with their heads moving to and fro . . . I was shocked at the sight of the camp when I walked through the bamboo fence. There were nothing but shabby-looking huts without roofs. The floors of the huts were covered with bamboo which was split in two. The floor bamboos were laid with the curved side up. On the rugged floor sick prisoners were shivering in soaking blankets. Rain oozed out from worn-out blankets every time the POWs, who were stricken with malaria, rolled over on their side . . .[10]

Incidentally, Nagase was posing as an inspector on this occasion, in order to get information from the prisoners, primarily by searching their belongings—which probably explains some of the sudden 'raids' of POW possessions about which Colonel Williams complained so often throughout their captivity.

Cecil Dickson may well have been one of the malaria victims the Japanese soldier saw that day in September 1943: he contracted the disease in May of that year, and had approximately 20 relapses to July 1944. He would suffer periodic bouts of malaria for the rest of his life. In his soldier's pay book, shown on page 122, Dickson also lists conjunctivitis, failing vision, infected sores and beri-beri, the last-mentioned from November 1943 through January 1944.

Dickson's greatest anxiety about health, however, may have been when his younger brother John contracted cholera in mid-1943 (the 'bad time' Dickson cryptically refers to in his letter). In later years he would often mention with wonderment how John, isolated in the cholera hut with half a hundred others, was one of just five men to walk out alive. Although John made a 'really good recovery', according to his brother, the younger Dickson's condition remained considerably weakened throughout the rest of their internment, and he was hospitalised immediately upon his return to Melbourne.

Barbara Clements remembered that: 'John and Cecil both had iron wills, and were full of stubborn determination. Nothing would break their spirit.' It had to be a large dose of determination which allowed John Dickson to walk out of that cholera hut, when no other medicine was made available to the POWs.

Colonel Williams would ask for volunteers to man the isolation hut, and some always stepped forward, despite the obvious risk. As a result, it was not uncommon for some to give their own lives tending to their mates. Leslie Hall summed up the situation this way: 'In the almost intolerable conditions existing in POW camps in Burma and Thailand, the word *mate* held greater significance than in any other sphere of life. Selfishness was rare. Few ever gave it a thought; 90% never knew the meaning of the expression.'[11]

In a bizarre twist, the only way the cholera patients could immediately reciprocate the risks their fellow POWs took in caring for them was to provide a sanctuary for precious items such as diaries, cameras and drawings. Ronald Searle tells how, whenever possible, he hid his sketches of camp life under the pillow of a cholera patient, because the Japanese were terrified of the disease and the cholera hut was the one spot in camp guaranteed not to be searched.[12]

Despite their drastic food shortages, the men of Williams Force at one point gave up their rations after Colonel Williams visited the 'hospital' at 55 Kilo camp and saw that the kitchen there had been without rice for two days. The Pioneers' commanding officer had made it a point to check the hospital camp, being aware of remarks made by Japanese officers such as: 'Your sick shall starve until they die or go back to work . . . no work, no food.'[13]

Was it possible the Japanese were making a mockery of Christian scripture, quoting the words of St Paul to his followers: 'If any would not work, neither should he eat'?[14] More likely, the Japanese were observing their own regulations, which held that sick soldiers were useless and should be abandoned or shot for failing to carry out their duties. Anthropologist Ruth Benedict, in her study of Japanese culture, cites instances in New Guinea and the Philippines where hospitalised Japanese soldiers were killed, and their medical officers committed suicide. She also quotes an American colonel, Harold Glattley, who told the *Washington Post* in a 1945 interview that during three years as a POW on Formosa, he saw no doctors for Japanese soldiers.[15]

It must have baffled the Japanese to watch POWs feeding their sick first, and tending to them constantly. Perhaps no single act more vividly contrasted the spiritual and cultural heritages of captor and captive, and no one dared to test that gap more boldly than 'Weary' Dunlop. Here, in his own words, is his account of a truly remarkable incident:

> I recall that the Japanese commandant in Chunkai Camp, court-martialled me summarily for operating on a Japanese soldier who failed to carry out his camp duties.
>
> He took a dramatic 'swish' at my neck with his gleaming Samurai sword, which however stopped quivering at my neck, then said, 'No, here is my sword, please honour me by killing yourself.' I returned an eloquent account of all the reasons why Australians did not commit 'hari-kiri'. His fierce brown eyes were locked on mine and he summed up, 'You mean that you are such a great coward you will not kill yourself?' To which I replied, 'You were right about one thing; I won't kill myself.'
>
> So I finished up in the 'box house' with my patient, Akimoto, that poltroon.[16]

A desperate situation was made nearly impossible to bear for the starving POWs as the local camp guards and their cooks insisted on confiscating, or at least taking a cut of, the rations which were being sent in for the prisoners. Just a week after the Railway was completed, Colonel Williams' diary reads: 'As ration carriers have to pass the Nip kitchen to get to ours, the fat Nipponese cook snatches what he wants from our containers. Hence, low rations for the prisoners . . . they took at least 100 men's potato entitlements from the last delivery.' By Armistice Day, 11 November, the CO's diary

The photo on the left shows brothers Cal (left) and Alan Mitchell, midway through a 136-mile training hike at Shepparton, Victoria, in July 1940. Right The Mitchell brothers, Alan (left) and Cal (seated) with Basil Ransome (standing) shortly after release, Bangkok, September 1945. Many ex-POWs sent similar photos home in advance of their arrival, hoping to assure families of their 'good health'. (COURTESY OF C.J. MITCHELL)

contains one of its starkest entries: 'We are completely out of food-stuffs. No meals can be served today.' Two days later: 'A herd of seven yaks all went to the Japs—not one cut for the prisoners.' On this occasion, his protest yielded 40 pounds of meat, but by then, they were down to one meal per day. And on 17 November, he recorded that the prisoners had to carry in rations for the Japanese, but none were supplied at all to the POWs.[17]

Reflecting four decades later on that desperate and debilitating year of forced labour in 1943, speaking with a sadness which must have been especially acute for a physician, 'Weary' Dunlop said in an interview: 'The trouble was that if you were sinewy, indestructible, if you were a good workman, you got sent back and back and back on these terrible tasks with utterly inadequate food. You could see these magnificently strong men with great hearts who slowly went to pieces, and died.'[18]

It should come as no surprise, then, to learn that when John Dickson finally arrived in Melbourne, family members were shocked at his condition. Dickson's older brother, Stan, was there with daughter Jeanette, who recalls: 'No one could believe how thin Uncle John was. He weighed just over three stones (about 50 pounds). Every rib was broken from malnutrition.' And despite Cecil's cheery assurances that he was 'practically as good as pre-POW days', when he docked in Melbourne after nearly two additional months of good food, Barbara Clements remembers that 'Uncle Cec still looked like a scarecrow'.

Of course, to the POWs who had been starved for so long, just the opportunity to eat three meals a day made them feel so robust, by comparison, that it didn't occur to them they might still look otherwise. Cal Mitchell, his brother Alan and their friend Basil Ransome couldn't wait to have a photographer take their picture in Bangkok, and they gleefully sent it home 'so our families could stop worrying', Cal remembered. 'That photo caused much distress and weeping about how thin we were, and how old we looked,' he added ruefully.

So while he tried to minimise his own health problems and those of his brother in this second letter home, Dickson knew that he had good reason to worry about his wife's condition. During their marriage, she had suffered several miscarriages, which left the couple childless—a great and lasting disappointment. Freda's doctor had detected a weak heart, and advised against further attempts at parenthood. And while Dickson was interned, his wife suffered a bout of rheumatic fever. It seemed to her niece Barbara that 'Aunt Freda was ill the whole time Uncle Cec was away. To us, as children, it was a period of terrible sadness. My father, Cam, died during that time; Aunt Freda was so ill; Uncle Cec was a POW . . .'[19]

Years later, Dickson would confide that when he first came down the gangplank from the *Circassia* on 3 November 1945, he moved along the walkway, chatting through the chain-link fence with a very pleasant lady for about ten minutes—before realising he was talking to his wife.

4

The Most Exciting Day

1 SEPTEMBER 1945: It has been fifteen long days since the camp bugler sounded reveille English-style, signalling the end of imprisonment—but not of confinement. For Dickson and his fellow POWs who remained at Nakom Nayok, patience was being strained not only by the priority departure of the Americans, but also by the continuing need to stay put and await word of their own travel arrangements. Today, at last, the strain had been broken by the arrival of supplies by air, and medical officers by truck—a sure sign that the countryside was becoming more secure.

Dickson was one of the lucky few to get a piece of airmail stationery from among the newly arrived supplies. He dared to hope that he would be home in time for his wedding anniversary.

Nakom Nayok Camp
Thailand
September 1, 1945

Dearest Old Binks,

Things are moving fast here now re our departure, which gives me a slight hope of being with you by October 2. Don't pin too much hope on it but there is just a chance. I have written to you already. This note, however, might beat the other home. An American friend, who left here a few days ago, was to send you a cable, also one to Stan re John's safety, so I hope these reached their destinations. Just to let the office know that I am still on the map I sent off, per another departed American, an account of how we received the news—which might & might not turn up. There is a very limited number of letters going on this air-mail. I was fortunate enough to get one, and would be glad if you would write immediately to the addresses on the back (or wire for preference) informing the people concerned that their husbands (respectively Capts. Edwards, Winning & Lovett, Flying Officer Matheson, Sgt. Dixon & Pvt. Redcliffe) and sons (Capt. Howitt & Cpl. Battye)

37

are well. On second thoughts, hang the expense and make it all
telegrams! Tremendous excitement to-day. First an American plane
dropped two Americans, a Thai, and then personal gear into the
camp, then a British plane circled round parachuting down books,
recent papers, cigarettes and a host of other stuff. There are two
schools of thought about the journey home. One is that we fly to
India via Rangoon; the other that we catch a ship at Bangkok for
Australia direct. A party of stretcher sick has just left the camp for
Bangkok to be flown to India. Cheerio old darling. Seeing you
soon—and won't it be magnificent!

Tons of love, Pop

'SECURITY; THINK BEFORE YOU WRITE' is printed across
the envelope's flap. What an irony! How he would have liked to
actually write letters home these past 44 months; but he could only
cross out inappropriate pre-printed lines on postcards supplied by
the Imperial Japanese Army. When he had been sick, he would draw
a line through the phrase: 'I have not had any illness.' And then he
could cram a dozen well-chosen words into two and a half lines of
space at the bottom of the card, and wonder whether it would ever
leave the camp.

Despite the fact that he was only allowed to date one card (in May
1944), Dickson cleverly found ways to signal when some were being written. The second card, for example, gives a traditional New
Year's greeting, and refers to Freda's upcoming birthday, 2 February.
Perhaps the most dramatic reference is his use of the word 'message'
instead of 'letter' in his final card, telling his wife that some of the
radio messages being sent by the Relatives Association were being
received over clandestine wireless sets.

Dickson would describe the situation some years later, in compil-
ing the 'Prisoners of War' chapter for his Battalion's history:

December 1943 was notable for one great event. It was the
arrival of the first mail that the prisoners received from home.
Much of it was written in July 1942, so it was almost 18 months
in reaching its destination. It had been written before messages
from relatives were restricted to 25 words, and the pages of
news from home were a wonderful tonic to the weary men.
They were in real need of a tonic then. Food supplies were at
their worst and the deathroll was mounting daily. The letters
revived thoughts and hopes of home, which now seemed so far
distant and remote. The men knew that to those dearest to them

in Australia anxiety would be their daily companion, for the men in captivity were behind a dark curtain and it would be natural for those who could not see behind it to fear the worst for their men. The sympathetic thoughts therefore flowed to, as well as from, Australia.

All that the prisoners could do to help allay the fears of their families at home was to take advantage of the opportunity, about once every six months, to send them a card. Most of these cards were already printed, and of course the words were supplied by the Japanese, requiring only the signature of the sender. They gave no hint of the real conditions that existed in the camps. They praised the captors for their treatment of the prisoners, who were alleged to be extremely grateful for the benefits being bestowed on them by their kindly and generous hosts. In return for these nauseating epistles the prisoners received 25-word postcards from home. These were written once a month, but they were released by the Japanese at very irregular intervals. It was not uncommon for 12 months to pass without an issue of inward mail, and some men received no word at all from home during the whole of their captivity. When mail was handed out by the Japanese, however, it had a tremendously uplifting effect on the morale of its receivers.[1]

None of his wife's long letters was delivered, but occasionally Dickson got a 25-word note. Fellow Pioneer Walter Summons compiled a record of the dates he remembers writing a postcard, and the dates his family received them in Melbourne:

Written October 12, 1942, received September 13, 1943
Written January 22, 1943, received October 6, 1943
Written May 31, 1943,   received November 30, 1943
Written February 1, 1944, received January 6, 1945

Ernest Gordon, a captain in the Argyll and Sutherland Highlanders, was one POW who received no mail at all during his entire captivity, a fact he attributed primarily to Japanese indifference to record-keeping and somewhat bureaucratic lassitude on the part of the International Red Cross. A member of a secret service group in Singapore, Gordon escaped with a handful of others on a sailboat, and almost got to Ceylon before being spotted and captured by a Japanese tanker.

Following pages *The six postcards sent home by Cecil Dickson, 1942–45. The first card was written from Java, before the Japanese distributed printed forms. Some arrived in Melbourne a year after being written.*
(PHOTOGRAPHED FROM THE ORIGINALS COURTESY OF MRS T.C. DICKSON)

VX19618, STAFF-SGT. T. C. DICKSON.

DARLING BINKIE,

VERY FIT. IN GOOD
SPIRITS. HOPE YOU SAME. LONGING
HEAR FROM YOU. TWO THORNS WELL.
LOVE OLD DARLING, ALSO MOTHER,
FAMILIES.

POP.

IMPERIAL JAPANESE ARMY.

I am interned at The War Prisoners Camp at
Moulmein in Burma.

My health is (good, ~~usual, poor~~)
~~I have not had any illness.~~
~~I (am) (have been) in hospital.~~
~~I am (not) working (for pay at~~ _____ ~~per day).~~
~~My salary is~~ _____ ~~per month.~~

I am with friends. MAY 1943 BRING HAPPINESS

OLD GIRL MANY HAPPY RETURNS OF FEB. 2.

LOVE TO MOTHER AND ALL THE FAMILIES

From POP.

IMPERIAL JAPANESE ARMY

I am interned at The War Prisoners Camp at
Moulmein in Burma.

My health is (good, ~~usual, poor~~)
~~I have not had any illness.~~
I (am) ~~(have been)~~ in hospital.
I am (not) working ~~(for pay at~~ _____ ~~per day).~~
~~My salary is~~ _____ ~~per month.~~

I am with friends (JOHN, McCARTHY, NOLAN)

RECOVERING FROM TEMPORARY SICKNESS,

OTHERWISE FIT. HOPE YOU WELL. LOVE OLD DEAR.

From POP.

IMPERIAL JAPANESE ARMY.

Our present place, quarters, and work is unchanged since last card sent to you The rains have finished, it is now beautiful weather. I am working healthily (sick). We receive newspapers printed in English which reveal world events.

We have joyfully received a present of some milk, tea, margarine, sugar and cigarettes from the Japanese Authorities.

We are very anxious to hear from home, but some prisoners have received letters or cables.

Everyone is hopeful of a speedy end to the war and with faith in the future we look forward to a happy reunion soon.

With best wishes for a cheerful Christmas.

YOUR FIRST LETTERS RECEIVED, SPECIAL RE-
MEMBRANCES ELLA + NEEDHAMS, LOVE OLD GIRL

From T. C. Dickson

IMPERIAL JAPANESE ARMY

Date 10-5-44

Your mails (and ——————) are received with thanks.
My health is (good, usual, poor).
I am ill in hospital.
I am working for pay (I am paid monthly salary).
I am not working.
My best regards to ALL. NOT ENOUGH SPACE TO GET

SENTIMENTAL! JOHN WELL, KEN BLOOMING. LOVE OLD GIRL

Yours ever,

Pop

IMPERIAL JAPANESE ARMY.

I am still in a P. O. W. Camp near Moulmein, Burma, There are 20,000 Prisoners, being Australian, Dutch, English, and American. There are several camps of 2/3000 prisoners who work at settled labour daily.

We are quartered in very plain huts, The climate is good. Our life is now easier with regard to food, medicine and clothes. The Japanese Commander sincerely endeavours to treat prisoners kindly.

Officers' salary is based on salary of Japanese Officers of the same rank and every prisoner who performs labour or duty is given daily wages from 25 cents (minimum) to 45 cents, according to rank and work.

Canteens are established where we can buy some extra foods and smokes. By courtesy of the Japanese Commander we conduct concerts in the camps, and a limited number go to a picture show about once per month.

FEELING FIT - JOHN ALSO - AND OF COURSE THINK-
ING OF THE OLD LADY A LOT. WILL BE THRILLED TO RECEIVE MESS

POP

The Japanese simply never bothered to add these few stragglers to the list of POWs they had supplied to the Red Cross, so Gordon was listed as 'missing in action and presumed killed'. His family had no inkling that he was alive until April, 1945 when, by some miracle, one of his pre-printed postcards was delivered to their home in Scotland.

A further twist to Gordon's story is that just one person *did* know of his whereabouts: a United States Steel executive with whom Gordon had become friends in Singapore. Once a month, the American sent Gordon a cablegram through the Red Cross, asking how he was doing. (Despite this regular contact, no one at the Red Cross thought to pass this information along to Gordon's family.) None of these cables reached him until one day, while Gordon was working on the Railway, a Japanese vehicle drove up to the worksite. Out stepped an officer, demanding that Gordon be identified.

'I thought, this is it; they've discovered my diary or something, and I'm going to be killed,' Gordon recalled. 'Instead, the Japanese hands me this cable, with a flourish, and they all thought I must be someone very important.' His family did not learn he was free until they received an official cable in September 1945, and he was not able to communicate with them until he reached Rangoon that same month.[2]

Freda Dickson could only guess whether her husband was still alive by the time she held each soiled, long-delayed piece of stiff manila paper, with just a few words in his handwriting. After all, she hadn't even heard that he was a prisoner until a year after the fact.

Her anxiety had increased tenfold, or so it seemed, over the past nine months—ever since some POWs being shipped to Japan had been torpedoed, then rescued, by the same United States submarines, in September 1944. Nine Pioneers were among those rescued and brought back to Stewart House, near Brisbane, on 18 October 1944. The stories they told intelligence officers about conditions in the Burma–Thailand POW camps were so appalling that for several weeks the dramatic rescue of these men at sea was kept secret, while the governments of Britain, the United States and Australia anguished over whether to reveal such atrocities to the public.

Finally, on 17 November 1944, Acting Prime Minister Forde addressed the House of Representatives in Canberra, as simultaneous announcements were being made in Washington and London. After he described the daily horrors the POWs were enduring, the public was outraged—but the families of those POWs were chilled beyond belief.

Leo Cornelius, one of the nine rescued Pioneers, described the tremendous burden placed on the handful of recovered POWs by anxious families: 'One of the greatest difficulties of my life was the meeting in Melbourne of relatives of Pioneer and [HMAS] *Perth* survivors, especially when the soldier concerned was deceased or ill when you last saw him . . . we were under specific orders not to release bad news, in particular, under any circumstances.'

As word spread of their return, the repatriated POWs were besieged with calls and visits from anxious families of those still held prisoner. The inquiries turned into what Cornelius describes as 'an avalanche, which caused some of us to go into seclusion'.

He describes the poignance of his personal experience, heightened by concern for the well-being of an elderly aunt with whom he was living: 'It was not unusual for her to wake about 7 a.m. to tell me there were several people waiting to talk to me. When I protested she occasionally broke into tears and said, "Some of them have been here for hours—in fact, since daylight." '[3]

Perhaps the only comfort for Freda Dickson at that time was to surmise that Cecil had *not* been selected for transport to Japan. The one dated postcard she received became especially significant, because it was written in May 1944, after POWs had been selected for that journey. This was the only time the Japanese allowed a date to be placed on outgoing correspondence; the concession was a direct result of International Red Cross protests earlier that year.

As her niece Barbara verified, reading and hearing first-hand accounts of such monumental hardships, especially from some of the men in Cecil's unit, made it very, very difficult for Freda Dickson and other POW relatives to sustain hope for their loved ones' safe return. But they tried to comfort each other with weekly meetings, where they shared information and offered mutual support. And they kept up their system of sending monthly postcards and radio messages, in the hope that some would be received.

No doubt Prime Minister Forde caught the sentiments of such families in his concluding sentences of that November 1944 address:

> The Government regrets that these disclosures have to be made, but it is convinced it is necessary that the Japanese government should know that we are in possession of the facts and will hold them responsible. All the rescued men speak of the high courage shown by their comrades. Everywhere and in all circumstances, the Australians have maintained matchless morale. They have shown themselves undaunted in the face of death. The many who have survived privation and disease in the jungle have

developed spiritual and physical powers to triumph over
adversity and their captors. Let us look forward to the day of
their release.

Now that day had come, and Dickson's efforts at spreading the
news about friends who survived would succeed. Apparently Freda,
being a good newspaperman's wife, contacted Mr Knox at the *Argus*
as soon as she received this letter, and the list of names appeared in
a story under Dickson's byline on 13 September 1945. Just over a
week later, on 22 September, his news account of the camp's activity
on 1 September was printed in the paper. A reproduction of the
article, obtained from the archives of the *Herald and Weekly Times*,
appears on p. 45 preceded by an editor's note explaining who has
filed the story; the text is printed below.

POW's MOST EXCITING DAY
Liberation in Siam Camp
From WO T. CECIL DICKSON, mining editor of THE
ARGUS before enlisting in 1940, who was recently liberated
from a Siam POW camp.
    The most exciting day at Nakou Nai POW camp, Siam, since
August 17, when 2,500 British, Australian, Dutch, and American
prisoners were told that the war was over, was September 1.
    Shortly after breakfast that morning a US transport plane
dropped packages into the camp from a height of 300 feet.
    An hour later a British machine, circling at a low altitude,
dropped package after package into a small square. Before the
end of the day the men had been issued with toilet and shaving
soap, razor blades, cigarettes, and other almost forgotten
luxuries.
    Meanwhile a third plane, having failed to find the camp, had
dropped four British medical officers with great quantities of
medical supplies into a paddyfield some miles away. They
reached the camp by motor-truck later in the day.
    One of the four, a 23-year-old English major, on landing,
screwed a black-taped monocle into his eye and asked a group of
Siamese 'where the deuce the prisoners of war were to be
found.'

34 AIF UNITS REPRESENTED
Five hundred and fifty Australians from 34 separate units, under
Captain J.J. Edwards, MC 2/3 Machinegun Batt, of Adelaide,
were among the personnel at Nakou Nai. The 2/4th Machinegun
Batt was represented by 63 men, the 2/2nd Pioneer Batt by 54,
and the 2/40th Inf Batt by 53.

POW's MOST EXCITING DAY

Liberation In Siam Camp

From WO T. CECIL DICKSON, mining editor of THE ARGUS before enlisting in 1940, who was recently liberated from a Siam POW camp.

The most exciting day at Nakou Nai POW camp, Siam, since August 17, when 2,500 British, Australian, Dutch, and American prisoners were told that the war was over, was September 1.

Shortly after breakfast that morning a US transport plane dropped packages into the camp from a height of 300 feet.

An hour later a British machine, circling at a low altitude, dropped package after package into a small square. Before the end of the day the men had been issued with toilet and shaving soap, razor blades, cigarettes, and other almost forgotten luxuries.

Meanwhile a third plane, having failed to find the camp, had dropped four British medical officers with great quantities of medical supplies into a paddyfield some miles away. They reached the camp by motor-truck later in the day.

One of the four, a 23-year-old English major, on landing, screwed a black-taped monocle into his eye and asked a group of Siamese "where the deuce the prisoners of war were to be found."

34 AIF UNITS REPRESENTED

Five hundred and fifty Australians from 34 separate units, under Captain J. J. Edwards, MC, 2/3 Machinegun Batt, of Adelaide, were among the personnel at Nakou Nai. The 2/4th Machinegun Batt was represented by 63 men, the 2/2nd Pioneer Batt by 54, and the 2/40th Inf Batt by 53.

The period between the end of the war and actual liberation was in some respects a trying one for the men. But their high spirits and morale averted what could have become an intolerable situation.

Although nominally free, they were still behind a high bamboo fence, forbidden to leave camp and taste the joys outside. Patience was the only course, especially as the district teemed with armed Japanese.

NOT VINDICTIVE RACE

Whatever the failings of the British race, vindictiveness is not one. Hardly a POW at Nakou Nai, or anywhere else for that matter, had but good cause in the preceding 3½ years to take violent vengeance when the day came against Japanese and Koreans.

But the day did come, and hardly a hair on a short-cropped Japanese head was hurt. Relief at their release banished the spirit of revenge from men's hearts.

Only one incident occurred at Nakou Nai camp. One of the newly appointed British camp police found himself face to face with the most hated Korean in the camp, by whom he had been bashed only a week before. The Korean, who was drunk, made friendly advances to the camp policeman, who felled him in one blow.

News article sent by Dickson to the Melbourne Argus *just after liberation, in late August 1945. It appeared in the 22 September 1945 edition.* (COURTESY OF THE HERALD AND WEEKLY TIMES, MELBOURNE)

The period between the end of the war and actual liberation
was in some respects a trying one for the men. But their high
spirits and morale averted what could have become an intolerable
situation.

Although nominally free, they were still behind a high
bamboo fence, forbidden to leave camp and taste the joys
outside. Patience was the only course, especially as the district
teemed with armed Japanese.

NOT VINDICTIVE RACE
Whatever the failings of the British race, vindictiveness is not
one. Hardly a POW at Nakou Nai, or anywhere else for that
matter, had but good cause in the preceding $3\frac{1}{2}$ years to take
violent vengeance when the day came against Japanese and
Koreans.

But the day did come, and hardly a hair on a short-cropped
Japanese head was hurt. Relief at their release banished the spirit
of revenge from men's hearts.

Only one incident occurred at Nakou Nai camp. One of the newly
appointed British camp police found himself face to face with the
most hated Korean in the camp, by whom he had been bashed
only a week before. The Korean, who was drunk, made friendly
advances to the camp policeman, who felled him in one blow.

The benign attitude of newly freed POWs toward Japanese camp
personnel was a source of continuing puzzlement and debate to some
officers, especially in view of how close all POWs came to being
executed.

Cal Mitchell remembered: 'Our hidden wireless sets picked up the
information that on August 22, the Japs planned to start executing
all POWs, beginning with the officers. We beat the deadline by just
six days! And of course, the non-commissioned officers were just as
well organised as the officers.'[4]

Harry Whelan loved to tell the story about how a Japanese interpreter, seeking to ingratiate himself with 'Weary' Dunlop, read him
the order that if Japan surrendered, all POWs were to be executed
first: 'Taking his turn to have a little fun, at last, at the Jap's expense,
"Weary" pointed out that since under the code of *Bushido* a Japanese
had dishonoured himself if he surrendered, and would be required
to commit hari-kiri, "Weary" and his fellow officers would have
liked to witness the ceremony . . .'[5]

Sir Edward, commenting on the incident in a 1992 letter to the
author, pointed out that 'All prisoners were to be eliminated, so that
my presence at the hari-kiri ceremony was impractical.'[6]

However, the Allies had for some months previously been parachuting commandos into the jungle near as many POW camps as could be located, with the purpose of training Thai villagers to assist in storming the camps at the first sound of gunfire. Interpreter Takashi Nagase recalled seeing those commandos arriving, and searching for them—mostly in vain, apparently: 'On full moon nights, Allied spies dropped by blue parachute in groups of five. We spent many nights searching for them throughout the jungle and grassy fields.'[7]

The POWs also learned through radio broadcasts that, since their campsites were presumed by British intelligence to be a location for Japanese troops, the RAF was planning to bomb them—on 17 August! As Ernest Gordon observed: 'Had the war continued for two more weeks, we would have copped it one way or another, at the hand of friend or foe.'

Echoing Dickson's report in the *Argus* story, Gordon wrote: 'Though we now held the power, it never occurred to us to raise a hand against them . . . The liberators wanted to shoot the Japanese on the spot. Only the intervention of the victims prevented them. Captors were spared by their captives.'[8]

But Mitchell was one officer who would not have been inclined to such leniency, had he been with his troops on the day of liberation. He emphasised: 'As regards the attention given to the Japanese after the capitulation I must say we were all rather surprised by the actions, or rather lack of action, by our troops. I brought this up with them at the time and they were greatly surprised. It could be summed up by the remark "What! And be as big a lot of bastards as them?"'[9]

Christian values wear many labels.

5

Undreamed of Luxury

5 SEPTEMBER 1945: Dickson finally located more paper to continue the letter he had interrupted on 30 August. Pages 317 and 318 of an accounting ledger, lined horizontally in blue with a vertical red margin column, served his purpose.

In the last couple of days, he had retrieved several letters from his wife, which had been brought to his camp from a more distant Japanese headquarters. Undistributed mail was found at almost every location (Nakom Nayok was an exception), and was handed out as quickly as possible to the eager POWs.

Trying to read his wife's letters in sequence, Dickson began to catch up on family news, and not all of it was pleasant. He learned for the first time that his brother-in-law, Cam, had died several months earlier. Many POWs experienced similar shocks upon opening those first letters from home.

There is no salutation on this letter, because Dickson was picking up where he left off six days previously:

> *Having gone so far, special small sheets of paper were issued for the letter on August 30, so I'm finishing the one I began on that day. None of our officers came to this camp, but I had letters from Capts Winning and Bishop, who had gone to other camps. Both were well.*
>
> *Yesterday was full of excitement. Three planes dropped a large quantity of food, etc. One's tastes have become so simple through having so little for so long that all of this stuff that is being poured in on us now is like undreamed of luxury. Everyone is putting on weight (including yours truly) as a result of the enormous improvement in food, vitamin tablets, etc.*
>
> *A couple of days ago I had the pleasure of walking out of the camp and experiencing the feeling of freedom. Two of the officers and a sergeant were also of the party. Hailing a Jap truck outside the camp, we went into town, about 8 miles [15 kilometres] away. Quite a fair place, although 20 miles [32 kilometres] from the*

railway. Friendly people, plenty of Japs and Koreans—and even armed Jap guards at the main corners—I think to keep order among their own people (troops). We ate lunch in the market surrounded by 20 or 30 Thais—one speaking good English interpreting for the rest.

Re mail from you. Five of the long letters did not reach me and I received most of the 25 worders up to May 1944. As you say, it is hard to imagine 50 Canterbury Road without Cam. I was very grieved to hear the news about the poor old chap. There will be an enormous amount for you to tell me about the doings when I reach home.

Latest report is that we are flying to Singapore, although officially our postal address, which I append below, is India. Unless you hear otherwise, write there, but I hope we will be with you before there is time for an exchange of letters. In the meantime look after yourself old darling. Remembrances to family and friends.

Your loving

Pop

Many POWs found mixed blessings when they finally received batches of mail from home. One of the most poignant accounts of searching in vain for familiar handwriting was told by Leslie Hall in his manuscript of family history, 'The Queen of Hearts'. Hall kept pestering the postal staff to look, and look again, for a letter in his mother's handwriting. Exasperated, the postal clerk said: 'Here's the pile; look for yourself.' In rapid succession, Hall found several pieces of mail addressed to him from various relatives, but still none from his mother. Finally, he opened one from his sister, only to discover that his mother had died a year and a half ago. How often he had pictured his reunion with her—he would lift his petite mother and swing her in circles, as he had done so many times. Now, all he could look forward to was a visit to her grave. Heartbroken, he wandered into the orderly room, and when a friend approached, Hall could only point to the sheet of paper in his hand.[1]

For quite a few returning POWs, the anticipation of arrival was mingled with apprehension about who might not be there to greet them at home. One POW returning on Dickson's troopship, the *Circassia*, got such bad news when he phoned home from Fremantle— the ship's first stop—that the poor soldier just quietly slipped overboard during the night on the way to Melbourne (see Chapter 16).

Arrival in Australia would also bring an unwelcome task to those, like Hall, who felt an obligation to seek out relatives of POWs who had died in the camps and try to offer words of comfort, as if details of a final rest in peace might help to assuage the searing news which many families had just received.

While he waited for passage home, nothing pleased Dickson and his friends more than encountering Japanese and Koreans trying to blend into the landscape, and forcing them to salute. To all military forces, of course, saluting is a required act of respect, to be displayed first by the one junior in rank. Since the Japanese considered all POWs to be of lesser importance than even the lowliest Japanese private, nothing apparently brought swifter retribution—or just a handy excuse to administer a beating—than the failure to salute promptly. Even among their own ranks, breaches of respect brought incredibly brutal responses.

The insistence on 'respect' was all the more galling to POWs, especially officers, not only because of the frequently brutal and temperamental behaviour of their captors, but also because the prisoners were often under the command of junior-ranking Japanese. At one location during 1943, the camp commandant was a three-star private!

As Harry Whelan explained: 'You had to be careful; if you did one thing to displease them, then they had it in for you. For example, if you wore a hat, you were supposed to salute; if not, you bowed from the waist. I saw a man kicked to death because he was too sick to stand up and salute.'

This exaggerated protocol was even demanded of civilians. One Dutch woman, interned in Sumatra with her two young children, was apparently 'marked', as Whelan would say, in the early days of her captivity. Perhaps she failed to bow correctly, 'Japanese style', during daily *tenko* (roll call). Every single day for the next three years, she was beaten, no matter how exemplary her behaviour might have been—and her children were made to watch.

In his diaries, Colonel Williams frequently referred to a 'saluting blitz', in which POWs were beaten repeatedly for allegedly failing to salute rapidly enough—usually when they were midway through a task. At one point, he noted, guards took to sneaking up behind working parties of POWs and using the element of surprise as an excuse to administer a fearful bashing.[2] One camp commandant even complained to the Pioneer CO that 'The Australian troops must conform as do the Americans and British, and salute the Great Nipponese. The Australian attitude is to treat Nipponese like cows and pigs. This must cease; saluting must improve.'[3]

Dickson found a brilliant way to beat the Japanese at their own game, and he managed to do it by combining the three priorities which, when breached, caused the greatest discomfort in Japanese culture: observing protocol; avoiding embarrassment; and never appearing to be taken by surprise. In one camp, he timed his morning rounds to coincide with the moment when a particular Japanese officer was standing outdoors in his silk bathrobe, concentrating on his image in a propped-up mirror as he lathered shaving soap on to his face. At that precise moment, Dickson would round the corner and salute smartly, forcing the Japanese to drop his razor (usually in the dirt) and return the salute, while dripping shaving cream all over his silk robe. This was one of Dickson's favourite stories, and just about every one of his friends told it with renewed glee nearly half a century later.

Because of their constant insistence on proper saluting, nothing apparently made the Japanese feel the reality of surrender more than the sudden requirement that *they*, and not the Westerners, must now salute first. Former interpreter Nagase confirms this: 'Shortly after the surrender, I was forced to salute an Allied group of soldiers in a busy street in Bangkok . . . I had to salute the Caucasians, who had been our prisoners until recently, in the local people's presence. I had never felt such a heavy saluting arm . . . then a real feeling of surrender struck me.'[4]

Apparently the post-liberation transition was more orderly at Nakom Nayok than at certain other locations. Hardly anyone in the Allied military forces, be they liberators or POWs, shared the confidence of the Supreme Allied Commander, General Douglas MacArthur, that the Japanese would lay down their arms once instructed to do so by their Emperor. It was a fortune of history, at least in this respect, that the American commander was so well schooled in Japanese culture. MacArthur insisted that the Emperor send his Foreign Minister to sign the surrender in public, aboard the battleship *Missouri* in Tokyo Bay. Some very tense days passed before Emperor Hirohito agreed to the terms of peace and arrangements for the formal ceremony.

As was his custom, MacArthur made sure of full media coverage (just ask any Pacific war correspondent how many times the General strode ashore in Leyte Gulf, the Philippines, in October 1944 to declare 'I have returned' for the cameras). He knew that once the Emperor's envoy was seen carrying out the ceremony of surrender in full view, it would be incumbent on his subjects to do likewise. More important to Allied troops, and especially to POWs in such remote locations, once Japanese military personnel, from general to lowliest guard, heard their Emperor's voice on the radio instructing them to lay down their arms, *they did so*, much to the astonishment and great relief of all.

By contrast, where word of the Emperor's actions had not reached his troops in Burma, the situation was dangerously different. Nagase tells of his experience accompanying British and Australian officers of the Allied War Graves Commission to Burma on 24 September, some five weeks after the surrender was official. In one of those little ironies of history, this incident took place near Thanbyuzayat, Burma, where the POWs were forced to begin construction of the Railway:

> The moment the train pulled in at the open platform the clicks of unlocking safeties of rifles were heard from every direction. Japanese soldiers . . . got up with guns at the ready. Their piercing eyes were focused on the Allied party. The surrounding circle was becoming smaller and smaller . . . The Allied party did not have enough time to get their arms, which lay in the next [rail car]. They did nothing but stand still . . .
>
> I shouted to the NCO: 'Didn't you get some news about us?' He gave us a blank look . . . [finally] the commanding officer showed up . . . I approached [him] and said in a low voice, 'Lieutenant Colonel, would you please salute the Captain of the Allies?' The Lieutenant Colonel looked offended.
>
> [Australian] Captain White had gotten off the rail car and taken up stance for taking the salute from the Japanese officer, who had turned up in full uniform . . . the Lieutenant Colonel . . . raised his right arm wearily and slowly to salute the Australian without approaching him, which might have been a sign of his resistance . . .
>
> Captain White received the Lieutenant Colonel's salute . . . [and] returned the salute by swinging his right arm from his side straight up above the shoulder in the typical Australian way. Then he made a big sound with both heels of his boots.[5]

Even in Thailand, not all Japanese camp personnel sat quietly waiting for someone in the Allied command to show up and collect their weapons. Possibly the most jittery days of August were endured by the POWs at Tamuan, a campsite in northern Thailand, near the mountains. Harry Whelan was there, as was Leslie Hall. Whelan describes the scene:

> For some weeks prior to August 16, we would awaken to find the camp surrounded by Jap soldiers with machine guns, etc. They had made us fill in all slit trenches in the camp, and it was pretty obvious that they intended harm to us . . . our lives were undoubtedly saved by the atomic bomb.

When the war ended the Japanese were still in force in the vicinity, and still occupied the guard house with a machine gun prominently displayed on a tripod. We were very wary for probably the first two weeks after news of surrender.

All officers, other than a few doctors, had been separated from us some months previously and Tamuan camp was, from a POW point of view, commanded by a British Regimental Sergeant Major named Edkins, who had been in the British army for over 20 years. He had plenty of common sense and did a good job—much better, in my opinion, than some of the officers had done.

Probably two weeks after the war's end a British paratrooper, Captain Ross, plus a corporal (I think his name was Phillips) drove into the camp. They had parachuted into the area, walked to a road and held up and commandeered a Japanese truck. I subsequently heard that he had gone to the Japanese guard house, demanded to see the senior Japanese officer and an interpreter (all prison camps had a Jap who could speak English). I understand that Captain Ross told Colonel Ishi, the Japanese commandant, that he, Captain Ross, was now in command, and that if Ishi did not do as he was told he would shoot him. I was in some minor position of authority in the camp, and had access to Corporal Phillips. I queried the wisdom of a two-man army talking to the Jap commandant in this manner. The corporal replied that Captain Ross was a mad bastard, but a brave one! Anyway, Captain Ross got away with it and from then on, things improved. Colonel Ishi was, I understand, executed as a war criminal . . .

Finally, a pink and white Australian officer arrived, and began to address the troops. Up piped a digger, who called out, 'What'd ya do, Mate, *walk* here?'

I remember that flags appeared from somewhere. We soon had the Stars and Stripes and the Union Jack flying over the camp. Later on, we flew an Australian flag . . .

Unfortunately, there were still a lot of very sick men in the camp, and I seem to remember there were deaths nearly every day . . .[6]

Leslie Hall wrote of the continuing deaths at Tamuan: 'The sad part was [that] for some, the unbelievable happening was just too late. The sounding of "The Last Post" was a solemn reminder all diseases and illnesses had not automatically ended the moment peace had been declared. Many had been too ill to even *learn they were free again* [before succumbing].'[7]

The raising of long-hidden flags was surely one of the greatest sights for sore POW eyes in mid-August 1945. Dickson remembered that one of his campmates had sewn a Union Jack inside his shirt, and its tattered, sweat-stained remnant was proudly hoisted at Nakom Nayok, while everyone sang 'God Save The King'. Even the Americans joined in, and one Texas farm lad came to Dickson with tears streaming down his face, put his arm around Dickson's shoulder, and sobbed: '*I sang* "God Save The King"! I cried tears as big as horse's turds when I did it, but *I sang it!*'

No flag was in the railroad car with Cal Mitchell in the marshalling yards at Bangkok: 'It was near midnight and we were a trainload of Australians and Dutch. When the announcement was made by a senior officer, the Dutch stood and sang their national anthem, and then we rose and sang "God Save The King". If there was a dry eye among us, it would have been an exception.'

The initial absence of their nation's flag caused much consternation among the Americans at Nakom Nayok, and Benjamin Dunn described how they laboured to create one:

> The Dutch soldiers had worn green straw hats with bright red linings so we collected some of those and salvaged the linings. I still had a single piece of white tenting large enough for a flag, and I had a piece of keel which was just the right shade of blue for the field. We carefully marked off the stars in the field and then colored around them with the blue keel, leaving the stars white. I still had a needle and some white thread I had unraveled from the canvas I had borrowed in Singapore; I helped to sew the red and white stripes together.
>
> We worked on the Flag for two days and finally completed it. A soldier and a sailor were appointed to stand at attention as the Flag was raised on the large bamboo pole that was erected in front of the American hut . . . I was chosen as the soldier . . . I remember the emotion that gripped me on that occasion. To see that Flag slowly raised to eminence over this camp of the enemy, at whose hands we had suffered for so long, was an experience the memory of which will remain with me forever . . .
>
> Our Flag was heavier than most because of the material in it, but a good breeze had sprung up and when the wind struck it and it rippled, it was absolutely breathtaking. It was the first American Flag we had seen flying for three and a half years, and when one was on the ground looking up at it, he couldn't see a flaw in it—and for what it meant to us, there wasn't a flaw in it or what it stood for.

When we got word that we were going to leave the camp, our First Sergeant took possession of the Flag. I haven't forgotten and won't ever forget that he took the Flag. I thought any of us who made the Flag should have had it . . . I hope he has it to this day and that he is as proud of it as we were . . .[8]

A homemade Australian flag, conceived by Pioneer Harold Ramsey in Japan, may have been the signal which brought the first relief supplies to POWs there (see Chapter 8).

Flags were among the precious items hidden in the hollow legs of those POWs who had endured amputations to avoid death from spreading leg ulcers. Kevin Nolan remembered British and Australian flags emerging from these novel hiding places, as well as his first post-liberation assignment:

Immediately Colonel Albert Coates, the northern equivalent of 'Weary' Dunlop, took command of the camp (Nakom Paton) and posted a piquet on the only gateway into the compound. This consisted of a sergeant (me) and six men.

Can you imagine how my knees knocked when, immaculately dressed in a loin cloth and bare feet, and armed with a bamboo stick, I had to explain to the two top Jap officers that they could leave the camp for the evening, but they must leave their pistols and swords in the guard house until their return! I am very proud of the fact that this order was accomplished mainly by sign language. I was completely astounded by the meekness of these formerly arrogant brutes who complied without argument.

These (same) two were two of about eight referred to in Cec's letter of September 29, '45, when I was detailed to escort them to a detention camp in Bangkok. Now dressed in jungle greens, and complete with boots and a hat, and armed with rifles, we sat them up on boxes on the back of a tray truck, whilst my two offsiders and I perched on the cabin roof very alert and watchful, maybe hoping they would do something foolish. They didn't; in fact they were so meek and mild, bowing and scraping, it was almost sickening. I handed them over to a Captain of a Ghurka regiment and left, feeling that they were in good hands—and that they had got the message that no nonsense would be tolerated![9]

Perhaps one of the most daring post-liberation forays was made by Ron Winning:

When the war ended, I was in Nakom Nayok officer's camp. About ten days after the end I was sent for by the senior Allied officer and myself, a British Captain and a Dutch Captain were ordered to proceed north with two trucks and two English-speaking Jap sergeants to find 1500 POWs somewhere in northern Thailand. We eventually found them, and took command.

Then an English officer, of Z Special Force parachuted in, and a few days later he gave me orders to take 40 unarmed men to the aerodrome at Takli and take over all the arms of the Jap aerodrome guard regiment. This I did, and ordered the Jap commander to hand over his sword. I still have it.[10]

Cal Mitchell recalled that the British had set up an underground headquarters in Bangkok, which was operating for quite a while before the war ended. When a young British major arrived at one POW camp, he was surprised to find that the Japanese there were still armed. So he had his signaller send a message to the headquarters in Bangkok, saying that the major was about to disarm all Japanese in his area. According to Mitchell, due to a lingering uncertainty on the part of Allied commanders as to whether the Japanese would abide by the Emperor's announced wishes, the headquarters sent a message right back to the major: 'Under no account disarm Japanese in your area'. The major replied: 'Have already disarmed all Japanese in my area', to which headquarters responded: 'Good show.'[11]

Good show indeed, all the way around, as POWs took their first bold steps of freedom.

6
A Would-be Correspondent

9 SEPTEMBER 1945: As a newspaperman, Dickson knew he was sitting on the biggest news story of the year, and he would have liked nothing better than to resume his profession right then, and cover the story as an eyewitness. The discovery, recovery and treatment of POWs had become daily page one news worldwide, and Dickson yearned to put his talents to use as a correspondent. But red tape would prevent such a transfer from taking place; he would have to be content with the slim satisfaction of learning, a couple of months later, that two of his articles did find their way into the pages of the *Argus*.

Dickson wrote this letter without paragraph indentations, in order to save paper:

Nakom Nayok
Thailand
September 9, 1945

Dear old Binks,

The mail position from this end has undergone a great improvement. We are now permitted to send four letters a week. If you don't receive the whole four from me you'll know that I've reserved an occasional one for 365 Elizabeth Street [the Argus *office]. Incidentally, I'm making an effort to have myself transferred to Bangkok on the news side. These things are not easy when one is still a member of the army, so nothing may come of it. But it's worth trying. In the meantime keep it under your hat. All of this does not sound much like going home! The position in that regard is at present obscure, and one can only hope that developments will be faster than would appear likely at present. Oct. 2 seems a rather forlorn chance! But however long it is I feel sure we both have the patience to see it out, old dear. The great excitement yesterday was a visit from Lady Louis Mountbatten. No other woman with her. She went down 'big' with the troops, and is certainly a charming*

57

personality. Pretty obviously she has been under a big strain but I should say she was a very capable woman. She was the first white one we had seen for more than three years! I saw Ken Kingston at Batavia, and last year at Tamarkan, where I spent 13 months. He left from there to go to Japan and I hope is safe. Ken Barrett also left on a Japan party, but as far as I can hear he was not on the ship that was sunk with a heavy deathroll among the prisoners. I was at Thanbuzayat, Burma, when the camp was bombed twice in June 1943. About 30 prisoners were killed in the two raids. On Nov. 29 last year, when the anti-aircraft positions close to the Tamarkan camp were bombed by 21 Liberators, the corner of the camp copped it and we lost 16 men. The A.A. [anti-aircraft guns] and bridge, also close to the camp, were raided several times in the following couple of months, but we were prepared with slit trenches, etc. and had only one more man killed. Most of these camps were slap up against military objectives. At Nonpladuk, 35 miles from Tamarkan, a railway junction, about 100 prisoners were killed in one raid. Another 40 were lost on a train that was attacked by aircraft. Taking these events into consideration, (with others not mentioned) and the enormous deathroll on the construction of the line itself, one is extremely fortunate to be kicking along still. However, enough of these unpleasant things. The food continues good & one is still laying on flesh. An RAF Dakota dropped more food to-day. It looks as if yours truly will be busy in the next day or two, as pay is expected to arrive from Bangkok. It's a great luxury, by the way, to smoke Players cigarettes, dropped from the air, after some of the muck, wrapped in any sort of paper you could get hold of, that we have had to put up with.
Love till next letter day my old darling,

Your ever loving

Pop

Dickson's frustration was compounded by the ability of a fledgling journalist, Rohan Rivett, who had been placed in an Australian Army officer's unit throughout his internment, to pull strings, get home first, and 'scoop' Dickson with a series of lengthy articles in the very newspaper at which Dickson was a staff editor! Because he was a civilian, Rivett was not troubled by military 'red tape' which bound Dickson to continue as a soldier.

Understandably, the editors at the *Argus* were only too happy to print Rivett's accounts. The series, which appeared in the paper in mid-September 1945, became the basis for his best-selling book,

Behind Bamboo, which Rivett managed to complete in November 1945, making it the first of many books published on this subject. At the time of its publication in May 1946, the *Argus* asked none other than returned Mining Editor T. Cecil Dickson to review Rivett's book. Here are some excerpts from his review, which appeared in the 18 May 1946 edition of the *Argus*:

> The tendency of some young writers to over-emphasize the first person is understandable. In this case the author's rather obvious efforts to portray himself as the war correspondent would have been more convincing had he shown greater concern for the accuracy of detail demanded by what, after all, is a job of reporting.
>
> Some of the errors which occur in this book are venial offences against a cardinal principle of journalism. Others, such as a grossly inaccurate statement of the time and place of a fellow-prisoner's death, which occurred more than 1,000 miles away and a year later than is stated, are unjustifiable. Working against time to catch the book market while it is still 'hot' is no exoneration.

Although he later became well known as a campaigning newspaper editor, Rivett was a controversial figure in the POW camps. He had been employed as a trainee at the Malaya Broadcasting Corporation for about three months when the Japanese over-ran Southeast Asia, and Rivett, along with many other British subjects, was captured in Sumatra. He was interned with survivors of the HMAS *Perth* and USS *Houston*, and eventually reached Java.

Rivett's father, a well-connected figure in Australian government and social circles, feared his son would be killed by the Japanese, who tended to view journalists, and especially correspondents, as spies. So the elder Rivett requested that Rohan be assigned to the Australian Army. Brigadier A.S. Blackburn agreed to place the younger Rivett under his command, giving him all privileges of officers' rank, including the Officers' Mess. This irritated many commissioned officers; as one reflected some years later: 'In our unit there were many young men from backgrounds of privilege or influence, but they chose to enlist in the ranks, like everyone else, and never tried to use family connections to gain special favors.'

More irritating than Rivett's sudden arrival in their midst was his tendency to offer his somewhat liberal points of view in lectures to fellow officers. One one occasion, a Pioneer officer recalls, 'Rivett concluded a speech with these stirring words: "It won't be the British who liberate us; it won't be the Americans either. The great Red

Army will liberate us!" That went down like a wet sock with the troops, of course.' Several former Australian army officers also noted that because of his civilian status, Rivett was never sent to work on the Railway or put in charge of a work force.

Far more welcome among the POWs was Lady Louis Mountbatten, wife of the British Admiral. This extraordinary woman insisted on visiting a number of POW camp locations immediately following the Japanese surrender, which was by all accounts quite a daring feat. She was tall and good looking; needless to say, her appearances were a great morale-booster to the weary POWs. Pioneer Lieutenant Gordon Hamilton, in a letter to his family just a day before Dickson penned his note, wrote:

> Lady Mountbatten paid us a visit yesterday together with her staff of two Colonels A.T.S. and numerous Army officers up to a Major General R.A.M.C., on a camp inspection. She was the most pleasant and natural person possible. Shook hands all round and chatted breezily for about half an hour. They say she is indefatigable, and already had visited some of our Jungle Camps inland. When communications were difficult, she wanted to be dropped by parachute, in lieu of any other means of coming. She arrived yesterday sitting in the very uncomfortable front seat of a battle-buggy, while her numerous retinue rode in comfortable limousines. It was a thrill meeting her, though.[1]

Lady Mountbatten visited Tamuan camp as the British POWs were being flown to India. Harry Whelan remembers the day: 'By this time we all had a shirt, a pair of long trousers and a pair of khaki sandshoes, so we were able to look fairly tidy for her ladyship. [She] visited the so-called hospital, which was just an ordinary hut with no medical facilities whatever. I believe she was appalled at the way the Japs had behaved toward POW.'[2]

On the eighth anniversary of the terrible Allied air raid at Tamarkan camp, Dickson wrote an article for publication, describing in dramatic detail the events he refers to in his letter. The published version has not been located, but his original draft was recently discovered by Mrs Dickson and it appears below in its entirety. The reader may note that the first person singular pronoun does not appear once, and only in the last paragraph does Dickson reveal that he was an eyewitness to the events:

OUR BOMBERS CAME
The 29th of November is a date which British prisoners of the Japanese at Tamarkan, Siam in 1944 have cause to remember.

Eight years ago to-day Allied aircraft launched a long series of attacks aimed at a railway bridge and Japanese anti-aircraft post just outside the camp boundary. It was the beginning of the end of a long captivity. But it added a new hazard, bombs dropped by friends, to an already hazardous existence rife with death, disease and malnutrition.

A week or so before the attacks began, Allied aircraft dropped pamphlets in the vicinity of Tamarkan camp. They were addressed 'To all British Prisoners of War'. They surveyed the successful progress of Allied operations in Europe and the Pacific, and concluded: 'Take heart; we are coming. (Signed) South-East Asia Command.' After November 29, when the ground shook with 1000 pound bombs exploding and machine gun bursts at the attacking aircraft, one wit at Tamarkan suggested that 'Take heart; we are coming' should now be amended to 'Take cover; we are here'!

Allied prisoners in Siam, survivors of the force that had worked on the Burma–Siam Railway, were at the time concentrated mainly in five large camps situated along a 35-mile stretch at the Siam end of the new railway. These camps were Tamarkan, Chungkai, Kanburi, Tamuan and Nonpladuk. And not far from Nonpladuk, which was at the junction of the new railway with the old Bangkok–Singapore main line, was Nakompaton, a hospital camp housing some 7000 sick P.O.W.'s.

A year had passed since the new line was completed by forced P.O.W. and coolie labour. Through heavy jungle country, it linked, for the first time in history, the railway systems of Burma and Siam. For 12 months the railway had been used by the Japanese to transport reinforcements and supplies to their army in Burma. Its construction, which cost the lives of 15,000 allied prisoners, had taken more than a year. Late in October, 1943, trains were traversing its whole length, and by the end of February, 1944, most of the survivors had been moved to Siam.

Like Chungkai, three miles away, Tamarkan held 4500 Allied prisoners. Mainly British and Australians, as well as Dutch and a few Americans, they were under the charge of Lt.-Colonel [C.G.W.] Anderson, the Australian C.O. who won the Victoria Cross in the Malayan campaign. Life at Tamarkan was bearable after those hideous months in the jungle. There was not much work, and there was enough food to live on.

For a year, Allied aircraft had passed regularly overhead on their way to bomb objectives in and around Bangkok and the coastal areas. It was a source of infinite satisfaction to the inmates that, although the Japanese anti-aircraft guns invariably opened fire on the passing bombers, not once did they score a hit.

During September 1944, an ugly rumour circulated among the prisoners at Tamarkan. It was said that there had been a raid by Allied planes at Nonpladuk, 35 miles distant, and that 100 Allied P.O.W.'s had been killed by bombs that fell in their camp.

So persistent did the rumour become that senior P.O.W. officers at Tamarkan announced on parade one evening that it lacked official confirmation and should therefore be disregarded. The rumour unhappily proved to be true. Allied aircraft had carried out a highly successful night raid on the Nonpladuk railway junction, yards and workshop. The last stick of bombs had fallen in the P.O.W. camp. There were no slit trenches in the camp, and in addition to the 100 killed a further 100 prisoners had been wounded.

At Tamarkan, the fear grew that the experience might be repeated there.

Evening parade was held just before sundown, when for the second time each day the prisoners were counted and checked by the Japanese guards. On the evening of November 29, 1944, the fall-in bugle sounded as usual and the 4500 prisoners formed up in their various sections on the parade ground.

Apart from patients in the camp hospital, a few prisoners were exempt from the parade—men sick in their huts and members of a late work party which had just returned to camp.

Officers and NCOs were checking their sections, when the sound of approaching aircraft was heard. Eyes turned to the north-west. There, in formation, at an altitude of about 6000 feet, were 21 Liberators. They were headed straight for the camp. First reaction among the assembled men was of admiration; through the ranks ran that thrill of excitement that the spectacle of friendly aircraft never failed to provoke.

The Liberators continued their straight course toward the camp. Suddenly excitement gave place to misgiving. This time, it was obvious, the bombers meant business. The peace of evening was shattered as they raked the ground below with their machine-guns and cannon. In the anti-aircraft post, the Japs were caught napping, but not for long. They sprang to action and quickly returned the fire.

Forty bombs rained down, and the earth shook again with the concussion of their explosions as they buried themselves in the soft earth. The Japanese had opened fire just in time to destroy the bombers' aim. Intended for the anti-aircraft post, only three of the bombs went near their objective. Most of them fell between the post and the camp fence. Four fell in the camp.

With shells still bursting around them and flak raining down on the camp, the bombers passed overhead. Their silver bodies

glinted in the rays of the setting sun as they banked in a wide
arc, formation unbroken, to return in the direction whence they
had come. At that stage of the war their base must have been at
least 1000 miles distant.

Before the sun had finally dipped below the horizon, the
inmates of Tamarkan had begun to count the cost of that brief
visit. Had the raid occurred ten minutes earlier two or three
hundred men must have been killed; every hut was partly
wrecked.

Daylight had gone when all men in the camp except hospital
cases were called on parade again. A count showed that 16 men
were missing.

Next morning a pathetic procession moved out through the
camp gate. It was bound for the cemetery, a mile away. On
improvised stretchers were the bodies of fourteen men that had
been recovered.

Two of the stretchers were draped with large flags. One was
the Union Jack; the other a red lion on a yellow background—
the Scottish standard. For more than two and a half years these
emblems had been carried around in the kits of their owners.
Despite many kit inspections, the Japanese had never seen fit to
confiscate them.

Fourteen men were buried in Tamarkan that day. But the raid
had reduced the camp strength by sixteen.

And so the air raid siren had frequent use during the next few
months. For, in the words of the troops, it was 'on again' every
few days as Allied aircraft hammered at the large steel and
concrete bridge that carried the supply line across the river on
its way to Burma.

During one raid a prisoner was killed by a machine-gun bullet
from a low-flying plane, and another man lost his arm. The
canteen and one of the large living huts [were] burnt down after
being set alight by stray incendiary bullets.

On the other side of the picture, severe damage was inflicted
on the bridge, and eventually four of the five anti-aircraft guns
were put out of action with the loss of 150 Japanese lives.

Lt.-Colonel Anderson protested several times to the Japanese
that such close proximity to a military objective was no fit
place to hold defenceless prisoners of war. The Japanese were
unconvinced. Lieut. Naguchi, the camp adjutant, better known
as Bluebeard, had what he considered the unanswerable reply.
'You are soldiers,' he said; 'therefore you should be prepared to
die at any time.'

To give Bluebeard his due, during air raids he was the only
person in the area above ground. His buck teeth revealed by a

wide grin, he would walk about, oblivious of flying flak and bomb splinters and stray machine-gun bullets, obviously enjoying the whole proceedings.

By the end of February, 1945, even the Japanese found the position untenable, and they ordered abandonment of the camp. The flags were pulled down; and the inmates were dispersed among other camps in Siam. Only the cemetery remained—a reminder that Tamarkan P.O.W. camp once stood there.

What about the two missing bodies that were not found after the raid of the 29th November? Not until after the war were the facts about them revealed. Two British prisoners had taken advantage of the confusion and escaped to a nearby village where American paratroops had been placed. There they remained secure until Japan signed the instrument of surrender.

If only we had known that such a haven was so close at hand! It was as well, perhaps, that we did not. With all the good will in the world, the paratroopers might have found some difficulty in accommodating 4500 escaped prisoners.

One Allied aircraft was a welcome, though somewhat mysterious sight, flying daily over the camps. It was a Mosquito reconnaissance plane, and it flew very high, out of the reach of Japanese anti-aircraft guns. Cal Mitchell recalled: 'It was so high, all we could see were the vapour trails. The Japs called it the "come-look-see, go-back-speako" plane. When we got to Bangkok, we found out that the pilot was Australian, from Scone, New South Wales. His brother was a POW in the camps.'[3]

The airman had especially requested that assignment, as his way of sending signals of hope to his brother, so far below.

7
Finally, Some Money!

9 SEPTEMBER 1945: Again, Dickson uses no paragraph structure in order to save space on his one precious sheet of air mail stationery:

Nakom Nayok
Thailand
September 9, 1945 (sent by air)

My old Darling,

This is an unexpected note out of the blue, and I was lucky enough again to land one, although there were not enough to go round. I don't know how the ordinary letters are travelling. I should think by air—but if not then this one should reach you ahead of some I have written earlier. Still no sign of a move, but we hope for an unexpected order any day. As pay sergeant I had a busy morning. With tikals [Thai currency] valued at 7d. each, we disbursed more than 85,000 tikals among the Australians at the rate of 170 tikals per man to those who wanted it. I took my share. Although there's not a great deal to spend it on except food, which is plentiful anyhow, it might come in useful, and represents only p.5 out of the paybook if it is deducted, which is uncertain. I might take another look round the town—perhaps to-morrow. Have not been out of the camp since I was in there eight days ago. More excitement to-day. Another plane arrived about mid-day and disgorged bundles of clothing and foodstuffs (including Guest's Famous Biscuits!), marmalade, IXL [one extra large] jam, etc. This time it was not one of the mere twin-engined Dakotas, but a large four-engined bomber (R.A.F.) which disgorged the packages (some with parachutes & some without) through the bomb doors. Having done so it swooped down to the camp to less than 100 ft. before returning in the direction of Rangoon. I have no doubt these displays have [left] a nasty taste in the mouths of our yellow friends, many thousands of whom are down the road a couple of miles away. We are right in the depths of the monsoon now. For the last couple of months the rain has been in very heavy thunderstorms, quickly over. But it poured heavily the whole of last night, and looks like doing so to-night. Fortunately the atap roof above me does not leak. Incidentally, I have not slept in anything but a bamboo and atap hut for 3 years, so look forward to a civilised home again. These atap buildings are pretty airy affairs, usually with low eaves and no walls, with bamboo sleeping platforms, but in this warm to hot climate that is no hardship. With the departure of most of the British and the Maylay [sic] volunteers I lost quite a few friends. The Dutch are not popular but I had some good friends among them also.

Tons of love,

Pop

Serving as paymaster for the whole Australian wing still in Nakom Nayok camp, Dickson was at last able to distribute some pocket money to his countrymen—a little over five pounds, or roughly US$15.00, was the allotment. His letter touches on what was to become a raging controversy between ex-POWs and the Australian government during the next several years: how much back pay was due to POWs, and whether they were entitled to a meal allowance for all the meals they *didn't* have while in captivity (see concluding chapter).

The issuance of pay was a double-edged thing. On the one hand, the military authorities couldn't arrange to ship POWs home very quickly, so the stranded ex-prisoners were entitled to some 'walking-around money' while they waited. On the other hand, officials were apparently reluctant to put too much at one time in the hands of ex-POWs. This policy denied the newly freed men some of the simple first tastes of freedom, and was much resented. As Cal Mitchell remarked, 'They treated us like children, really; never wanting to give us much at a time. Some time elapsed before any pay was issued, and then only one pound per week [under $3.00]. Perhaps it was thought that the substantial sums in our pay books would be splurged on wine, women and song. It was most frustrating having so little money. A bottle of whiskey (so called) was one pound. However, it was discovered that banks in Bangkok would accept cheques and many of us availed ourselves of this benefit. The money was shared out and settlements were effected upon our return home.'[1]

In this letter, Dickson gets around to describing the grass huts in which he had been living for the past three and a half years (see the

The photo above was taken secretly by an Australian prisoner at Kanchanaburi, Thailand in early 1945, before it became exclusively an officers' camp. Prisoners are standing outside the rear entrance to long huts, constructed of bamboo and foliage. (COURTESY OF C.J. MITCHELL, AWM P1502/08) The photo below was also taken by an Australian prisoner, inside a hut at Tamarkan, Thailand, in early 1944. All POWs are clearly aware that the picture is being taken. The camera and film will then probably be buried in the ground at a spot known only to the owner. A prisoner risks severe beating or death if either the camera or film is discovered by the Japanese. (COURTESY OF C.J. MITCHELL, AWM P1502/03)

Australian prisoner gets his comrades to look toward the camera for another secret photo, Kanchanaburi, Thailand, 1944. Note the POWs' possessions hanging from the rafters and along the aisle. (COURTESY OF C.J. MITCHELL, AWM P1502/06)

two photos, taken in captivity, which show the interiors of these structures, pp. 67, 68). With characteristic aplomb, he claims that, given the climate, this hut structure was 'no hardship'. Nevertheless, a fairly clean hut, with intact roof, must have been a vivid contrast to the dilapidated ones he had often encountered along the way.

Although Dickson acknowledged he was looking forward to a 'civilised home' again, some ex-POWs took a while to get used to beds and mattresses. Harry Whelan remembers being given a kapok mattress to sleep on in Bangkok, but he and his companions all wound up on the cement floor, preferring the hard surface to which they had become so accustomed!

In his closing sentence, Dickson emphasises the unpopularity of Dutch POWs. As mentioned in Chapter 2, POWs of other nationalities, who had been put under Dutch command on Java, bitterly resented the swift decision by the Dutch to surrender there. In his book, Benjamin Dunn reflected the anger of many:

> On March 8, 1942, a Major . . . said in effect . . . 'The Dutch
> High Command has agreed upon terms for capitulation to the

Japanese. You are all to lay down your arms and surrender.' He continued with tears in his eyes, 'It is not the choice of the Americans—but the Dutch.'

This came as a real jolt . . . none of us had even seen a Jap . . . we were being forced to surrender by the Dutch and Javanese because they didn't want to defend the island. That Dutchman, who gave us that talk back at Camp Singosari, had lied when he said, 'We will fight shoulder to shoulder with our American, British and Australian allies and inflict severe losses on the enemy!'

The decision to surrender made by the Dutch probably did save the lives of many Australians and Americans, but it was held against them [the Dutch] for the duration of the war.[2]

In later years, discussing his quartermaster duties as a POW, Dickson would remark to his family that, despite his efforts to be scrupulously fair in doling out equal amounts of a pitifully small yak carcass to each unit, the Dutch would nevertheless frequently complain about their portion—'As if they somehow felt entitled to more than anyone else,' he would add in bewilderment.

Invariably, this attitude would provoke some POWs to grumble: 'It was you who got us into this mess in the first place . . .' And the Dutch did not exactly boost their popularity when Colonel Williams, on one occasion, discovered that the Netherlanders had eaten not only their own share of rations, but had consumed the provisions for the Australians as well.[3]

Leslie Hall noted that, oddly enough, although many of the Dutch captives had lived in Southeast Asia for several years, most were repelled by the version of rice served in the camps, so they tried to get more meat instead. He believed that Australian eating habits were a key to their higher rate of survival: 'The Australians ate everything available and sought more. The American troops despised rice and consumed less than their issue. The Dutch, although avid rice eaters normally, ate less than anyone.'[4]

As for the British, many soldiers had grown up in the cities of England, without access to a lot of fresh fruits and vegetables, so their diets had not been as well-balanced as those of Australians or Americans. Worse still, they were quite unaccustomed to rice; some even found it hard to swallow. Possibly these factors were key reasons why the British death rate was higher than that of any other POW nationality in the camps, according to figures from the Australian War Memorial and the Allied War Graves Registry.

Probably the most serious incident involving a Dutch POW

occurred at Tamarkan camp, when a Dutch interpreter was found to have turned in three Americans who smuggled several copies of a propaganda newspaper, *Bangkok Chronicles*, into the camp. As a result, the Americans were tortured and beaten for several days by the *kempe tai*. One of the Americans caught up with the Dutchman after liberation, and beat the daylights out of him. The American stopped short of killing the interpreter when told that the Dutchman was scheduled to be tried back in Holland as a Nazi collaborator.[5]

Of course, the Dutch were well aware of the resentment, and sometimes outright contempt, aimed in their direction by fellow POWs. Benjamin Dunn wrote of a touching deathbed confession made to him by one young Dutch flying officer, as both lay in a hospital hut: 'Knowing he was dying and being still rational, [he] talked to me of the shame he had of his fellow countrymen for their failure to resist longer and harder in the defense of Java. He said he thought Americans had a lot more courage than the Dutch and that we helped each other more in times of trial.'[6]

Dunn also credits a Dutch physician, Dr Han Hekking, with keeping the death rate remarkably low among American POWs. Dr Hekking, who had been born and reared in the Dutch East Indies, was assigned as camp physician to survivors of the USS *Houston* and the Texas 131st Field Artillery, who constituted most of the 668 Americans toiling on the Railway. (Dunn and 17 fellow members of the 26th US Field Artillery were assigned to the Texas unit in Java.)

At least one Australian found a plus in the Dutch outspokenness about entitlements. J.G. 'Tom' Morris recorded in his diary an incident when the Japanese Commander of all POWs in Thailand, Lieutenant Colonel Y. Nagatomo, visited the miserable 55 Kilo hospital in November 1943. 'The Senior Dutch officer, [speaking] fearlessly and in good English, took the occasion to berate Nagatomo for failing to distribute Red Cross parcels and mail, and demanded to have them. It was a great boost to our morale.'[7]

Within a month, that brave Dutchman was dead from starvation, disease and parcels sent but not distributed. He was laid to rest at Thanbyuzayat cemetery, along with 437 of his countrymen.

8

All This Mail!

Nakom Nayok
Thailand
September 12, 1945

*P.S. did I tell you that thanks to the RAF I now bathe with the
old favourite Lux soap?*

Dear old Binks,

*You'll be getting almost sick of receiving letters from me! I spent
yesterday in Nakom Nayok with John and another. On returning to
camp about 8:30 there awaited me three cards from you—July 23,
November 19 and December 31 (all 1944). Prompt mail service,
what! One of the Jap methods of being unpleasant seemed to be to
procrastinate over the censorship and handing out of incoming mail.
Had quite a good day in the town. Did nothing much more than
wander about, poke into about every second shop (of which there
would be quite 200, although the place is only a glorified village),
and dawdle over a couple of meals. Chicken is the usual motif,
served in open cafes in the roofed-in market. The usual buying of
'souvenirs' goes on but I have seen nothing as yet that I should care
to take home. One of the features of Nakom Nayok (which we
pronounce Nakom Nai) is the fast-flowing river which divides it
roughly in half. One crosses it in small boats propelled by one oar,
at 10 cents a crossing. Keeping it up against the swift current is a
work of art. John, as usual, was frequently surrounded by large
numbers of kids, who are legion, and who up to the age of about
five wear only their birthday suits. They all have the expression
'OK—, No. 1' with which they give the thumbs up. With my new
shorts and shirt I wore the old webbing belt, which I have managed
to preserve! Before setting out I had to let it out a hole in each side,
and it was still a little tight. The East doesn't seem to cater for No.
10 feet, so I had to wear clogs, which are simply a wooden sole
with a single strap across the toes. The last pair of socks I possessed*

was the one I bought at the Leviathan. You might remember the favourable comment they produced on the beach at Pt. Lonsdale from Mesdames Pratt and Purcell. They have, however, been defunct for more than two years now. I was very pleased to hear that [Leo] Cornelius was safe home. He, [Vic] Clifford and [Jack] Hocking I knew. They are the only three of whose return we have heard. They were certainly very fortunate. I was not considered for the Japan parties, being at the time classified as sick and over 40. We expect a move to Bangkok in two or three days—thence, let's hope, it won't be too long before we continue to Singapore and so home. And, let there be no moaning at the bar when I step ashore! That, perhaps, does not convey what I want to say, which is—a quiet reunion somewhere with the old Missus without any beating of drums or fanfare of trumpets. I'd like to arrive unexpectedly and walk in through the door. But whatever the circumstances, it will be the best day ever, and I won't really mind how it occurs. Cheerio, old darling.

Pop

The most recent communication Dickson had received so far from his wife was penned on New Year's Eve 1944, as she faced the beginning of a fourth year without a glimpse of her beloved husband. Several accounts by ex-POWs indicate a remarkably efficient delivery system by the Japanese High Command, considering the remote location of most POW camps. The cruelty was on the part of local camp commandants, who simply refused to distribute incoming mail, and who were consistently lax in sending out the pitifully few post-cards POWs were allowed to write, judging by the arrival times of those cards in Melbourne.

Newly-liberated POWs in other locations found large sacks of undistributed mail; often they knew just where to look. As Dickson remarked, this was just 'one of the Jap methods of being unpleasant'.

Along with undistributed letters, POWs and their liberators frequently found unopened Red Cross boxes, the contents of which were often rancid or rotted beyond use. Failing to distribute these parcels, which usually contained lifesaving medicines as well as food and clothing, went beyond 'unpleasant' and crossed over to criminal behaviour. Perhaps because prisoners had only recently been moved there, no Red Cross parcels were stored at Nakom Nayok; clothing was in especially short supply, and the first new clothes arrived by air-drops.[1]

An Australian prisoner dares to carry his camera outdoors, while POWs of all nationalities line up at a canteen, Kanchanaburi, Thailand, 1944. 'Coffee' was usually burnt rice and hot water. Note the remnants of uniforms and makeshift utensils: no new clothing or supplies had been issued in over three years. (COURTESY OF C.J. MITCHELL, AWM P1502/07)

Efforts by the prisoners to preserve, patch and mend their clothing for three and a half years were a true test of ingenuity. As mentioned earlier, most of the Pioneers' gear was on a second ship, which steamed for Australia while the *Orcades* deposited the Battalion on Java. So when captured, members of the unit had only the clothes on their backs, and whatever spare articles they might have in their backpacks. Luckily for the Pioneers, they were not inclined to trust the assurances of the Japanese, who told all POWs that everything would be provided in new locations, and they need not trouble themselves to carry such things as utensils or first aid kits. Unhappily, many British soldiers did take those assurances at face value; as a result, the Australians felt obliged to share suddenly precious utensils, so that fellow POWs might at least have a container to hold food rations. And the contents of small, personal first aid kits became prized like gemstones, until they gradually disappeared.

Probably the most foresighted of newly captured POWs was Harry

Bishop, a member of Dickson's C Company. After the surrender in Java, Bishop spotted a Chinese businessman who sold cloth. 'I thought maybe it might be useful to have some military cloth with us, so I bought a bolt from him, signed for it, and told him I would pay for it later, *which I did*,' he emphasised proudly. 'I carried it with me from Java to Burma, and it certainly came in handy. Quite a few men were able to patch up their garments with pieces of that cloth.'[2]

Although Dickson mentions in this letter that he wore clogs to town, once his boots rotted in the jungle he was barefoot during most of his captivity. Years later, Margaret Dickson marvelled at her recollection of how intact Cecil's feet were. 'There wasn't a mark on them, in spite of all the years of tramping over rocks and thorns and what-have-you. Even Cec wondered at his luck of never scratching or cutting his feet while building that infamous railway!'[3]

Dickson also told about how a tailor in one camp advised him to cut his trousers into shorts, which he did, salvaging the extra cloth to serve as two pillows. One by one, the 'pillows' were used to patch his shirt, in an effort to keep the scorching sun off his back.

Predictably, the subject of clothing became a sore point between the Pioneer Commanding Officer and Japanese authorities; equally predictably, the Japanese withheld needed items, even when available.

As early as February 1943, Colonel Williams already painted a desperate picture regarding clothing for his men. A diary entry reads:

> A general warning, 'If any man received any clothing and still had some in his possession, he would be punished'. How they expected men to work in any kind of weighty cloth in the tropical heat, is beyond anyone's imagination. But, the Nipponese did!
>
> In day time, and especially out on the line job, the temperature feels anywhere in the vicinity of 120 degrees Farenheit, as men haul the ropes to pull up the piledriver or swing a pick and/or shovel.
>
> As the line of men moved along and they were seen to be wearing any kind of rag at all, no shirt or shorts were issued.
>
> If what they were wearing was torn or worn out they were told to mend the article concerned. The fact no needles, cotton or material of any type was on issue, mattered not. As far as the (well named) Economy Officer cared, if they were wearing something, that was it. They were clothed, even if it was merely a 'G' string that only protected one's modesty, it was sufficient.
>
> The fact it was completely beyond the point of repair due to climatic conditions still did not matter . . . A lad, wearing a pair

of shorts that could only be accepted as a grass skirt, was refused a replacement. Not one man in the whole camp had received any clothing replacement for over twelve months. The shorts, or part thereof, they wore had been issued to them in the Far East, being their last issue of clothing (one pair of shorts each); no shirts since the Middle East. Every pair of shorts now worn had long since lost identity as such. What they wore was merely rotted material.[4]

By mid-September of that horrible year, writing from the filthiest camp conditions yet encountered, Lieutenant Colonel Williams fairly exploded with words in his diary:

> Time and again Force commanders have made appeals to the Jap. authorities for an issue of suitable footwear to all POW. On rare occasions clogs and rubberised slipper type of footwear have been made available, but never in a quantity. In any case what [were] issued were not suitable for the work being done and were so fragile they soon wore out.
>
> Major Meagher was aware boots were stored at the Base camp and were to remain there until the rainy season was over. So much for the vaunted kindness of the Nipponese![5]

It probably would have been no consolation to POWs if they had known that 'G' strings were the common attire for Japanese peasant farm labourers, an observation made by women prisoners on Sumatra, as they noted that Japanese soldiers who guarded them reverted to their customary garb of civilian life. Women prisoners were even ordered to sew such loincloths for use by their captors, but they sweetened the task by sewing pins inside the hems, and embroidering an occasional thistle on the corner, as an exquisite subliminal message.[6]

The enforced daily toiling of POWs in the jungles of Burma and Thailand probably marked the first time that people of northern European descent had been used as coolie labour in such a tropical climate, and the lack of proper clothing cost many dearly. For the rest of his life, Dickson would be plagued by cancerous skin lesions, which were periodically removed.

The Japanese were aware that fair-skinned Caucasians were at greater risk of developing such problems, and Dickson's light complexion, together with his age and health at the moment of selection, spared him from a hazardous voyage to Japan, and a new experience of forced labour. The selection of POWs to work in the factories and shipyards of Japan was another clear violation of Article 31 of the 1929 Geneva Convention, since the locations to which prisoners were sent exclusively involved the manufacture of products for use in the war.

A total of 115 Pioneers were picked to be shipped to Japan, in a move which journalist and former United States submarine officer Clay Blair Jr recognised as particularly cruel—plucking POWs at random from the midst of their friends, and throwing them among strangers to perform yet another type of hard labour in their captor's homeland.[7]

On 24 June 1944, a ship carrying fifteen Pioneers was torpedoed and sunk; nine members of the unit drowned. The remaining six continued their journey to Japan on another vessel; they were all recovered there at war's end.

An even larger contingent of Pioneers, 73 in all, left Saigon on 4 September 1944. Eight days later that ship was also sunk by United States submarines, near Formosa, and 55 Pioneers drowned. The luckiest survivors included those mentioned by Dickson in his letter: Leo Cornelius, Vic Clifford and Jack Hocking. They were among nine Pioneers who were finally pulled aboard the very submarines which had attacked their convoy.

As mentioned in Chapter 4, great secrecy surrounded the rescue of these men. When they passed through Guadalcanal on their way to Australia, security was so tight that no one stationed there had any idea of the ordeals the POWs had just endured. Edith Monks Stark was a 28-year-old American Red Cross worker, helping to operate a service canteen on Guadalcanal at that time. She remembered:

> A truck passed us, carrying a group of Australians. They were skin and bones—such scarecrows—and they looked so sad. I was told they were prisoners of war who had been rescued. I asked why they looked so sad, if they were on their way home. I was told it was 'because nobody expects them'. When we pressed for more information, we were told their families didn't even know they were alive, and some of the wives might have remarried. So they were going home to a very uncertain future. I never saw the group again, after they passed by in the truck.[8]

For 48 years, Edith Stark's puzzlement about the sad-looking Australians remained, until a chance conversation in Shelter Island, New York in May 1992 brought forth the truth.

By an odd coincidence, another nine Pioneers were rescued from the same torpedoed ship, the *Rakuyu Maru*—but by a Japanese vessel. Typically, the Pioneers had found each other, and most managed to cling together, floating on real or makeshift rafts, until they were allowed to climb aboard a Japanese cruiser.

Probably the luckiest Pioneers selected for what they termed 'Japan Parties' were the 27, including their Chaplain, Padre Kellow, who remained in Saigon after the Japanese decided not to attempt another shipment of POW labour to Japan.

Several detailed accounts have been written about the incredible experiences of those Japan-bound POWs; quite a few have been sought out and interviewed over the years. However, no one ever tracked down George Carroll, who along with Bill Mayne, Harold Ramsey and six other Pioneers, was among those hauled aboard the Japanese cruiser mentioned above, to continue their fateful journey.

Here, for the first time, is Carroll's story, as told in a lengthy interview in Melbourne in October 1991. Carroll's narrative is augmented by the recollections of Bill Mayne, who shared the same experience, both at sea and in Japan, for ten months in 1944–45:

> The ship was sunk at 2 a.m. We jumped overboard, then got back on the ship during the day, till evening when it sank. The torpedo missed the hull. Only one person was killed on the ship. He was a Jap!
>
> We scrounged supplies. The Jap escort vessels came back. The lifeboats were adrift. I was one of the last ones off the ship. There was a small dinghy with two Japs in it. It sank. I and one Jap got back on it. We thought the escort vessel would pick up POWs. By nightfall we got 14 lifeboats rounded up. There were about 20 to a boat. I was with Rowley Richards and Vic Duncan. We tied the boats together. A typhoon came up, and we cut loose. Three boats stayed together, but when we woke up we were all by ourselves. We heard machine gun fire; we thought a Jap sub had surfaced.
>
> We saw ships in the distance; they passed. We thought they were mirages. On the fourth day, we saw three ships. They were Jap cruisers. They picked us up. As each POW climbed aboard, we got a hit in the head or back with a baton or rifle butt, or whatever they had handy. I fell back into the lifeboat from the force of the blow, and had to climb up and get another whack. They put the POWs in front of a double-barreled gun. The captain spoke English. The Japs had no rations, hardly. They gave us broken biscuits soaked in brandy.
>
> We went to a port, Sangai, in Hainan Province, China. We were put on an oil tanker. There was an air raid that night. The bombers missed us—bad shots!
>
> We were on a US whaling vessel which had been captured by

the Japs and re-named the *Kibibi Maru*. There were 150 POW on
board. Everyone was packed below deck for three or four days.
They were steel hatches. We were being constantly fired upon
by Allied ships. On the fourth day we were allowed up for fresh
air. We met the commander—he hadn't been home for eight
years! He was in charge of troops going to Japan. He improved
our conditions.

There were 20 ships in our convoy. When the shooting began,
our ship turned to avoid a torpedo, and a boatload of Japanese
women and children got the torpedo. Finally, we saw Japan. It
was a thrill! We had just half a cup of water and a rice cake per
day. As we came into Tokyo Bay, the ship behind us got
torpedoed.

By the time we got into Moji, I could hardly stand up. I was
half blind, and covered with oil. The Japs gave each of us a
small box of rice and a turnip—that was it!

Mayne adds:

We boarded a train at Moji and travelled northwards we
thought, although the blinds were drawn and we were told not
to look out. We managed to peek now and then. We arrived at
Yokohama station where we detrained amidst a crowd of curious
Japanese workers who just stopped and stared at the bedraggled
men who got off the train. Some of us were naked; some had
on only a pair of shorts. Eventually the guards produced some
blankets for us; apart from our nakedness, the day was very
cold. [The winter of 1944–45 in Japan was the coldest in 42
years.]

Fifty of us were sent to Kawasaki, a camp in a compound
with a bamboo fence containing a long hut, Jap sergeant and
guard quarters, communal bath, kitchen, store shed and small
parade ground. Everything was constructed of bamboo. The
camp comprised mainly American and Dutch POW.

Carroll continues:

Kawasaki was not too bad. We walked to Yokohama to work,
at 4 a.m. We worked till dark, making submarine fans and
wheels for trains. We got two meals a day. If you worked well,
you'd get one cigarette a day. This—*Pommy*—tried to get us to
follow this work incentive. *We—didn't—want—to—do—that!* The
British were in charge of our workforce. There were civilian Jap
guards in our camp, and military ones at the factory. The
Aussies had to follow what the Pommys said.

Mayne remembers an especially hard rule:

A rule of the camp regarding sickness: you had to report to
the doctor the night before to be excused from work, and still
have to front the Jap sergeant for his OK. On this particular
morning, I awoke with a fever and high temperature; but
because I had not reported sick the night before, I marched
off to work. On arrival at the industrial works I asked the guard
could I lie down on one of the benches in the canteen where we
had our midday meal (I had a temperature of 103). He said OK;
I had just lain down when the Boss guard (we nicknamed him
Rubberneck) started laying into me with a five foot hectonal
(an inch-thick stick he always carried); after that he bashed me
around the head and told me to follow him. He took me to the
section where I worked (I was in a section where we made
condenser tanks for submarines; my job was to take the buckles
out of quarter-inch and half-inch 20 ft. by 15 ft. steel plates,
with an 8 or 16-pound sledge hammer). Rubberneck spoke to
my Jap foreman and the next thing I was told was to swing
this 16 pound hammer all day, non-stop. I was afraid to stop,
because after we finished work for the day we were taken
upstairs to a disused canteen, and if you had been noticed talking
to the Japs or not working, your number was called out. Then
they practiced jujitsu on you. Some terrible beatings were
received there.
    A lot of the boys had trouble holding their water after being
fed a diet of rice and very watery soup three times a day, every
day; so by the time we were ready to start our walk to work
(approximately three miles), many had bursting bladders. After
walking in the snow with only sandshoes for footwear, blokes
would begin relieving themselves as we walked along, leaving a
telltale trail in the snow. The Japs did not like this; if you were
caught you got a bashing. To overcome this, those with severe
problems carried a tin or bottle in their overcoat pocket and
emptied it at work.[9]

It is interesting to note that British, Australian and Dutch women
held captive on Sumatra were repelled at the constant sight of Japanese soldiers relieving themselves at will, anywhere they happened
to be, in front of whoever might be around at the moment.[10]
    Carroll's narrative continues:

Toward the end of 1944, the air raids began. Tons of ammo
were blown up. We heard bombs being dropped. We saw
Tokyo burnt to the ground. There were 800–900 planes one
night. They dropped canisters of fireballs. Everything wooden

between Yokohama, Kawasaki and Tokyo was burned. We lost
a few POWs in those raids.

The Japs took us to a market yard. We didn't know what
would become of us. We went to a factory at Kawasaki. We
slept and worked there. It was 24 hours a day of work. We
thought surely the bombs would come, and they did. We went
to another factory, at Yokohama, after the first one was bombed
out. We made submarine plates there.

In Yokohama there was snow. We had no boots. We were
given shirts and pants made of material like hessian bags, dyed
green, to wear. The more dirt and grease we got on us, the
more it kept us warm. We wore caps with our names and a
number on the back. We would sweep the snow off the
equipment, but it was snowing so hard, it came right back.
The hessian cloth was thin, like paper. Things got bad; there
were more guards.

A Jap general gave each of us a Red Cross parcel, with a
pair of boots and some clothes in it, because Prince Konoi was
coming to inspect our factory. They took back the clothes after
the Prince finished his inspection.

On Christmas, we got half a day off. We had a Red Cross
box, shared by six people. I saw the interpreter shaking the Red
Cross boxes, and taking what he wanted, before we got them.

Mayne remembers more about George Carroll and Red Cross
boxes:

Christmas 1944 we received one Red Cross food parcel between
three men. That was the only food parcel we got in Japan apart
from the two we got illegally; this came about through an air
raid. One night we had just finished our evening meal when the
sirens started. We were ordered to get into our bed and we just
laid there and listened to the krump of the bombs falling; they
were getting closer. All of a sudden we were told to grab
everything we could and get out quick. When we got out the
sky was bright with the glow from the fires, which were
engulfing us as far as we could see. We had only gone about
100 yards when a stick of incendiary bombs fell on our camp;
all went up in flames as we watched. After walking for miles
dodging the fires, we rested in an oil refinery for the night.
In the morning we marched through the burnt out streets of
Yokohama and surrounds. Eventually we got back to our work
factory where we settled down in another disused canteen.
While we were looking at what belongings we still had, George
Carroll produced two Red Cross food parcels, which he shared
among a few mates, myself and Harold Ramsey included. It

appears that while everybody was in a hurry to leave camp, George went to this shed where the parcels were kept and helped himself. He carried them all night at the risk of severe beating or death.

During air raids we were ordered down into the shelters, such as they were, very little ventilation and only room to stand. Nobody could sit, and to pass the time we would start a discussion on our main topic: food. If our mothers and wives could have listened in, they would have heard how their meals were appreciated and missed. We had Dutch wanting to know how Aussies cooked; Yanks asking how the Dutch prepared food; and so on. We all had a special recipe we were going to try when we got home. Hunger was always with us.

Carroll tells how things began to change for the better, as 1945 began:

On New Year's Day, 1945, they came around again and transferred the healthiest of us to Niigata, a rural town farther north. It took us three or four days to get there. The POWs were allowed to listen to radio news and to read the [local] papers. We were astonished till we figured out why—there was no news of the war in their papers. The people didn't even know there was a war on!

It was a pleasure to walk to work, between the seaport, the airport and the factory. There were much easier conditions. We dug a hole under the fence and got food. It was worth the little bashing if we got caught.

Once again, Carroll has omitted his role in a truly remarkable episode. Mayne gives the details:

[Niigata] was an industrial city straddling a river. Had the Japs not surrendered, we learned later, Niigata would have been next on the list for an atom bomb. [It] was a more relaxed camp, with electric light that the occupants made good use of, by making frypans and many other electrical gadgets. Just about every second night we would have a blackout—somebody was testing another invention!

During our stay there, [Pioneer] Harold Ramsey had a birthday. He wanted something special for his meal on that day. One day just before his birthday, while walking back to camp along the main road, we passed this vegetable garden. Harold suggested that we raid it that night. Our camp was surrounded by a high wooden paling fence, and every night each man had to do one hour fire picquet; a guard came around and asked your number. When your turn was up, you woke up the next person. We asked a mate, [fellow Pioneer] Jim White, to stand picquet in place of the bloke who should be doing the shift. We wanted him to stand guard and wait for us to come back. What we did was dig under the fence after the guard had done his round; then after we had crawled under the fence Jim filled in the hole and waited for our return. Outside the camp was a large railway siding where shunting was going on all night. We had to keep away from the fence because a battery of anti-aircraft guns were emplaced there. Having got past these obstacles, we had to go about 1000 yards to a highway; we crossed that and came into the field where the vegetables were. Trying to find what vegetables we wanted was quite some job in the dark; every so often we had to drop flat whenever a car or truck passed. Eventually we got enough to satisfy us and we headed back to camp where we gave our signal, hoping the guard had not noticed the disturbed soil—or perhaps was not standing right there, having a quiet smoke. Luckily, Jim returned our signal, so we started digging and finally got under the fence and back to our bunks. Harold got his special birthday meal!

While we were at work one day, word went around that the Commandant's chickens had been knocked off. Guards had been ordered to search all POWs to find the chickens. As it happened, a Canadian used to trap rats overnight and cook them up in the morning. This particular morning he was doing just that, when the guard came in and saw the can bubbling away over the brassière. He accused the Canadian of stealing the Commandant's chooks. The Canadian said they were rats, but the Jap, not believing him, set about eating what he thought was chicken. No more was said about the chickens, and the Commandant never did find out who pinched them.

Carroll reveals, among other things, another way the POWs supplemented their diet, at the expense of some university students who were helping the war effort:

There were 60,000 Japs employed in the factory. It was *very* big, and manufactured submarines. There were university students by the hundreds who also came to work here.

We were feeding the furnaces at a coke, coal and iron foundry. They gave you a basket of scrap iron—some of it was from Australia! You had to fill the basket, run up and stack it in the feeder. We sat down and began working much more slowly —we didn't want to help their war effort! We said we couldn't stand the pace—this worked! The Japs laughed at our Australian foolishness.

Ramsey and I got a job pushing two Japs around taking stock orders. This lasted one week; then we got the Japs to push, by bribing them with stolen food, and so the Australians sat in the cart.

The students came in groups of 50. They left their lunch boxes in a certain spot. The POWs stole their dinners. We ate 20 and threw the rest in the sea. Our baskets of rice were all dirty from the factory soot. When you went home at the end of the day, you weren't searched. We had enough tobacco and cigarettes copped from the students for 20 or 30 people! Jobs were allotted every day, but two Japs picked me and one mate, Ramsey, for the same jobs each day.

Soon the Yanks started dropping 10-ton sea mines. One landed in our camp, and went 15 feet down into the ground. One plane crewman who was shot down, gave info about how to defuse the bomb. He defused it, and the Japs made him part of our workforce.

We stood at the dock one night, and watched two ships go out and hit mines and sink. All crew were lost. We didn't work for four days while the bodies were cleared from the harbour.

We could see Nagasaki across the way, when we walked to work. One day as we were going to the factory, the air raid alarm sounded, and we took cover. When the all-clear sounded and we came out, we looked across and all you could see were just two chimneys standing. I'll never forget that sight. It was the result of high-explosive firebombs, *before* the atom bomb was dropped there.

Mayne adds that, during the final week of the war, 'Leaflets [were dropped] on our camp showing what damage a big bomb did, and underneath that a drawing of a small bomb and the amount of damage that did; so we knew something big had happened.'

Carroll's story resumes:

The bombing was stepped up. We had to help dismantle the factory to be shipped further north. The bigger bombs missed us—we were lucky. One day we looked and saw three planes from the USS *Lexington* strafing our camp.

The raids began in the daytime. We made an Australian flag —I'll have to give Ramsey credit for that one—to fly in the camp, hoping the planes would see us. We saw an aircraft carrier. [After the announcement that the war was over] All the Japs left the camp. Planes from the carrier dropped a parachute.

We raised our flag. Then they came again and dropped
everything they could from the ship! Guess they saw our flag!
Then five planes a day dropped 10 tons of supplies to POWs—
clothes, boots—they dropped one load five miles away. When
we got there, the Japs had scavenged all of it. There was a
population of 50 million Japs, and 200 POWs. We had to put up
a fence again to protect ourselves from the scavengers. We made
the Jap guards and police come back to protect us. For 10 days,
we began getting haircuts and boot shines from the Japs. It was
just like heaven!

A British official parachuted into our camp. He had a two-
way radio. We did not know another British POW camp was
15 miles away. They never got a thing. They were captured in
the Aleutians and were in desperate shape. We found them and
shared our stuff.

Mayne adds a poignant note about sharing:

[When the Americans dropped food supplies] There were
always some chocolates or cigarettes broken. All food was
now controlled by our quartermaster, and we had already taken
charge of all the rice the Japs had been holding, so by now we
had plenty to eat. Any broken biscuits, chocolate or cigarettes
we could help ourselves to; not many blokes were bothering
about them because we had all the food we could eat. A British
friend and I decided we would give some to an aged Jap who
had been our foreman. This Tommy and I had been on a gang
pushing small rail trucks around this vast area of railway tracks,
picking up all the different pieces of moldings from around the
various furnaces. Our Jap foreman did not harass us; he just let
us get on with our job, and just before our lunch break he
would allow us to go and collect grass which we would boil up
and eat with our rice. Other times he would give us a pipeful of
hair tobacco each, to smoke.

Armed with broken biscuits, chocolate and cigarettes, we went
to the factory and found out where this old Jap lived. We gave
him our gift, and he could not thank us enough; like us, he had
not seen these things for some time. He invited us to have a
meal with his family. We accepted, and when we left, both of
us gave him a note with our name, unit, number, etc. to give
the occupation forces, in which we outlined the humane way he
treated us. After we arrived home, we received word from the
American forces that he had been granted a double ration of rice,
for the kindness shown toward us.

Right after the Japs told us the war was over, they said they

Recovered Australian prisoners at Yokohama Railway Station, Japan, late August 1945, displaying a handmade Australian flag. Pioneers in the photo are Pte. George Carroll (far left); Pte. Jim White (fourth from left); Pte. Harold Ramsey (centre); and Pte. Bill Mayne (second from right). Unfortunately, in the confusion the flag was left behind in a US Army truck. (AUSTRALIAN WAR MEMORIAL, AWM 19202)

would have to stay and guard us from the civilian population. We were told to stay in the camp, but we had other ideas. My British mate and I went for a walk into town, and had a shave and haircut. The barber did the job with a cut-throat razor, and a few thoughts went through my mind as he was shaving my throat; but all went well, and he did not charge us for his services. In wandering around town, we came across a brewery, so we walked in there, picked up a case of beer and walked out. This was the first alcohol we had had for three and a half years, apart from a small glass of sake the Commandant had given us very soon after the cessation of hostilities, during a display of dancing by geisha girls.

It seems as if the Pioneers in Japan had a more pleasant, and less frustrating, post-liberation experience than their fellow members of the unit in Thailand, and a quicker start to their trip home. Carroll describes the stages of that exhilarating, final path to Australia:

At the end of August 1945 we travelled for one and a half days to Tokyo on a clean train, with Jap servants and white towels. When we got there we saw millions of civilians and Yanks. They escorted us to the airport. In the confusion, we left our handmade flag behind us in the US truck. I've always regretted that.

All our gear was burnt in the air raids. They gave us soap and a towel to shower, then we had a medical inspection and clean clothes. We went home either on a hospital ship or by plane. I flew out in a B-29. When we left Tokyo, the pilot took us over the A-bomb site at Hiroshima. We landed in Okinawa, and were there a month. The Japs were still fighting. We took off from Okinawa in a C-54, and crash landed in a snowstorm in Luzon. We landed in a field. For two weeks, while they fixed the plane, we were treated like royalty. Then from Luzon, we flew to Manila. We had to circle the airport, so they took us hedge-hopping through Corregidor.

When we landed in the military airfield in Manila and saw all those planes, we laughed remembering that in the factory [in Japan], we had five minutes of propaganda every day. They gave us figures of how many US planes had been shot down the day before. We knew the figures were so exaggerated, because if they were true, we knew there wouldn't be a plane left in the world!

Mayne remembers one thing about the Manila airport: 'When we landed there, a band started playing "Waltzing Matilda"—what a lovely sound! We realised at last we were going home!'

Carroll continues his homeward-bound recollections:

Prisoners of all nationalities were in Manila, at a holding camp where you got the OK to be shipped home. We were under American command, and we were treated real good. There were just six men to a tent, and a real mattress to sleep on. Someone made your bed and washed your clothes. The Americans waited on us hand and foot, and prepared whatever we wanted for breakfast. They gave us the privilege of making the Jap prisoners work, picking up litter while kneeling. If they didn't do it properly, we'd tip it over and make them do it again.

A doctor visited the sick all the time. We saw movies, and they issued us three sets of clothes. One rainy day, we were handed over to a British officer, because we were to be transported home on a British ship. He stood us at attention in the rain. An American officer came upon the scene, chewed out that Pommy real good, and sent us back in our tents and told us to rest.

A typhoon held up the boat which was to ship us home. We went out in pontoon boats to a British aircraft carrier, the *Formidable*. The waves were 10 feet high, and we lost some men trying to get aboard. I couldn't figure out why they didn't wait a while to have us board, but the captain of the carrier said he had to rendezvous with his fleet, and he was in a hurry.

We sailed into Sydney in November '45. I took a train to Albury, where I had worked and lived in a boarding house. I had no family, and the old lady who ran the boarding house had been notified that I had been taken prisoner and presumed dead, so she got rid of all my clothes and belongings.

I got two months leave, then came to Watsonia. I got 12 months leave, then got out of the Army. One of the first things I did when I got home was to get a set of false teeth. I had broken mine on Java just before we were taken prisoner—so I had no teeth at all for over three years!

Looking back, I can't emphasize too strongly my gratitude to the Americans, and their decision to use the atom bomb. I'm convinced it saved our lives, and the US saved Australia from the Japanese.

Just about every ex-POW interviewed during the preparation of this book has expressed that same sentiment, using almost the exact words spoken by George Carroll.

9

Moving Out

14 SEPTEMBER 1945: Almost a month to the day after hearing he was free, Dickson had finally started the first leg of his trip home; at last he was writing from Bangkok. Unfortunately for the ex-POWs at Nakom Nayok, their camp was located right in the middle of Japanese defensive positions in northern Thailand, and was described as a particularly difficult place to reach safely from points south.

For the first time, he refers to a specific major act of brutality about which he had just heard, committed on a Pioneer.

Bankok [sic]
Thailand
September 14, 1945

Darling old Binks,

Note new address! Day before yesterday we had a sudden order to be ready for the move next day. As everyone was becoming very 'browned off' at things, to use the Tommies' expression, the news was extra welcome. Travelled the 80 miles from Nakom Nayok yesterday by motor-truck with Jap drivers. Very unkind, perhaps, but I had a certain amount of pleasure in ordering the offsider of the truck of which I was in charge out of the front seat, which I occupied with another staff sgt. who was in the party, while his nibs climbed up in the back with the troops. Also a certain amount of pleasure in receiving the salutes of Jap. soldiers and officers en route. What a change! They do realise, I think, that they have lost the war, and have knuckled down pretty well to the changed conditions. The trouncing they have had in Burma, as well as closer to their homeland, no doubt has helped to make them see the light. Their attitudes toward us had eased considerably in the latter stages of our period as their guests, but some of them, even up to the last, were pretty truculent. The story has reached me in a letter from one of our officers of the bayoneting to death on August 14, last day of the war, of a Pioneer, after he had been kept tied to a tree for 23 days and fed on rice and water for 18 of them. If that story is true, which I believe it is, the Japs responsible will pay dearly for it. The journey down to Bankok [sic] took me back to many a run down the Geelong road in Lea. It is flat country, with paddy-fields as far as the eye could see on either side of the road. One different note was a narrow canal running alongside the road of a fair distance, up & down which an occasional barge, propelled by sail or oar, passed. We are in quite good quarters here. I believe it is the Chinese School of Commerce, recently occupied as Japanese Kinpie (military police) H.Q. Post-war mail has begun to arrive. Only A's to C's have been sorted so far. Look out if there isn't one from you in the D's! Last night we (John, 2 others & myself) went in to the city per the local taxi service, the vehicle being rubber-tyred tricycles, with a hooded seat for two at the rear. The place was rather dark as the electricity supply is not yet fully restored, it having been put somewhat out of joint by our bombs. Power stations, railway workshops, docks etc. here were hit hard, and the bombers used to pass straight over us at Tamarkan on moonlight nights to do it. There was little else to do than find an eating establishment, and wash the meal down with a bottle of beer each at the enormous price of 17 tikals (10/-) [shillings] a bottle. But it was the first for a long time, and it was good. Some of our convoy from Nakom Nayok yesterday were cut off & sent to another camp, at the University. Sixty of them left by air for Singapore this morning. So perhaps I might be next!

Lots of love,

Pop

The incident mentioned here by Dickson was detailed by fellow Pioneer Gordon Hamilton in an 8 September 1945 letter to his family. Hamilton also alludes to a second incident, involving another sick Pioneer:

We have just heard after the death of Pvt. Durkin of our Battalion. He had a bout of malaria and wandered off from a working party in north Siam, and was caught 2 days later. He was chained to a tree for 21 days, tortured and beaten, cigarettes butted on his face etc., and on the 14 Aug. last (2 days before surrender signed) was taken out and bayonetted to death after digging his own grave. One case of *many* such!

Poor old Lew Whitfeld died as a result of kicks in the stomach by one of our guards.

Not only was this extreme brutality inflicted on someone from their own unit but, as in so many other cases, the torture was inflicted for an act which had a perfectly reasonable explanation. And thus was drawn the line between major and minor war crimes: Private Durkin was not trying to escape; he was not concealing a wireless radio or a camera. All of these infractions were recognised risks. But this POW was delirious with fever.

The other death mentioned by Hamilton, that of Lewis Whitfeld, was especially devastating because it occurred right in the middle of their hut. Cal Mitchell told how it happened:

At the 131 Kilo camp, Lew was a walking skeleton and was also virtually blind. The blindness was caused by dietary deficiency [read: malnutrition caused by starvation]. He had big brown eyes, and he could hardly see out of them. I can still remember those beautiful big eyes. He had just come out of hospital and was sitting near us—we were playing cards on one of the bunks—when this Korean known as 'The Maggot' appeared. Of course Lew couldn't see him, and was beaten and kicked (for failing to stand and salute the guard). He died three days later of cerebral malaria.

Together with others I forwarded a statutory declaration to the War Crimes Tribunal. Just recently, in a book I read where, in 1947 in Singapore, 'The Maggot' was hanged for this crime. I had not until then known what had transpired at his trial.[1]

There is evidence to suggest that some Japanese military personnel sent to staff the POW camps considered themselves deeply humiliated and insulted by the assignment. It has been stated that they were, all too often, those who for some reason had been found inadequate to offer more active service to the Emperor. British writer Lavinia Warner, for example, interviewing a group of women who had survived Japanese internment, learned that their camp commandant had often expressed his feeling that to be put in charge of prisoners was humiliating enough, but to be placed in charge of *female* prisoners was doubly so.[2]

However, former interpreter Takashi Nagase pointed out in a 1992 letter to the author that many camp commandants were reserve officers, called back to serve in that capacity, and it was his observation that most seemed content with their assignment. But he acknowledged that some camp officers, especially younger ones, may have been disappointed at not having more glorious military

opportunities—and thus a greater chance for promotion in rank—
and concedes that they may have tended to take out their frustrations on the prisoners.[3]

Cal Mitchell noted that: 'Mention of the poor types of Japs and
Koreans in charge of POW was quite true. However, I am sorry to
say that this could be said of most nations. It is a natural thought
[for a commanding officer] when asked to supply personnel for other
units, to get rid of all the most useless or unpleasant people.'[4]

The most consistently vicious camp personnel were, by all accounts, Korean guards. Nagase, who had frequent contact with staff
personnel at many POW camps in Java, Burma and Thailand, states
that Koreans: 'All volunteered to be Japanese soldiers, but I am so
sorry that against their expectation, their treatment by the Japanese
[was] not good, and the training was so severe that they were much
disappointed. But they tried very hard to become true Japanese
soldiers . . .'[5] However, information supplied to Benjamin Dunn by
fellow American prisoners reveals that, toward the end of the war,
several Koreans relaxed a bit and began conversing with POW
officers. Some Koreans admitted that they were serving as camp
guards as their own prison sentence, having been convicted of some
crime back home. This revelation appears to give the term 'criminal
behaviour' a truly double meaning. As Dunn put it, 'Woe be to the
poor prisoners who happened to be in a camp guarded by Koreans
who were being punished or disciplined.'[6]

No doubt POWs took little solace in occasionally seeing the Japanese use swift brutality on one of their own staff. In a retrospective
1985 radio broadcast, one Australian ex-POW recalled standing in
the camp guardhouse and watching, in disbelief, as a Japanese officer
knocked a sergeant to the ground for a 'backtalking' remark. The
officer began kicking the sergeant, who never uttered a sound as he
was slowly kicked to death.[7]

The slightest appearance of insubordination brought such swift
punishment that it kept everyone's nerves on edge. Colonel Williams
noted in his diary: 'The guards are particularly vicious today, and
one lad had his head split open when struck with a heavy piece of
wood. When the Force Commander protested vigorously he was
told the cause of attack was due to a smile at the guard by the man
concerned. Prisoners are not allowed the privilege of smiling.'[8]

Of course, most POWs had no way of knowing that in the Japanese
culture, children are taught from an early age that expressions of
familiarity, even smiling, are regarded as acts of insolence, and must
be avoided.[9]

According to the Rescript for Soldiers and Sailors, written by Emperor Meiji in 1882, one's 'sincerity' made one's acts acceptable, as long as the act was carried out to fulfil duty to the Emperor. By the time a Japanese soldier finished his training, he had repeatedly been subjected to the situation he feared most: surprise and humiliation, because 'hazing' at the hands of upperclassmen was frequent. For the rest of his life, the recruit would look for a way to settle the score with an individual tormentor—but at the same time, he often couldn't wait to pass on similar humiliations to anyone who might come under his control. He was likely to graduate with a heightened insistence on respect; in his own training, a sudden blow was often used to teach 'insight', and a failure to show respect frequently led to disastrous reprisals.[10]

Even the continuing brutality of relentlessly driving POWs to work on the Railway far into the night, with no sleep, appears to have a precedent in Japanese military training. A British colonel who was allowed to observe Japanese training methods in 1934–35 once questioned the captain in charge of some recruits why he was driving the soldiers to a new task, after three days and two nights without sleep. Why not let them rest up and be fresh for the next day, he asked. 'They already know how to sleep,' the captain replied. 'They need training in how to stay awake.'[11]

The Japanese recruits in that training exercise may have been learning a form of discipline for a few days, but their exercise was not stretched for months on end while they were being starved and beaten daily. Colonel Williams observed that for the POWs under his command, 'On the Burma Railway we had no time to ourselves. We were building a railway for the Japanese and never at any time did we have any more than six hours sleep. On one period the men worked 72 hours without a break.'[12]

Some of the most baffling aspects of Japanese behaviour, as far as the prisoners were concerned, may have occurred in the weeks following surrender. Quite a few ex-POWs told stories similar to the one Cal Mitchell related, which occurred in Bangkok when a Japanese officer approached an Australian officer, extended his hand and said: 'Now we are friends.' Mitchell still seemed astonished at the recollection, even after a lifetime. 'Imagine! All the brutality and starvation was just to be put out of mind—he wanted the fellow to shake hands, just like that!' He snapped his fingers.[13]

One United States-educated Japanese woman has summed up her countrymen's outlook in a way which may offer some clue to the abruptly changing attitude which ex-POWs found so hard to fathom.

Michiko Asano, who has served as Vice-President for Education in the College Women's Association of Japan, recently wrote to a Wellesley College classmate: '. . . We Japanese . . . try to hide the things past which are not comfortable to talk about. For decades we have been doing this . . .'[14] Mrs Asano sees this pattern of behaviour beginning to change, but she recognises that for nearly half a century it has prevented young Japanese from learning much about their country's role in World War II.

For Railway survivors, the memories were too searing to dismiss with a handshake.

10

In Touch With Things Again

Bankok
Thailand
September 15, 1945

Dear old Binks,

Another day nearer home! Last evening one Sgt. Dixon and I paid a visit to Bankok's Chinatown, and had lots of fun. We dropped in at Chinese wedding feasts, private mah-jongg clubs—in fact anywhere giving forth sounds of life. The old (and not so old) Chinks dispensed hospitality in the shape of iced lemonade, cigarettes, and China tea, and we didn't remain long enough anywhere to outstay the welcome. I haven't yet located New Bankok, which I believe is quite modern and not unlike Haifa in Palestine. Perhaps to-morrow I might get there. One of the troubles in finding one's way about is that unless you take French leave you don't leave here until about dark. It is then raining & continues to do so for a couple of hours, so it's pretty dark with no street lighting in operation. Another handicap is financial. Owing to shortage of power the trains are not running at night, and the run into the city by jarru [tricycle taxi] costs at least 5 tikals. Meals begin at about twice that price. Cigarettes cost at least 20 cents each—that is the smokable ones. The Odeon theatre puts on pictures for the troops free every second night. The films are flown over from Rangoon. There is an excellent and substantive theatre in the grounds here to seat 500–600. It is being rewired for sound. To-night a concert is being held there. As I write I can hear the band rehearsing—the best music I have heard for years. I now have thank goodness a new pair of boots. A perfect fit. Put them on for the first time when I went out last night, and suffered none of the ill effects usual with

new footwear. My last pair konked out two and a half years ago.
We are gradually coming back into touch with things again. There
was a parade for General Shin (I think that was the name),
commander of the 14th British army, which did such good work in
Burma. He was driven out of that country by the Nips in '42, and
has been doing battle with them ever since. Knowing them as he
does, and knowing their treatment of prisoners, he is not letting
them down too lightly in Malaya and Singapore, where his army is
in occupation. Owing to the fat condition of the Jap major-general
who had charge of prison camps in Malaya and the somewhat
lighter condition of some of his former guests, he [Gen. Shin] told
us, he has the aforesaid major-general on a 'controlled diet'. That
gentleman is also doing a strenuous course of exercise in his bare feet
very close to the point of a bayonet—just to let him know what the
'exercise' he has given his former prisoners was like. Gen. Shin
remarked that he thought the Nip's physical condition would be
greatly improved at the end of a week's treatment! We also had an
Australian lieutenant along this morning who left home since the
war ended. He told us about conditions in Australia generally and
answered a lot of questions. Love to you old dear and remembrances
to family and friends.

Pop

Next to the rare religious services they were allowed, the equally
rare musical performances and outdoor concerts kept feelings of
hope and humanity alive for the POWs during their endless months
of degradation and death.

If one picture is worth a thousand words, the photograph on
p. 96 taken secretly in captivity and, like the others displayed in
these pages, buried, dug up and re-buried at constant risk of death
for so many years, says more than any verbal description could
possibly accomplish about what the opportunity to hear music meant
to these men who were starved in so many different ways.

For example, one Australian (wearing hat), seated in the right
foreground next to the man standing closest to the camera is so sick
he cannot hold his head up—but he is there. Further down the
line, another POW, seated, leans on a friend's back for support. According to donor Cal Mitchell, the picture was taken at Kanchanaburi
(also called Kanburi) camp in early 1945, when conditions had
improved somewhat, but the men are still pitifully thin. Note that
many are looking towards the camera, apparently aware that their

*This photo taken by an Australian prisoner at Kanchanaburi, Thailand,
in early 1944, shows mostly Australian and some Dutch POWs
assembling for a rare outdoor concert. No matter how sick, every man
attended. Note the POW seated in the foreground, wearing a hat, too
weak to raise his head. Several POWs look toward camera; photographer
was especially bold to attempt a snapshot at such a large gathering. The
low railing was also used as a communion rail for the equally rare
religious services.* (COURTESY OF C.J. MITCHELL, AWM P1502/02)

photograph is being taken, and probably wondering if it will ever be
seen by anyone. No doubt few dreamed that it might one day be on
display at the Australian War Memorial in Canberra.

In the POW exhibit at the War Memorial, several musical instru-
ments are displayed. They were crafted, hammered and pieced together from various materials, as Mitchell attests: 'At Kanburi, some
fellows were really quite ingenious. They made violins, using cat
and other animal gut; carved flutes from bamboo, wrote musical
scores from memory, and created an orchestra of sorts. When the
commandant was in a good mood, the orchestra was allowed to
give a concert now and then. Of course everyone came.'

Colonel Williams proudly describes one concert, on 20 November 1943, during the worst of the days on the Railway, as 'A
professional refreshing show that proved, beyond doubt, no matter

the suffering, there is always a group who can minimise miserable moments and build up morale'.[1]

If the entries in the Battalion commander's diary can be taken as a gauge, the November 1943 concert may have been the first since February 1943, which in turn was the first since November 1942. So 'every now and then' seems to have meant every six months or so.

Another POW, Australian Driver Thomas Fagan, also describes a rare 1943 concert, given by and for sick prisoners: 'Last night was a great lift for all of us; the Nips allowed the boys to put on a concert. Hard to believe how sick men can change so rapidly. A bit of a sing-song, some laughter, a joke or two and one's anguish is, for a few minutes, gone. We enjoyed the show even though those who rendered items did so only with a great deal of willpower. They, too, suffered from various ailments and a few propped themselves up on bamboo crutches. What a fantastic lot!'[2]

Leslie Hall mentioned that a frequent request at concerts was to hear a rendition of the 'Colonel Bogey March', commonly used in British training drills, and therefore one of the more accurate touches in the film, *The Bridge Over the River Kwai*. But most of the time, he noted sadly, the only music POWs heard with any frequency was 'Taps' or 'The Last Post'.

Prisoners were often punished if they whistled or sang on the Railway, but frequently at night some found a way to cheer up everyone within earshot by whistling tunes softly, or by daring to sing. Hall remembers one musician called 'The Tiger Rag King', who was apparently allowed to wander from hut to hut at the 55 Kilo hospital camp, playing his mini concertina. Far beyond the light recreation usually associated with wandering minstrels, his music meant so much because it was literally the only medicine available to those who lay and listened in the dark.

By contrast, the Japanese sometimes indulged in light recreation by picking POWs at random, and subjecting them to various forms of torment to fill idle moments, such as lunch breaks along the Railway. Artist Ronald Searle captured such a moment for all time in his drawing, titled 'Lunchtime Games', which is now part of the Imperial War Museum collection in London, and which is reproduced in his book of sketches and text, *To the Kwai—and Back*.[3]

On this particular day the selectee was an Australian, judging by his hat. All his friends could do was to gather nearby and glare or scowl at the tormentors, which they are certainly doing. Seated in a ridiculously out-of-place upholstered lounge chair (probably appropriated from a nearby prosperous Thai household) is the

Japanese camp overseer, with a red star on his pith helmet. His boot is propped against the prisoner's thigh, and he holds a sharpened bamboo rod to the POW's back. The emaciated prisoner, wearing only a loincloth and a bandage over his leg ulcer, is being forced to stand in the noonday sun, holding a heavy rock above his head. Of course he will soon waver, causing some amusement among his tormentors as he reacts to the bamboo piercing his skin. No doubt he will drop the rock before being signalled to do so, because he is too weak to hold it for long. This act will be an excuse for a beating, which a guard stands ready to perform, leaning on a cudgel like a minor-league baseball player who waits his turn at bat. After the beating, as a gesture of appreciation for providing them with this noontime diversion, the Japanese will allow the prisoner to have a cigarette, before sending him back to work on the Railway.

No wonder Dickson enjoyed hearing the British general's description of having the Japanese major-general do, as he phrased it in his letter, 'a strenuous course of exercise in his bare feet very close to the point of a bayonet—just to let him know what the "exercise" he had given his former prisoners was like'.

He was referring [not having quite heard the name correctly] to General Sir William J. Slim, who was very popular among the Australians, and later served as Governor-General to Australia. No doubt the general's talk to so many ex-POWs, gathered in Bangkok on their way home, was a well-planned event to assure them that those who were directly responsible for their suffering would not go unpunished. Like the carved artwork so often seen on court buildings, the general's speech was a welcome reminder that the scales of justice are still the best way to restore mental equilibrium for innocent victims of crime.

11

This Accursed Lack of Pence

16 SEPTEMBER 1945: Dickson displayed some rare peevishness as he struggled to keep up his morale, and wondered if he would *ever* hear from home—or get there!

Bankok, Thailand
September 16, 1945

My old darling,

In yesterday's letter I suggested that I might make an early visit to New Bankok. Funds not permitting, I have not done so yet. This accursed lack of pence hampers activities considerably, and according to latest reports there will be no pay for a week, when we receive 250 tikals or its equivalent in Singapore dollars, if we move before then. The tikal rate has jumped from 34 to 60 to the £1 sterling, but even with the increased amount it doesn't go far with prices at a high level. As in all of these countries, we are fair game for the local business people, large and small. Last evening, in search of cheap entertainment, Dixon and I walked across to Chinatown. Peering into the doorway of a Chinese theatre, we were invited in by the doorkeeper, so had an interesting hour or so for nothing. The colour scheme would have intrigued you. Almost every hue was represented on the stage and its surroundings. They should have clashed, but didn't. Costumes and headdresses glittered. The actresses were all young girls of the doll-like Chinese variety, while the male members of the cast were mainly long-bearded villains who posed and strutted and declaimed until retribution overtook them and the sword removed their heads. Leaving there, we drank iced coffee and ate fancy cakes at a restaurant with a European flavour. It was a typical sticky tropical night, and after wandering about watching the sights for a while we retraced our steps. Nearer home we dropped in

*an open air market cafe and sipped more iced coffee. Close at hand
we found another Chinese theatre, and spent half an hour there.
The show was comedy, which had the audience in a continuous
simmer of laughter. And so home. Today I had a daylight dash
about Bankok in a car with a Jap chauffeur in search of small
change for a few hundred tikals of canteen profits to be distributed
among the troops. This evening looks like free pictures at the Odeon
theatre. Nothing came of my effort to crash into the news gathering,
as the place is now teeming with correspondents. I hear there are
two 'Aussie' men here, including a photographer. Have not yet
contacted them. I don't know if you have seen the jungle battle dress
we are fitted out in. It is 'jungle' green drill. Trousers are similar
pattern to the Tommy khaki battle dress, with plenty of pockets
about them. The shirt when not tucked into the trousers is a tunic,
with four pockets and a belt of the same material. Boots are black,
with short puttees or gaiters. It's a good outfit and will be improved
when the hats turn up. The old one is battered—just a bit! Tell
Keith I was talking to Charlie Poulton today. Have also seen
young Mac Kingham, and we have here also Bob Kevinan of
Patchewollock.*

Love till next time,

Pop

No letters from you yet, but hoping!

Since none of Dickson's letters mentions the cheque arrangement
with local banks referred to by Cal Mitchell, it must be assumed that
perhaps only a few commissioned officers had discovered this source
of financial relief, or that the courtesy was extended only temporarily.
Mitchell arrived in Bangkok before Dickson, and departed sooner
for home. As late as 29 September, Dickson reported that 'The
banks are not operating on exchange yet'.

Most American ex-POWs were flown home before Bangkok's
inflated prices became an issue. But for the Australian and British
troops who had to wait for available ship transport, the euphoria of
freedom became increasingly edged with a new form of confinement,
dictated not by a guard but by an empty wallet.

So the hospitality of local people was much appreciated, and in-
vitations to private homes became prized commodities. Best of all,
such moments not only gave former prisoners something positive to

write home about, but also assured loved ones that they were capable of sliding into normal social activities with some ease, after all they had been through.

Gordon Hamilton (who came home on the *Circassia* with Dickson) wrote home about such a visit:

> The family that I met have been wonderfully good to me, and several others of us from this Camp. They are the kindest-hearted, most happy and hospitable people that you could wish to meet. They quite took us to their hearts and did everything they could to make our stay here as happy as possible. The family is: Mr and Mrs Serm. Saligupta, two daughters (the eldest seventeen), two younger sons, all from his first marriage, and a little daughter aged three. Then there are Mrs Serm's cousin, a very fine woman, well educated, been to America (her sister married the present Premier of Siam, lately the Siamese Ambassador to America), his uncle and their adopted daughters, all aged about eighteen. In my last letter I told you we had been out there to dinner the previous night with two A.B.C. [Australian Broadcasting Company] men. Well, they so thoroughly enjoyed the night, that they decided to make a recording of the party to broadcast in Australia. So last night we all went out there again with recording apparatus, and did the whole thing again. You will probably hear it in a fortnight or so. I hope to be home by then!
>
> We had a grand time—lovely food, Siamese dancing and music, and the fun of making the recordings. Today they came out to lunch with us at the camp—I think that they enjoyed the fun, but not the food. We had tomato soup straight out of tins, and I must admit that it was rather strong; cocktail sausages in tomato sauce; sheep's tongue with tinned peas and carrots; finished with tinned peaches and evaporated milk. It was rather a funny mixture and must have been very peculiar to them, unused as they are to European food. Then they took us out on a shopping expedition, and we made our fond farewells.

An even greater disappointment than the continued lack of funds, perhaps, was Dickson's revelation that he had not been able to cut through red tape and resume his status as a working newspaperman. His hope of being allowed to contact the *Argus* or another news organisation to receive such an assignment while still a member of the military ranks had apparently been dashed by the sight of so many civilian correspondents, newly arrived from all over the world. The best he could do as he later describes, was to assist in the professional news-gathering.

For ex-POWs, maintaining morale in Bangkok was a matter of battling some frustrations; as prisoners, maintaining morale in the camps had been a daily battle against despair, and finding ways to remember who they were.

During the grim days of October 1943, as the exhausted, rain-soaked prisoners struggled to complete the Railway, Colonel Williams made this entry in his diary: 'They return [from a long shift] weary, hungry, but defiant, as one man demonstrates when he brazenly whistles a tune entering the camp. He is real morale builder.'[1]

Turning harassment by the Japanese into an act of absurdity was a more subtle form of defiance, and any opportunity was quickly seized. Cal Mitchell recalls one such occasion, at Kanburi camp: 'One night, in the pouring rain, the Japs said there had to be another roll call. We were all in bunks, with clothes off. One man stood up and started to leave the hut naked. The others said, "What are you doing, going out like that?" He said, "Why should I get my clothes all wet, and have them soggy all night and into tomorrow?" We all decided that made a lot of sense, so 800 men went outside naked, and it was the Japs who got their clothes all wet.'[2]

Another time: 'We had to all line up and at 11 a.m. all face the north and bow and send our mental salutations to the Emperor on the occasion of his birthday. As we straightened up I heard the chap in front of me say, "If that old bastard receives my message he'll burst into bloody flames!"'[3]

Birthdays, anniversaries—indeed, any special occasions—were looked forward to with determination—a milestone to strive for, a certainty to count on. Defiance was still in his voice, a lifetime later, when Pioneer Jack D'Argaville said: 'We always knew we'd win, and we always said we'd be home by Christmas, by my birthday, by Easter. When that day would pass, we'd say, "next year".'[4] Many around him nodded in agreement.

Towards the end of the war, as the rumours became more persistent that the Japanese were about to capitulate, some POWs became openly defiant of the Japanese. American Ben Dunn was one:

> We were standing around a tent where some [Japanese] officers and non-coms were having a meeting. While we were waiting for them to put us to work, Henry 'Bull' Barbatti, a sailor [from the USS *Houston*], who was getting pretty cocky, decided he wanted a smoke and walked brashly in their tent and interrupted the meeting and asked for a cigarette. One of the officers gave him one and Barbatti said, 'No, I want three more for my friends.'

Almost any other time, this boldness would have earned him a good bashing, but this time, the officer simply gave him three more cigarettes. Barbatti came out grinning and distributed them among the three of us, but since I didn't smoke I gave mine back to him. He had earned it with his courage.

A few minutes later a guard came out of the tent and told us to move some 100 kilogram sacks of rice . . . I'm certain he knew that none of us could carry a 220 pound sack of rice, but he looked at me and told me to pick one up. Even when I had been in perfect physical condition, I could never have shouldered one without help.

Thinking how stupid the guard was to suggest such an impossible feat, and remembering how successful Barbatti had just been in his bold request for cigarettes, I couldn't resist replying, 'Pick it up and carry it yourself, you son-of-a-bitch!' I was positive he couldn't understand English because we hadn't heard any of those Japs say a word to us in English—just their gutteral Japanese.

As soon as I called him a son-of-a-bitch, he grabbed a bamboo pole, hit me in the head with it, and said in perfect English, 'Don't you ever call me a son-of-a-bitch!'[5]

If the struggle to keep spirits up was a daily task for POWs, it was equally so for their relatives back home—especially because of the sparse mail distribution. As Cal Mitchell put it, 'The contact with our people, or lack of it, was one of the most difficult crosses to bear.'[6] His sister-in-law, Eileen, remembered attending meetings of the Pioneer Battalion Relatives Association:

Jean [Cal's wife] and I used to go every Tuesday lunch time to the Battalion Women's Auxiliary meeting in the Railway Building [Melbourne] where wives and mothers gathered to share news and to chat. Being only a fiancee and not next of kin, I never held any office or did anything of note, but it was lovely to go and talk and listen. The mothers all seemed old and very gallant . . . The lack of all news was so appalling—hard to believe in this day of instant communication that it could happen. That fact speaks loudly of the utter disruption the war brought. I was absolutely thrilled when the first card came for me, at the end of 1943. There had been silence since March 1942 [when the unit was captured on Java]. The card was apparently written at the beginning of 1943—it had no date. Al had crossed out the printed words—sick, in hospital, etc., and left in 'well'. He said he was with three friends, Harry Bishop, Pemberton and Tranter. It was a good idea to mention names as we could then let other people know. The cards came at random and we all shared the joy of whoever had just got one—they came very seldom. Some men wrote things like: 'Tell this to the Marines', after saying they were well and happy.

Only three cards ever came for me. Much later, in January 1945, two came almost together. One was dated May of 1944. They were the same kind of printed cards. Al told me years later that at the time of writing one of them he was delirious with an attack of malaria. I have studied the cards to try to work out which one was written at that time [without success]. My memory of the women in the little club rooms is so much of the patient middle-aged mothers; some seemed very old. The wives I saw on different Tuesdays—I suppose everybody young had a job, but I suppose the mothers stayed [at the gathering] all day. I remember at least two Christmas parties for Pioneer children; all [of us] working together for a happy afternoon.[7]

In utter contrast to the deprivation of contact between POWs and their families, an American airman stationed in the mountains of Burma at Christmas 1944 not only had a typewriter at his disposal, but a mimeograph machine as well. He even had coloured pencils to shade the Christmas newsletter he composed, to duplicate and send to a list of friends and relatives back in the States. William Palmer Goetz, of Buffalo, NY, composed his Christmas message on 12 December 1944, in full confidence that it would reach everyone in time to act on his request: 'Be sure on Christmas Eve to step outdoors and lift your eyes to the Heavenly stars above. Find the Big Dipper—for on each star I will have planted a very warm and sincere wish for your good health, happiness and good fortune throughout 1945, and it will be just 12 hours before!'[8]

For thousands of prisoners confined a few hundred miles away from Airman Goetz, their only communication was to gaze at those same stars, silently send their prayers and wishes aloft, and hope that next Christmas would come for them.

12
'You Understand?'

Bankok
Siam
September 26, 1945

Dearest old Binks,

Note that we are no longer in Thailand, the new Prime Minister having announced that in future the country will go under its old name of Siam. I was corrected at the Publicity Dept. yesterday where I went to collect a map of the city, and referred to 'Thailand'. 'No Thailand,' the clerk said. 'You understand—Siam.' We've been talking that sort of language so long now that it will be a pleasure to hear English unadulterated again. The expression, 'You understand?' was a common one with our former hosts when enforcing their point of view. One of the standing jokes was that, whether you replied yes you did understand, or no you didn't, you received a wipe over the chops just the same. 'You understand?' 'No.' Bang! 'Now you understand?' 'Yes.' Bang! It usually didn't hurt much—just an open-hander—but was somewhat lowering to the dignity. One of yesterday's pleasures was a civilised haircut in a comfortable chair in a clean saloon, with electric hair clippers. Having cleaned up the pay, I went out early, alone for a change, took a train to the other side of the city (New Bankok), where I had some stripes sewn on my shirt, lunched, and wandered about looking at things. On the way back I tried to buy some pencils, but the Chinese business people are having a sit-down strike at present and all they would say was 'No sell!' On the previous evening, the curfew was lifted, as there had been no shooting for a day or two, and we were allowed out until 11 p.m. With another man I walked down to the Odeon theatre, having to avoid certain thoroughfares that were picqueted, but with no street lights, and all the Chinese shops in darkness, and hardly anyone about except a few scared-looking young Siamese soldiers, the prospect was rather gloomy.

105

*Last night rain came down heavier than I've ever known before,
and to-day there are heavy monsoonal showers. Rather a bad day
for drying my jungle greens, which I washed this morning. Capt.
Winning, whom I'd not seen for eight months, came in to see me
to-day. I am driving with him to-morrow. He and I have got on
well together over the last few years. Of that more when I return.
This evening I am driving with Felix von Kispal, born a
Hungarian baron, now a naturalised Dutchman, who was a good
friend in the leaner times. While confident that you have written,
I have not yet received a post-war letter from you. A lot have
received mail, but many others have missed out so far. Better luck
in the next day or two perhaps.*

Love from your old

Pop

Had a vaccination to-day!

As mentioned earlier, the constant bashing to which any POW
might suddenly be subjected kept everyone's nerves on edge. Because
many beatings seemed to happen for petty reasons, these incidents
might be classified as 'petty brutality', if only to separate them from
more prolonged savagery which brought a prisoner close to death.

The incident Dickson describes, being slapped in the face for who-
knows-what minor infraction of protocol, was quite a common form
of torment; its main purpose probably being, as he says, 'somewhat
lowering to the dignity'. What he *doesn't* mention is that, before his
punishment began, he was made to kneel. Fellow Pioneer Bob
Adolphson recalls: 'Cec was so tall, [over 6'4"] that the Japs made
him kneel for "discipline", so they could reach his face to slap him
around, or to give him a bashing.'[1]

Australian POW artist Murray Griffin sketched an incident from
memory, showing a kneeling Australian being beaten; his drawing
hangs in the POW exhibit at the Australian War Memorial, Canberra.
Even though the Australian is on his knees, his head is still almost
level with the caps of the two guards, who are taking turns thrashing
him. As an added torment, he is being made to kneel on a freshly
cut wedge of wood, which has just been hacked out from a Railway
construction log. While the beating goes on, he has to hold a heavy
metal pipe aloft, perhaps to remind him how weak and emaciated he
is. Soon he will simply collapse and fall prone, unconscious, as his
fellow POW in the background has done.

A tall prisoner has been made to kneel on a chunk of wood freshly cut from the Railway construction site, so that two guards can more easily reach his body, to take turns beating him. He is made to hold a heavy pipe aloft. Soon he will collapse, unconscious, as his fellow POW in background has done. (MURRAY GRIFFIN: *AN INCIDENT ON THE BURMA RAILWAY*, BRUSH AND BROWN INK WITH WASH OVER PENCIL, 35 × 50.8CM. AUSTRALIAN WAR MEMORIAL AWM 26525)

Dickson's way of maintaining his dignity at moments like that was to stand up, dust off his knees, and go about his business as best he could. Long before their capture—in fact, shortly after they had enlisted as Pioneers back in Melbourne—Alan Mitchell labelled the tall, unflappable man from Geelong 'Dignity'. In a letter to his fiancée Eileen, written from bivouac camp in the summer of 1940, Mitchell remarked that even when bedding down under the stars during field manoeuvres, Dickson insisted on wearing his hat.

Walter Summons claimed that Dickson 'Had the ability to appear dignified under any conditions, and was one of the few who could invest a loin-cloth and wooden clogs with a little of the "dignity of man". He, and his brother, who was known as "Gentleman John" because of his faultless manners, were a grand pair to have in the same camp.'[2]

Many years later, Gordon Hamilton still recalled: 'He had an innate dignity of bearing and behaviour whatever the circumstance, and that is how I shall always remember him.'[3]

And, after half a century, Leo Cornelius was still trying to figure out why Dickson joined the Pioneers: 'How such a gentle, urbane person could have come to roost in a tough old battalion as ours has always seemed to me an absolute paradox.'[4]

On one occasion Dickson's friends remember him losing his cool—but that was because his brother was being savagely beaten. Finally Dickson couldn't stand watching any longer, and he tried to intervene. (John was much shorter and smaller in build than Cecil.) Of course, the guards then turned their attention to Cecil, and beat him too.

Harry Bishop pointed out that: 'The Japanese appear to be very susceptible to alcohol, and periodically there would be trouble with guards and NCOs for this reason.' Several ex-POWs have said that some of the worst sudden beatings were at the hands of Japanese or Korean guards who were drunk. Bishop continues: 'I can remember when I had a run of ten bashings over ten weeks, all of which were to do with my duty as cook house *shoho* (officer). One was because a cook set fire to a chimney; another was when I was standing in front of the cookhouse—I saw a guard coming and moved to the back so I wouldn't have to salute him.'[5]

Dickson may have joked at dinner parties about still enjoying rice, after consuming over 3800 consecutive meals of it; but surely in his mind there was the flashback of being on the brink of starvation for that whole period—and gratitude for the creative genius of cookhouse personnel like Harry Bishop and Harry Whelan. Getting a cookhouse going, and searching for food to supplement their dwindling rations, was of vital importance. Whelan remembers working with Dickson:

> Both Cec and I had jobs in the quartermaster's store at Tamarkan camp, which was the camp near the two bridges. (The wooden one later became known in the movie as 'The Bridge Over the River Kwai'.)
>
> The number in this camp was usually 2000–3000 men. But when the wooden bridge was washed away in a flood in early 1944, soon after it was completed, the Japs brought about another 2000-odd men in to quickly rebuild it. At one time we had about 5000 in the camp. In order to feed everybody we had four kitchens: one for the Dutch, one for naval personnel, one for officers, and one (the biggest) for everybody else.
>
> We used to issue the rice direct to the kitchens; in other

words, they at times had up to a week's stock of rice. The entitlement or ration was 500 grams of dry rice per man, per day. We did not always receive this because some of the bags had split or were holed, and did not contain 50 kilos. This was the cause of an argument with the Japs, who insisted that a bag was 50 kilos, although it may be only half full.

A daily record was kept of the numbers eating from each kitchen, and transfers of rice from one kitchen to another were constantly being made. In other words, the quartermaster's store controlled all stocks of food, although the stock may be in the hands of individual kitchens.

You will appreciate the fact that everyone was hungry, and every effort had to be made to ensure that everybody got his fair share and appeared to be getting his fair share. Hunger turns men into beasts, and I have seen fights develop if one man thought he was getting less than someone else. Doling out the cooked rice and the soup was always a source of much argument.

Eldon Schmidt [of the 131st Field Artillery, Texas National Guard] lent me his slide rule, in a leather case, with his monogram on it, to assist me in splitting up the vegetable ration. That's how exactly we tried to measure out everyone's fair share! I kept it all these years, hoping to find out his address and return it. [As a result of the research for this book, Whelan was put in touch with Crayton 'Quaty' Gordon, long-time secretary of the Lost Battalion Association, as the 131st came to be known. To his dismay, Whelan learned that Schmidt had recently died.]

The Japs had supplied us with a platform scale. The vegetables used to arrive each day by river barge, and be carried into the camp by POW. I used to supervise the weighing, and being armed with the numbers eating from each kitchen, I would use the slide rule to work out the number of kilograms to go to each kitchen. I believe we were supposed to get 400 grams of vegetables per man, per day, in addition to the 500 grams of rice.

In Tamarkan, we also got a meat ration. I think it was 20 grams per man per day. We never actually got any meat as such, usually just enough to flavor the soup, [but] it made the soup more palatable. Cecil used to supervise the killing and splitting up of the meat ration. The killing was done in the camp by POW who had been butchers in civil life. [Dickson often remarked in later years to his family, how vividly he recalled trying to portion out the 'miserable carcass of some half-starved yak'.]

Here an Australian prisoner has photographed a team of fellow Australians drawing water outside a cookhouse, Kanchanaburi, Thailand, 1944. The water will be used for a 'stew', which will contain rice and whatever vegetables, meat scraps or bones the cooks have been able to acquire. (COURTESY OF C.J. MITCHELL, AWM P1502/04)

The kitchens were built of bamboo, with roofs made up from atap leaves, as were all other buildings in the camp.

The rice was cooked in 'kwalis'. A kwali was a cast iron dish about four feet across and one foot deep in the middle. A mud frame would be built up to support the kwali, with an opening in the mud frame about one foot wide to enable a wood fire to be built under the kwali. The only other cooking equipment we ever had were 44 gallon drums (British measure, about 20% larger than US measure). The soup, whatever it consisted of, was always cooked in these drums.

In Tamarkan, we were also supposed to get 20 grams of salt and 20 grams of sugar per man, per day. We did not always receive salt or sugar. We occasionally received some tea, but not often. Compared with what we had received in the jungle, while building the Railway, the rations in Tamarkan were quite reasonable. You were always hungry, but not starving.[6]

Some POWs who surely would have been starving, except for the constant attention of their fellow prisoners, were those confined to the camp 'hospital'. As mentioned earlier, the Japanese tended to cut off rations for 'non-productive' POWs; Colonel Williams routinely notes in his diary how rations were cut back in order to provide some for the sick. Sometimes 'healthy' prisoners did without a meal entirely so the sick could be fed something.

If a particularly nourishing bit of food came their way, POW cooks always made sure it went to the sick first, so prisoners were always on the lookout for an enhanced opportunity to find such morsels, particularly if possessions did not have to be sold clandestinely to natives in order to acquire them.

Cal Mitchell provided one vignette which could be considered high comedy, if its underlying purpose were not so grave. An Australian, passing the Japanese kitchen, spotted a bullock liver, unguarded for the moment. Thinking of its exceptional nutritional value for sick men, he grabbed it, plopped it on his head, and covered the oozing innard with his hat. As the liver blood began running down his face, a Japanese officer came upon him, and immediately sent the Australian to the camp hospital for treatment of his 'injury'. So the liver got a direct trip to its destination, the hospital stew pot.

The prisoners also supplemented their diet with literally anything that moved, or happened to slither within range. In later years, Dickson would joke to his family and friends: 'In the jungle, I found that I *could* eat snake!'

Harry Bishop remembered some of the ways cooks found to supplement rations during the leanest days, while constructing the Railway:

> When my party, Java 5A, started in Burma we were getting cattle for our beef ration and we had butchered them in the camp; rice and vegetables were delivered by truck. Six months later the cattle we were getting were so thin that they were dying in the yards before we killed them. The Japs tried a whole range of alternatives as conditions became worse (supplies couldn't be trucked in during wet season). They slaughtered the cattle in Moulmein and packed it in boxes after cooking it in a way to preserve it. They also got local dried fish, including white bait and dried slices of a big fish. These were good, but they were not enough.
>
> Motor trucks began to buck up on the roads and they got Burmese farmers with drays drawn by oxen to supply the camps. Very few got back [to the camps] after the wet season set in. Apparently they were susceptible to cholera. The end result was wagons abandoned along the road and the oxen were

An Australian prisoner has photographed another vital daily task at Kanchanaburi, Thailand, 1944, as a crew of Australian prisoners chop and saw wood for cooking fires. During the worst days of rain and constant moves in 1943, the prisoners were sometimes unable to gather wood, so no food could be cooked on those days. (COURTESY OF C.J. MITCHELL, AWM P1502/01)

turned loose. They could be seen in the forest by our wood cutters—always there were wood cutting parties. We had two butchers, one American, one Australian, who found that it was possible to catch the oxen and bring them in one at a time to butcher, close to the camp.

We also asked permission to collect edible plants to put in the stew. I simply picked leafy plants that were free of toxic tastes and didn't have too many fibres. It worked, but it only made a small difference to our stews. We could only get small parties to gather food, and there was a lot of walking between plants.

The Japanese engineers had a different approach. They took explosives and looked for pools along the only river in the area. They got fish and they had a few POW with them to carry the fish back to camp. By chance I walked along the river with a jungle greens party next morning. There were still a lot of fish floating belly up, and sitting on a rock was a beautiful otter, which dived in when we came by. The fish were beginning to smell, so we left them for the otter.

However, we made arrangements that the next time the engineers went fishing, one of their carriers would join a party of jungle green-seekers and lead us to the site. It worked; there were quite a number of fish floating, and we cleaned them straight away and hurried them off to the kitchen.

I had that job for the whole period I was on the Railway, and this continued until the last six months of the war, when all the officers were concentrated at Kanburi and I had a row with the British. During much of the time, I shared cookhouse space with the 131st Texas Regiment and USS *Houston* survivors, and also with the Dutch.[7]

Bishop's resourcefulness extended beyond buying the bolt of military cloth in Java, and creative measures to supplement POW diets. He also dealt in a practical way with the Japanese hierarchy:

This was part of the drill in the Japanese army: officers bash NCO; corporals, privates; and first-class privates, recruits. If this was accepted then there is less likelihood of them getting really nasty. The best outcome is to stand to attention until it is finished. I had one [Japanese] corporal tell me that I was a very good soldier when he finished slapping me. The worst thing to do was to dodge, or to fall down.

On the Railway the guards were Koreans but with Japanese officers and NCOs in charge of administration. However, there was little difference between them in the way they operated.[8]

That the prisoners could keep up their spirits despite constant harassment was a source of wonder and curiosity to many Japanese who witnessed it. Reflections on the POW attitude prompted Henry Shigeru Yagake to write an essay many years later on the subject. It appeared in the January 1992 issue of *Rafu Shimpo*, a Japanese-language newspaper published in Los Angeles, California. Yagake described how, towards the end of the war while at Phet Buri airbase in Thailand (adjacent to the camp where Dickson spent the first six months of 1945), his curiosity got the best of him, and he initiated a dialogue with three POWs whose work he was supervising. One prisoner was an American, the second was British, and the third was a Malay. The Japanese called them 'New York', 'London' and 'Calcutta' respectively:

'New York' was always very cheerful. So one day I just had to ask them the question that was utmost in my mind, because [we] were inculcated to believe in the *Senjin-kun* [Combatant's Code] of the Japanese Military, that said in part: 'One should not shame oneself by being taken alive as a prisoner; one should die instead and not shame his name for posterity of one thousand years.'

When I said to the POW: 'the Japanese men think it is a great shame to be taken a prisoner. What are your thoughts on the subject?' The answer came back promptly. 'No. We fought to our best of ability in the front line until we were captured, so we don't feel ashamed at all.' I then understood why they were so sunny.[9]

Probably the most hated harrassment was when POWs, especially after working long into the night on the Railway, were ordered to perform some service for the Japanese when they returned to camp—such as building a shower house or trimming their captors' hair. This form of abuse might be classified in a category by itself, if a suitable name could be found for it.

Even the most unreasonable order, if refused, brought swift retribution. Ron Winning, who was so brutally tortured for over a month in Java, remembered many examples of 'lesser' brutality as well:

The senior NCO sent for me and demanded that sick men in the camp be sent out to work. I refused, and he beat me with a heavy wooden waddy, breaking one of my ribs. When I still refused the Jap C.O. ordered all men in the huts be on the parade ground. He went along the lines, pointing his cane to any one he considered fit to work—even men carried out on bamboo stretchers were sent out.[10]

It would probably be safe to say that every ex-POW has memories of what he saw and endured very close to the surface. Sometimes a recollection, or flashback, is triggered by a phrase or gesture made at another time and place, as was the case with Dickson when the clerk in Bangkok used a phrase, in broken English, which had so often been the prelude to a beating in the camp.

Too often, though, the memories bubble up at unwanted moments, like the middle of the night. Many years later, Dickson confided to his second wife: 'When I was first in Bangkok, I drank a whole bottle of whiskey every night, and slept like a baby. I never drank that way again.'[11]

But like many of his friends, especially in his later years, Dickson relied on sleeping pills, just in case a troublesome scene from POW days haunted his night.

Even so, he could never predict when some image would intrude on his pleasant life. One such unwanted intrusion occurred during a visit by the Dicksons to the United States during the 1976 Bicentennial year. As part of the festivities, tall ships from all over the world had been invited to sail into New York Harbour, and then up the Hudson River on Independence Day, 4 July.

Knowing how much Cecil had enjoyed sailing during his younger days, Margaret's daughter and son-in-law, Susan and Ralph Gross, had arranged to take the Dicksons on Ralph's sailboat up to Newport, Rhode Island, where the tall ships were assembling for their parade down Long Island Sound, past the Statue of Liberty, and into the harbour. It was to be an overnight outing, and in deference to the Dickson' comfort, Susan and Ralph had booked a nice hotel room with a waterfront view in Jamestown, just next to Newport.

During the night, many of the tall ships put into port, and as luck would have it, the captain of a large sailing vessel from Japan dropped anchor directly in front of the Dicksons' window. The next morning, Cecil opened the draperies to greet the sunlight, only to find the Rising Sun flag waving in front of his nose.

Later, at breakfast, he confided to his family: 'Of all the flags I would rather not have slept in the shadow of, it was *that* one. It brought back a flood of memories, of my unwilling tenure as a guest of the Emperor.'[12]

13

News From Home!

29 SEPTEMBER 1945: Dickson was so full of news and happiness that, despite squeezing two sentences on each line and omitting paragraphs, he still used ten pages torn from an accounting ledger to complete this letter. At last he had received mail from his wife and sister—and funds wired from a bank officer in Melbourne to which, regrettably, he did not have access.

Chinese Chamber of Commerce
Bankok, Siam
September 29, 1945

My dear old girl,

Two very exciting days just past. After writing to you on the 26th your cable arrived—first post-war intimation that you were all right. For which three cheers! Then yesterday morning I received your letter of September 16, and one from Marie of the same date. Then in the afternoon I had the opportunity of saying a few words into a microphone, one of 30-odd who were allowed to send a verbal message home. The recordings are being flown to Australia, where it is expected they will be broadcast from national stations in about a week. It is possible that I might be in another broadcast, as the A.B.C. correspondent here has asked me to assist with a programme he is planning. I expect a ring from him this morning. If anything comes of it I shall certainly let you know the details. Facilities and conditions are not good enough here at present to broadcast direct, so the discs will probably be sent home, the same as with the personal messages. At this stage I was called away to receive a new 'hat'. It is one of the green berets that go with the jungle green battle dress. Very acceptable, as the old khaki fur felt, which was passed on to me early this year by Cal Mitchell, had outlived its period of usefulness. The last two days have been busy with pay again. It comes once a week at the rate of 60 tikals, which at 5d. Australian to the tikal goes like the wind. After balancing out yesterday

afternoon I took the surplus cash back to the field pay office away
out the other side of Bankok by truck. It was quite an interesting
run, taking me through parts I had not seen before. I was dropped
eventually at the Oriental Hotel, where the surplus officers are
quartered, and went out to dine with Ron Winning and an English
M.O. [Medical Officer] who had spent most of his POW days as
doctor in coolie camps. What appalling stories he had to tell. The
Chinese strike continues, which means that it is difficult even to get
a meal. But we did manage to dig up fried eggs and German
sausage. Went on to a newly opened cabaret called the New World.
It's quite an attractive place as these turnouts go, but as there had
been some trouble over the band, and there was no music, it was
rather flat. On our way back to our respective abodes we called at
another cabaret, where dancing was in full swing, but the 11 o'clock
curfew cut that rather short. As Ron had just come down from
up-country where there wasn't much chance of spending, and I had
personally paid the M.O. 490 tikals that afternoon, the evening
cost me nothing! The banks here are not operating on exchange yet,
so I do not hold out much hope of receiving any money in response
to Mathers' cable. It would have been handy to buy a few things
before leaving here. Latest information about the move is that at
present the planes are being used to fly the 861 Australians out from
Petburi, which I left on July 4. That should be complete by October
1, when movement from Bankok is expected to be accelerated. Some
time in October should see me home. The evening before last spent
with Kispal (aforementioned). He has been busy preparing reports
on a number of Japanese offenders, with whom he had extensive
contact. To-day he is leaving with a commission that is going up-
country to investigate Japanese treatment of coolies. After the last
war, in which he fought as an officer for the Hungarian army, he
accompanied the commission which fixed the new boundaries of
Hungary. Kev Nolan, whom I had not seen for two and a half
years, and with whom I spent leave in Damascus and Tel Aviv,
came in a day or two ago with an escort to a couple of Japanese
who are 'on the list'. He is looking exceptionally well, his only
imperfection being that one leg has not quite straightened out yet
as a result of a bad ulcer he had behind the knee. It is very little
handicap to him now and is expected to come good with treatment.

Well, it was great to receive your letter. Give my love, of course,
to the family at 50 Canterbury Road and regards to all other
friends. I'm looking forward to making the acquaintance of the new
grand-niece. Great thrills! Good old Jay! Now whatever you do, old

girl, don't run yourself thin over the house-hunting business. I'm well practised in the art of living anywhere. Being with the old Missus again will be sufficient, whatever it might be. Incidentally, the chest swelled with pride at some remarks in Marie's letter about a certain person's doings in the last four and a half years.

You'll be bored if I don't stop prattling. So cheerio, old darling, till next time.

Much love,

Pop

Having been denied contact with loved ones for so long, Dickson absolutely revelled in the thought that, although not directly, his wife may actually hear his voice the following week—then surely she would have no doubt that he was all right, too!

Cal Mitchell also recorded a message from Bangkok, but he beat it home:

> I recall the radio messages being sent to our people from Bangkok in October 1945. In fact I sent one to Jean and my father. They were recorded on platters. When I arrived home on October 23rd, I asked if they had heard the message but no, they hadn't. About a fortnight after I got back, Jean received a message to say that if she listened to the radio at a certain time and date, she would be able to receive a message from her husband in Bangkok. At the appointed time we both sat and listened to me from Bangkok![1]

In one of his preprinted postcards from POW camp, Dickson apparently tried to signal his wife that some of the radio messages, broadcast monthly by relatives, were getting through. It must have been a real lift for the Relatives Association members gathered in the Melbourne Railway Station meeting room, when Freda Dickson shared that bit of confirmation, albeit many months after it was written.

Although clandestine wireless radios were set up in almost every POW camp, most units were equipped only to pick up news broadcast by the BBC. Unfortunately, for quite some time messages from families were beamed to Java, since it was over a year before most relatives learned that their loved ones had been shipped to Burma and Thailand.

Cal Mitchell confirmed that the handful of Pioneers who remained on Java did receive several messages directed to them, but he did not

*Australian officers standing inside a hut, Kanchanaburi, Thailand, 1944,
photographed secretly by a fellow prisoner. Hollow bamboo poles
sometimes concealed radio wires. Hanging bags of belongings were often
stolen by Japanese or Korean guards while prisoners were out. The POW
in the foreground, looking at the camera, has managed to keep a table,
marked with initials 'R.S.'.* (COURTESY OF C.J. MITCHELL, AWM P1502/05)

recall hearing of any along the Railway, for Pioneers. One lucky
exception seems to have been Ron Winning, who described how
two men at a nearby camp risked their lives to bring him a message
from his wife just before Christmas 1943:

> I was in a different group from the Pioneers, but two men
> risked their lives to contact me and give me the message . . . The
> work camps at this stage were fairly close together. They were
> not fenced. However, the Jap orders were that anyone caught
> outside [his assigned] camp would be dealt with. The two men
> who brought me the message slipped out at night, and walked
> about five kilos to my camp.[2]

Several POWs have described how wireless sets were hidden. A
favourite spot was the lower section of a water bottle, in which a
false bottom had been placed; one such contraption is on display in
the POW exhibit at the Australian War Memorial. Bamboo poles
which supported the huts were a handy conduit for wires. A strict

security system was devised, to pass information by word of mouth, and POWs made it a point to visit the sick first with news of an Allied victory, to boost their spirits and give them the will to live.

According to Mitchell, one of the more ingenious methods of hearing regular newscasts was hit upon in Java by a British aviator, who managed to keep his helmet intact when captured. He never took it off, because the earphones inside were still working fine. He was able to acquire an iron bed, to which a wire could easily be grounded. Mitchell could still visualise the Englishman, nodding and smiling a greeting at the Japanese guards inspecting the hut, as he sat and listened intently to the latest BBC news summary.

Of course, keeping a wireless operating without a ready supply of batteries was a challenge, and by war's end many 'nightingales', as the sets were called, had stopped 'singing'. However, resourceful POWs often took advantage of the presence of Japanese motor vehicles parked in the camps; many a truck parked for the night was the victim of a quick battery switch, and puzzled drivers would wonder the next morning how the battery had run down so much overnight.

Gordon Hamilton told his family with evident pride that: 'Despite danger, two British officers have kept a set going [in his camp] throughout, and the effect on the Japanese when they produced the set after capitulation was ludicrous. We had just moved camp, been subject to a stringent search; but the set travelled packed up with the Jap camp commander's personal electric equipment! Such a joke.'[3]

But in the same letter, Hamilton mentioned that two British officers caught operating a wireless in 1943 'were beaten to death in the most brutal manner'. Although quite a few pieces of wireless equipment were found during the 'blitz' searches of POW belongings, it could not always be established to whom they belonged. Various punishments were always meted out, but the incident to which Hamilton referred took place at Kanchanaburi in late 1943, and was even remembered by certain Japanese for its severity.

Interpreter Nagase recalls that the equipment was discovered in a surprise inspection:

> When all suspects were brought to the Military Police, they had already been beaten up badly. Most suffered broken bones and were gasping for breath. One prisoner had been beaten to death in camp. This well-known case was called the 'Shortwave Incident'. After the war ended, the officers and non-commissioned officers . . . who had been involved in the affair

were indicted as B and C class war criminals. Some of them were condemned to death.[4]

Nagase's role in helping to secure data for war crimes, and the lasting effect these memories have had on him, are discussed in the next chapter.

Towards the end of his letter, Dickson cheerily mentioned that his friend Kevin Nolan's bent leg was 'expected to come good with treatment'. But the restoration to reasonably good health was a long path for many POWs, and for most it was never complete.

Nolan detailed the onset of his leg trouble, and its impact on his immediate postwar plans:

> It was in Niki camp that I began to develop the ulcer to which Cec referred in his letter. After a nightmare trip by train to Kanchanaburi we were expected to walk to Tamarkan, where a large number of Pioneers were gathered. Nothing would stop me from reuniting with some of my old mates, some of whom I hadn't seen for a year or so. The uselessness of one leg, combined with a recurrence of malaria contracted on the train on the way down, allowed me to walk about half a mile before collapsing. Two burly Dutchmen carried me back to Kanburi, where I spent three and a half agonising months before being transferred to a new 'hospital' camp at Nakom Paton, where I remained as a hut commander until that magical day in August 1945 . . . Like Wally Summons, I had to endure the seemingly endless medical examinations, and a two month sojourn in a 'Thomas splint' getting the offending leg 95% straightened. [This treatment forced temporary postponement of his wedding plans.][5]

Summons, who died in 1990, was among the most severely ill of the POW survivors. Harry Bishop recalled:

> Wally Summons had a bad run on the Railway and was sent back to a hospital camp in 1943. Later on he was transferred to the camps in southern Thailand, where Australians were concentrated over a period in 1944. Wally had recovered a lot in the previous year, but he was far from fit and he was held in hospital for a couple of years after he got home.[6]

Despite Dickson's upbeat assertion, in an earlier letter, that his brother John was 'in fine fettle', the younger Dickson spent considerable time in the hospital once he arrived in Australia. He recovered remarkably well, but suffered increasingly severe arthritis as he got older, and when he underwent emergency surgery in October 1991,

Cecil Dickson's pay book, showing the list of known illnesses he contracted during captivity, written on pages which should have been a record of his daily pay as a soldier—blank for three and a half years.
(PHOTOGRAPHED FROM ORIGINAL COURTESY OF MRS T.C. DICKSON)

surgeons speculated that scar tissue they discovered could well have dated back to ulcers developed as a POW.

The illnesses Gordon Hamilton described in his first letter home were probably quite representative:

> Our captivity is something we are fast trying to forget. I have not space to tell you any details, but as you can guess, we had a very thin time, especially for the fifteen months after leaving Java. Burma was a hell hole. Fortunately we were brought down to Thailand at the end of '43 and conditions improved considerably. I survived dengue, and bacillary dysentery in Batavia September '42, and in Burma got malaria and amoebic dysentery. Went down to 6 stone 6 [about 85 pounds] in August '43 but pulled round . . . We will all be rather a bad bargain for a while though. Mentally we have become very slow and stagnant, and have developed queer habits and outlook—hope that diet and environment will soon correct that, but the past three and a half years must have left its mark. It is only when we come in contact with outside people that we realize our peculiarities.[7]

Eileen Mitchell says that, although she and her husband enjoyed a full and active life raising their family, 'Alan was never really well again, though—often back in hospital with an anxiety state, a strange heartbeat and amoebic dysentery for years and years. [But] he was never embittered.'[8]

The recurrence of strange tropical illnesses, sometimes unfamiliar to—and therefore unrecognised by—local physicians, plagued virtually all ex-POWs, and shortened the life span of many. Ernest Gordon observed during his ministry at Paisley Abbey in the immediate postwar years, that a disturbingly high number of ex-POWs died within ten years of their release from captivity, due to lack of proper medical treatment for illnesses contracted in the POW years. He credits his own vigorous recovery to a physician in Leith, Scotland, who established a wing for tropical diseases in the local hospital, and took it upon himself to become educated about the proper treatment for these illnesses. Most importantly for Gordon, this physician offered treatment to ex-military personnel. Gordon felt that the Socialist British government took very little interest in the individual health of ex-POWs. 'They seemed *angry* at us,' he mused, and showed a rare flash of pique as he remembered the offhand attitude of one 'rank-conscious' British military physician. When asked what he meant by 'rank-conscious', the Rev. Dr Gordon replied: 'Oh, you know, "Yes-sir, no-sir, three-bags-full-sir"'.[9]

Gordon estimated that about 10 per cent of ex-POWs returned to very good health following their release, and about 10 per cent remained in somewhat precarious shape, suffering from repeated neurological breakdowns, kidney failure, increasing blindness and limited use of limbs due to severe arthritis. Skin cancer was a common ailment for many, including himself and Dickson.

Sir Edward 'Weary' Dunlop agreed with Gordon that a premature death rate among ex-POWs may have seemed disturbingly high, but he pointed out that a survey taken some ten years after the war purported to show roughly the same death rate among ex-POWs as in the general population. He commented in an April 1992 letter to the author:

> This study [was] flawed in that the comparison should have been with a controlled group of young men selected as fit for war service. However, the death rate at that stage [approximately 1955] was not alarming . . . Nevertheless, an early survey, which I obtained, did reveal quite a lot of residual disease and disability . . . As regards Australian Prisoners of War, in rough round figures of 22,000 POW, 8000 died in prison camps due to disease, starvation, or drowning at sea. A few were executed. Of 14,000 who were recovered, recent Veterans Affairs [figures] state 5,300 still surviving. I suppose one could conclude that of the selected men fit for service, those who survived were very tough men.[10]

Because physicians like Dunlop and Lieutenant Colonel Albert Coates had been in charge of large numbers of POWs, they became effective spokesmen to underscore the need for immediate follow-up treatment, having kept detailed records of their efforts to provide care despite the lack of medicines. And, as mentioned earlier, Colonel Williams spent nearly ten weeks between September and December 1945 providing authorities with a complete medical record of each Pioneer. He also kept notations about each POW, regardless of nationality, who passed through his camp.

When over 14 000 Australian ex-POWs returned to their homeland, they and their relatives made a powerful lobby group indeed. And if the government faltered in its response, the Returned Services League and the newly forming Ex-POW Association of Australia were there to prod the bureaucrats along!

As a result, Australian ex-POWs have probably received more enlightened, comprehensive and lasting health care than those of any other nation. The War Veterans' Villages, designed and supported by the Returned and Services League, are unique in the world. They provide security, camaraderie, subsidised housing and medical care, in a most attractive setting, serving as a model of how to say 'thank you' in a very practical way. However, the government's financial response to POWs and their families is another story, discussed in the concluding chapter.

In terms of after-care, American ex-POWs fell somewhere in between British Socialist government indifference and Australian personalised attention, provided by both government and private groups. Like the Rev. Dr Gordon, many American ex-POWs lamented the difficulties some of their friends had in trying to deal with postwar life: higher-than-average rates of alcoholism and suicide, and lingering health problems. Although the United States does have a Veterans Administration system, which operates hospitals and clinics throughout the nation, the burden of discovery has primarily rested with the individual, in terms of identifying needs and getting treatment.

As was true among Australian and British POWs, the Americans had several medical personnel in their number, among them a surgeon, Commander William Epstein of the USS *Houston*. According to Otto Schwarz of the USS *Houston* Survivors Association, a personnel profile of each survivor was kept by a yeoman from the *Houston*, which he turned over to the Department of the Navy at war's end. In 1946, the yeoman happened to discover his records stuffed in a Navy office desk drawer, virtually discarded. He retrieved them, and gave the files to Schwarz as a memento. Schwarz still has the documents.

14

Another Anniversary Apart

2 OCTOBER 1945: It was the Dicksons' nineteenth wedding anniversary; and although he did not mention it, Cecil's 43rd birthday was to come in just four days.

Chinese Chamber of Commerce
Bankok
Siam
October 2, 1945

Dearest old Binks,

That most important anniversary has come round again, and here I am still in Bankok. The business of getting started seems a bit slow, but it would appear now that within a week at the outside I should be on the way, and the journey should not take long. With ordinary luck, say, home by the end of October. Meanwhile the time is passing pleasantly enough. In the evenings there is not much to do but sit about in cafes, which are innumerable, except on nights when there is something special on, such as a performance by the ex-POW party two nights ago, and to-night another dance at the Alliance Française, which I might attend. The alternative to going out is being eaten by mosquitos in camp, where they abound. Incidentally, I sleep under a mosquito net again. Although I had not been using one, I had been remarkably free from malaria. Only one attack (three months ago) in 16 months. Previous to that I had had a consistent run of attacks for more than a year. Yesterday I took the day off. Met Ron Winning at the Oriental in the morning, called on a friend at Diethelm & Co., a large Swiss importing house, then visited the Royal Palace which is open to the public in the day time. The young King has not yet returned from Switzerland, where he has been receiving his education. The palace buildings are

very ornate in the Siamese fashion, but unfortunately the most
interesting part, the shrine, was closed. We then drank iced coffee in
the lounge of the Ratanakosin Hotel, where we met again Simpson,
the A.B.C. correspondent, and a bunch of Dutch officers known to
us both. One, Lieut. Bom, a very pleasant fellow, invited us to
join his party for lunch to celebrate his wife's birthday. The result
was the best meal I have had in Bankok. After strolling the hot
streets for a while we drank more iced coffee, then separated. I
immediately ran into Kispal, with whom I drank more iced coffee
while listening to his experiences at identification parades, where
he has been helping to single out offenders among Jap prisoners.
Having been an interpreter, he has had close contact with many of
them and knows their form. The colonels and what not who have
wielded the power of dictators in prison camp administration, are
now performing the manual work that we have been doing for
them—their clothing being one pair of shorts and no footwear. They
do not walk about the gaol—all movements are done on the double!
Have received cables from Pardew, Orbost & Keith Pearson. The
mail position here as far as inward letters are concerned gives no
cause for cheers. I have had only the one letter from you and one
from Marie so far.

   Much love old darling

   Pop

Japanese interpreter Takashi Nagase, like Kispal, was put in close
contact with the hierarchy at several camp locations, especially when
prisoners were being interrogated. In fact, it is chilling to note that
as soon as Java fell to the Japanese, Nagase was sent there 'in order
to collect information', as he puts it. Thus he may have been in one
of the rooms where Pioneer Captains Winning and Handasyde, or
the Commanding Officer, Colonel Williams, were being so brutally
interrogated for 30 days non-stop.

   And, as previously noted, Nagase was familiar with the details
surrounding the wireless radio incident, discovery of which brought
about the immediate death of two British officers. He was at
Kanchana-buri and Ban Pong for over a year, beginning in August
1943.

   Although he was a soldier of lower rank, the necessity to be present during prolonged torture of POWs deeply affected Nagase, and
flashbacks have haunted him through all the years since. In his book,
Crosses and Tigers, he candidly admits that Westerners are always

puzzled by his rationalisation that absolute obedience to orders was required, because the directive may have come from the Emperor himself. Japanese soldiers, he says, were told in no uncertain terms that if they disobeyed orders, they would face court-martial. But perhaps worse still, their families and all relatives would face reprisal, because the soldier's disobedience would immediately be reported to his home town. His family would then be ostracised, and suddenly find themselves unemployable. Ruefully, he acknowledges: 'No matter how earnestly I tried to explain this to Westerners, I have never been successful in convincing them. This might be because of the environment in which they were brought up and educated. The respect for fundamental human rights seems to be rooted in the minds of people in the West. I have never seen any Western reporters look satisfied with my explanation.'[1]

The only time such strict obedience to orders worked to the advantage of POWs was when the Emperor issued the direct order, over the radio, for all Japanese military personnel to lay down their arms. One of the points Colonel Williams was able to prove, by documentation, at the Major War Crimes Trials in Tokyo was that the general treatment of POWs was carried out on direct orders from the highest level.[2]

After the capitulation, Nagase was at the Japanese Army War Termination headquarters in Nakhon Pathom, trying to control his panic at rumours that Japanese soldiers were about to be put to work on the Railway, as reprisal, under the same conditions they had imposed on POWs. Apparently word of the regimen being undergone by camp commandants, described by Dickson in this letter, had reached Nagase's ears—and had become embroidered with the threads of fear.

He was also terrified that some ex-POWs who had been tortured would recognise him as having been involved in these procedures, and turn him in as a war criminal. So it was with considerable apprehension that he learned, on 22 September 1945, that he was to accompany members of the Allied War Graves Commission on a seven-week trip through Burma (which was not yet fully secured), to recover the remains of POWs, in order that they might be reburied in official war cemeteries in Thailand and Burma. An equally important purpose of the expedition, Nagase was to discover, would be to gather evidence for War Crimes Tribunals. Composed entirely of ex-POWs who had worked on the Railway, the expedition was headed by British Captain Bruce and Australian Captain White. Non-commissioned officers and soldiers were all Australians.

Nagase was as frightened to be among this delegation of thirteen ex-POWs as he was to be entering the domain of the legendary fierce tigers who roamed the Burma countryside. His fears did not abate when the two captains pointedly reminded him that their sketch maps of gravesites had been confiscated during searches of their personal belongings. As mentioned earlier, Nagase had participated in some of these searches, posing as an 'inspector', to gain tidbits of information about the prisoners.

On 25 September, the party arrived at a spot near Thanbyuzayat. Captain White had a compass, and seemed to know just how many paces he needed to take to find what he was searching for. Then he found it: part of a rotted wooden cross, and another, and another, as the party made the Japanese clear the graveyard overgrown with two and a half years of thick jungle foliage.

As the party moved by railway, progressing in its search, advance word of its arrival resulted in the appearance of already-cleared graveyards, because the Japanese had removed foliage from known spots. On 28 September the group arrived at one such cleared POW cemetery in the Apalon district of Burma. Captain White paced over and over again in a certain direction, holding his compass. He knew just where to order the Japanese to start digging. Nagase tells why this spot was special:

> Teams of two or three Japanese continued digging very deep by turns. The depth was nearly two metres, but the captain did not order them to stop. The other officers were looking at the hole, holding their breath . . . Soon a rotten blanket covering a body came in sight. The color of the blanket was hardly distinguishable from that of the dirt . . . white leg bones poked out of the dirt.
>
> 'The other way round. Dig again on the head side,' ordered the officer. Soon the hoe made a sound over the chest of the body.
>
> 'That's it.'
>
> The Captain ordered them to stop, and he jumped into the hole. He pushed dirt aside. A reddish, rotten 20-litre petroleum can came in sight. The can had lain over the body for two and a half years. The body was quietly awaiting the War Graves Commission in the depth of the weird jungle. I stood there in silence.
>
> Captain White came out of the grave with the can in his hand and put it on the ground like a precious thing. He ordered a Japanese soldier to break open the can. With a blow of the hoe, coal tar splashed in all directions . . .

The Captain ran up to the can, thrust his hand in the coal tar and took out a small round tin. It was a sealed container of fifty navy-cut cigarettes . . . Cold silence continued between the Allies and the Japanese.

What they explained to me later was: 'He suffered from malaria and was unable to walk any longer during the march to the back regions. He asked the Japanese for permission to leave the march, in vain. He ended up dying in the jungle.'

What he had on his chest for the period of two and a half years was a sheet of paper which said the names and ranks of the Japanese commander, a medical doctor, an interpreter and a soldier in charge who were responsible for his death, as well as the marching conditions and his wage statement [soldier's pay book—see illustration p. 122].

'We were not allowed to carry any documents with us. We did not have any other means than what you saw just now. The evidence lay hidden with the body for future reference.'[3]

Nagase goes on to quote Captain White explaining further:

It is necessary that we show [the Japanese] what justice really is . . . There would not have been this many deaths if the Japanese had been a little more humane. When there was an epidemic of cholera, they did not even give us any lime to spray over the latrines. Of course, the Japanese had enough. I suspect there were very few Japanese who died of cholera. The disease is easy to prevent. We could only watch our comrades die in great pain. Things were no different with tropical ulcers. With a little mercury medicine, most patients could have been cured easily. Many of them had to have their limbs cut off [in order to live].[4]

Nagase was profoundly impressed that the prisoner who died, as well as his friends, had complete faith that his remains *would* be found one day, and that those responsible for his death would be brought to justice. It took him another 30 years of meditation to realise that this faith was centred in firm convictions about the nature of God.

The withholding of medicine, particularly when it had been de-livered to POW camp locations in Red Cross parcels, was just about in a class by itself as a war crime, and seems especially anachronistic. Article 108 of the third Geneva Convention, which governs the rights of prisoners of war, dictates that, among other things, pris-oners must be able to receive and send mail, and to receive one relief parcel monthly. Although the Japanese government apparently en-dorsed the general principles set forth in the Conventions, when it came time to ratify this particular Article, Japan declined to do so.

The Article would have made little sense to a nation so dominated by its military élite, thoroughly trained to believe that captivity was too dishonourable to consider. Perhaps the assumption was made that soldiers of other nations would surely feel the same way. In other words, Article 108 just didn't fit into their thinking. As a result, the Japanese High Command probably did not anticipate having to deal with thousands of military personnel and civilians who had chosen to live.

Although the Japanese government did honour Article 108 to the extent of assisting in the delivery of Red Cross parcels to POW campsites, either their public statements did not mirror written instructions to camp officers or local commandants were less zealous in following orders than some would have us believe. The result was that lifesaving food, medication and clothing intended for prisoners was either stolen by Japanese camp personnel, or allowed to rot, unused.

At the War Crimes Trials in Singapore, Australian physician Colonel Albert Coates testified that Red Cross medicine and supplies were actually known to be on hand at Nakhon Pathom camp, and that failure of the local commander to distribute them caused the death of many men who would otherwise have survived.[5]

A specific charge against Japanese Major Totaro Mitzutani at those trials was that he withheld Australian Red Cross supplies which were delivered to the camps under his command along the Railway, when conditions were at their very worst between January and November 1943. Attempts were even made to obscure the names on packages, which in many cases were individually addressed, witnesses stated.[6]

Benjamin Dunn obtained a list from the office of the United States Provost Marshal General of the items contained in Red Cross parcels which were being sent for *weekly* distribution to prisoners: 16 oz. milk powder, 8 oz. processed cheese, 6 oz. liver paste, 12 oz. corned beef, 16 oz. oleomargarine, 12 oz. pork luncheon meat, 8 oz. salmon, 4 oz. sardines, 8 oz. sugar, 12 oz. prunes, 4 oz. concentrated orange juice, 1 oz. coffee, 4 oz. chocolate, 1 oz. salt and pepper mixed, 3 packages cigarettes, 7 oz. biscuit, and 4 oz. soap. Dunn comments:

> If these foods were ever sent to the prisoners of the Japanese in Burma and Thailand, the Japanese must have used them. One time in Burma we were given a can of butter or cheese to divide among six men. They were old and rank and ordinarily would not have been eaten, but under the circumstances we were glad to get what little we did. That was the only commodity of Red Cross supplies ever issued by the Japs in any camp in which I was interned on the Railroad or in Java, Burma or Thailand.[7]

According to a report prepared in 1943 by the Liaison and Research Branch, American Prisoner of War Information Bureau, 50 per cent of the Red Cross supplies sent to Thailand were known to have been kept by the Japanese, and very few reached their destinations. Red Cross parcels were usually distributed through the Swiss Consulate in Bangkok. The consul there requested receipts signed by POWs; at first the Japanese complied, but soon informed him that they would not continue to do so. An additional problem for international relief agencies was that it was the stated policy of the Thai government not to recognise the existence of Allied POWs within its borders.

The report also stated that, 'despite repreated requests by "neutral authorities" (including the Red Cross), the Japanese have categorically refused neutral visits to prisoners "on the reason of military purpose" '—the main reason being that the building of the Burma Railway was supposed to be a secret project, as well as the fact that they were violating the Geneva Conventions by using prisoners of war to construct it.

Corroborating Ernest Gordon's view, the report quotes the Swiss consul as having seen Japanese officers inspecting POW camps at Nonpladuk, where prisoners of healthy appearance had been placed near the railway line for propaganda purposes.[8]

Most unfortunately for the more than 600 American POWs on the Railway, this 1943 report listed just three Americans known to be prisoners in Thailand. It was not until a few 'Japan Party' survivors disclosed the information in October 1944 that the world learned about the USS *Houston* survivors, Texas 131st Field Artillery and other American military personnel who were prisoners there too.

Cal Mitchell remembers being aware that Red Cross supplies were delivered, thorough the Swiss, to Tamarkan. They were big cartons, containing medical supplies, clothing, food—even phonographs. Almost everything was kept by the Japanese, he says.

In the Battalion History, Dickson recorded the one occasion at Tamarkan when Red Cross medical supplies were distributed, in May 1944. The shipment included valuable drugs and surgical dressings, he noted, which 'Saved the lives of many very sick men'.[9] One can only guess at how many more very sick men might have recovered and returned home had they received the many parcels so carefully packed for them.

Although the indifference of the Japanese to pleas for available medical supplies and food was a source of anger and heartbreak to prisoners, the basis for this attitude can be traced to the Imperial military training code, which teaches that the deprivation of food is an especially good test of how 'hardened' one is. The lack of calories is ignored, and the correlation of nourishment to strength is not recognised. Even civilians were expected to accept this teaching: during the war, propaganda on Japanese radio told people in air raid shelters that callisthenics would make hungry people strong and vigorous again.[10]

In view of such daily hardship, it is easy to see how acts of kindness, when they occurred, were appreciated. One of the most famous expressions of appreciation took place at the Tokyo War Crimes Trials, when a British officer, David Boyle, testified *on behalf of* Teruo Saito, who was adjutant to the Commandant at a POW camp, and who had been sentenced to death along with the Commandant. Boyle confirmed that Saito had done everything in his power to ameliorate conditions for POWs and, as a result of Boyle's statement, Saito was spared.[11]

Saito was probably just as astounded at Boyle's appearance as Nagase was to witness Captain White and several other Australians in September 1945 rushing to greet a Japanese lance corporal at Niki railroad station with smiles and handshakes. They presented him with cigarettes and some precious tins of food, then Captain White explained to Nagase: '[The corporal] was very kind to us. He often gave us cigarettes and told us jokes . . . in those days, our only pleasure was to go out [on a work party] with him.'[12]

The scene witnessed by Nagase is somewhat reminiscent of the gesture of gratitude displayed by Bill Mayne and fellow POWs in Japan towards the elderly civilian who had been kind to them in the factory (see Chapter 8).

Gordon Jamieson recounts the story told by a fellow member of the Ex-POW Association of Australia, an airman who was captured in Java:

> His Commandant was a very harsh person, a high-ranking
> naval person who was demoted to his position [as a POW camp
> commandant] due to the loss of his ship. He was very harsh
> until he heard of the event, following the [Japanese] midget
> sub attack on Sydney Harbour on the 31st of May, 1942. The
> Australian Government honoured the dead Japanese sub-mariners
> with a Military funeral and sent their ashes back to Japan in the
> midst of war. The story is that the Commandant, on hearing
> this news, paraded the POW and informed them of the gesture
> of the Australian Government, and from that time, he became
> lenient in his behaviour towards them. Unfortunately, this was
> short-lived due to the [fact that] most of the inmates [were]

shipped for work on the Burma-Thai Railway, where they met with very harsh conditions.[13]

As time went on, POWs noticed that it was not uncommon for the Japanese to display considerable brutality and indifference to their own ranks, as well as to prisoners. Never was this more apparent than towards the end of the war, when the Japanese military units were in disarray; with capitulation imminent, POWs were being moved about as well. Trainloads of POWs would be alongside trainloads of sick and wounded Japanese soldiers, to whom no apparent care had been given. Several ex-POWs described scenes like the one Ron Winning remembered: 'Towards the end of the war, all POW were transferred to camps north of Bangkok. Our train was stopped by a bombed bridge and a trainload of wounded Japs pulled in alongside us. They had no food and begged water from us to drink. They had been over a month coming from Burma. Five corpses were pulled out in the morning.'[14]

Ernest Gordon tells about encountering a similar scene, possibly even the same trainload:

> The wounded men looked at us forlornly as they sat with their heads resting against the carriages, waiting fatalistically for death. They were the refuse of war; there was nowhere to go and no one to care for them. These were the enemy, more cowed and defeated than we had ever been.
>
> Without a word, most of the officers in my section unbuckled their packs, took out part of their ration and a rag or two, and, with water canteens in their hands went over to the Japanese train to help them. Our guards tried to prevent us, bawling, 'No goodka! No goodka!' But we ignored them and knelt by the side of the enemy to give them food and water, to clean and bind up their wounds, to smile and say a kind word. Grateful cries of 'Aragatto!' [Arigato] ('Thank you!') followed when we left.[15]

In view of how Korean guards were remembered for their brutality, Harry Whelan's anecdote is all the more remarkable:

> The Japanese disarmed and refused to feed a number of Korean members of the Japanese army, who had acted as guards in prison camps. They were desperate, as the local Thai population would have nothing to do with them. The Koreans appealed to Sergeant-Major Edkins [at Tamuan camp] for help. He offered to put them under the protection of the British Crown, provided they were prepared to work and to cause no trouble. They accepted with gratitude and shared our rations.[16]

And perhaps most remarkable of all is Kevin Nolan's story about kindness toward a particular guard who had been known for his viciousness to POWs:

> Most of the guards we had along the line had nicknames, some of which were 'Gold Tooth' (had a gold-capped tooth); 'Silver Tooth' (two prominent amalgam fillings); 'the Boy Bastard' (baby-faced); and 'The BBC' (Boy Bastard's Cobber, or pal). These were four of the most vicious specimens.
> Late in the war [again, possibly in that same trainload described above] Silver Tooth was found among a trainload of sick and wounded Japs and Koreans. He was very emaciated, sick with dysentery, and malaria to the point where he could barely stand. Sgt. Hal Saddler, who had good reason to hate him, with aid of a friend, lifted him off the train, cleaned him by a roadside pool, gave him a banana and settled him back on the train. This was one of several cases of men not seeking 'a tooth for a tooth', refusing to sink to the level of the opposition.[17]

But the guard Cecil Dickson remembered best was one who found a subtle and very meaningful way to lift the POWs' spirits during the darkest days of Railway work. A guard would have direct responsibility for a certain number of prisoners along the line; the same guard might be assigned to one work party every few days. Dickson and his friends noticed that whenever this particular guard was in charge of their group, he was especially easy on them, making sure they had regular breaks, and time for a cigarette or a sip of water.

Communication was strictly forbidden by the supervising engineers, and a guard could be punished just as severely as a POW for breaking this rule. One day, however, the guard, without making eye contact with any of the POWs, began whistling a tune, softly. After he repeated the refrain a couple of times, several Dutch, Australian, British and American POWs looked up at one another, exchanging glances of recognition. The tune the guard was whistling had been written especially for the 1937 International Boy Scout Jamboree, for which 28 000 Scouts from 54 countries, including Japan, had gathered—in the Netherlands! Apparently the guard was among them, and he correctly guessed, from their ages, that some of the POWs might have been there, too. His reminder of international brotherhood gave that handful of prisoners a bucketful of hope to carry back to camp on that day.[18]

15

Free to Shake the Shackles

3 OCTOBER 1945: In what was to be his final letter from a Southeast Asian address, Dickson allowed himself a wonderful thought: maybe he would celebrate his birthday by leaving for home! He even celebrated the thought of not having to skimp on paper any more, by indenting paragraphs.

The letter opens with an abbreviation of the Crusader's forward cry: '*Dieu Veut* [God willing], We Prevail.'

Chinese Chamber of Commerce
Bankok, Siam
October 3, 1945

Dear old Binks,

D.V.W.P. I look like celebrating October 6 by leaving Bankok for home. According to Major Kerr, the camp commandant, that date will see the closing down of this 'camp' and we shall then be free to shake off the shackles of the East. Singapore is about 6 hours by air from here. What the rate of progress will be after arriving there remains to be seen. If by air, which I believe is a possibility, it will be a matter of days; if by boat a couple of weeks—say three at the most. So it looks as if, whichever way we travel, this is the month! Our 19th anniversary passed uneventfully until the evening, when I went to the Alliance Française dance. Despite the worries of Madame——, President of the Alliance, it was a great success. The beginning was unpromising. About 7.30 rain began, and continued for 2 hours. A few minutes after the rain set in, the electric light failed, and remained blacked out for an hour. The bus to bring the English nurses and VAD's [auxiliary volunteers] had disappeared, and Madame's two chief assistants were nowhere to be

135

found. When we left here by truck she was here in her car. When we reached the Alliance she was at the top of the stairs receiving the guests. She flew about like a streak of lightning, never sitting in the one place for more than three seconds. Then everything came good. I believe that Madame even influenced the ending of the rain and the restoration of the city's electricity supply. She is the English wife of a Frenchman, and has done a tremendous amount for the ex-P.Ws. One of her greatest achievements last night was to get yours Truly to dance, twice.

Was just called to the telephone. Ron Winning reporting that he was leaving for the aerodrome. Our daily useful [servant] placed my boots in position and gave them the final polish, and off I went round to the Oriental to say good-bye and relieve Ron of his final few hundred ticals, which would be of no use to him once he left here. A later word from the C.O. re: the move is that we leave here for the aerodrome at 11 a.m. on the 5th and fly to Singapore on the 6th. That, he says, makes us too late for the next ship, which is due to leave there on the 6th. So the last party, 75 of us, he says, will fly straight on to Australia. We'll see!

To return to the dance—despite Madame's whirlwind personality, the undoubted pièce de résistance of the evening was Lady Louis Mountbatten's chief-of-staff, who is here carrying on the good work while Lady L. is in Batavia. She is 6 feet high, about 30, and a good looker. The RSM [Regimental Sergeant Major] here (Sunny Lay), Peter Cutter (Pioneer Sgt.) and I had half an hour's chat with her after the guests departed. She has been all over the place with Lady L., including Russia. One result of the talk was that a consignment of Cadbury's chocolate has already reached here and been distributed.

I do not remember mentioning that I went to 7 o'clock Communion last Sunday morning at Christ Church, Sathorn Road. The inside differed not the least from a parish church at home, about the size of Christ Church, Hawthorn, except that instead of gothic windows in the side walls there were gothic doors, all of which stood wide open, letting in the fresh morning air. A plate inside the church records the fact that the site was given by King Chulalongkorn on condition that it should be used by all Protestant Christians, irrespective of nationality or creed.

Well, old girl, this might be the last letter from overseas, and furthermore I might even beat it home. You can guess how I have been looking forward to and longing for the great day. Now it's coming close I can't realise it. The sight of the old Missus again will do the trick!

Cheerio

Pop

Article 108 of the third Geneva Convention provides that a prisoner is to have 'Whatever spiritual assistance he desires'. It appears that the Japanese started out with a willingness to allow services of worship on a regular basis in Java, but soon found an excuse to ban them. The excuse given was that the prisoners were being unco-operative about following instructions to sign a pledge saying, among other things, that they would not attempt to escape. Even after the commanding officers reluctantly ordered troops to do so, the privilege was not restored.

Cal Mitchell wryly reflected on the result of this ban: 'If ever the churches want to have maximum attendance, they should declare churches out of bounds on Sunday.' He noted that on the Sunday following the Japanese announcement that henceforth church parades would be prohibited, 'Instead of about 100 turning up as usual, hundreds turned up; many of them no doubt had never attended church voluntarily in their lives.'[1]

The chaplain to the Pioneer Battalion, the Rev. Frank Kellow, an Anglican priest, was captured with the unit on Java, and remained with them until the spring of 1944. He is always referred to as 'Padre', and his presence among POWs of all units meant a great deal, by all accounts.

Mitchell chronicled the various efforts to meet spiritual needs in the camps—always at the whim of whoever happened to be their commandant at a particular site:

> In so far as regular services go, whenever we were in a settled camp, services would be held, but on the Railway of course only brief Communion services could be arranged. It basically depended on the Japanese commander at the time. On the Burma side of the Railway there were a number of chaplains, with the exception of the Group 5 force, which my brother Alan was in. This was the force commanded by Colonel [Blucher] Tharp who commanded the American [131st Texas] Artillery unity in Java. They had a very bad time. Their doctor, Captain Lumpkin died and they had a particularly vicious Japanese commander. There was no chaplain with the force. We had two

brothers whose name was Hovenden; Bernie, who was a
sergeant with our force, and his brother whose Christian name
escapes me. They were Methodists, I think, not that this
mattered at all, since all services were ecumenical. Bernie's
brother, after working on the Railway would, when he returned
to camp, perform the duties of the chaplain with hospital
visiting, burials and other acts of Christian charity. These acts
were of course a great strain on him, and he eventually died.

After we had finished the Railway we moved to Tamarkan.
Services were held weekly, but when the movement of officers
from the other ranks took place in early 1945, the officers were
moved to Kanburi where the commandant was a sadistic
psychopath. Any group of more than six people standing
together was making plans to escape [in his view] and were
punished. This led to clandestine meetings for services. Before
we reached Kanburi, we had lost Frank [Padre Kellow], who
had been selected to go on one of the Japan Parties. We were
fortunate to have other good men including our two Royal
Australian Navy Chaplains.

[Generally] no religious services were permitted in the camps.
This would depend on a general direction by the Japanese Camp
Commandant, or the passing whim of one of the guards who,
possibly becoming bored, would decide on some action to either
silence the tedium, or just to show his superiority.

I am only too happy to tell you more about Padre Kellow,
whom I looked upon as a good friend. Frank was a very fine
man, who had until he injured his knee, been a top sportsman,
playing football and cricket at high levels. Frank was second
wicket keeper for Victoria, (somewhat akin to the catcher on a
baseball team).

He had a little parish in a tiny country town in the northeast
of Victoria. The name of the town was Corryong. He enlisted
from there. When Frank was posted as chaplain to our unit in
1940, he was dubbed 'Pearly Gates' by some of the irreverent
young officers, and to us he remained 'Pearly' from then on. I
think he rather enjoyed it. It became so commonly used that
when Jean [Mrs Mitchell] first met Bettye [Mrs Kellow], she
said, 'How are you, Mrs Gates?'

On the Railway, Frank was a tower of strength. In the early
days, Frank built a small chapel, open air, rails to sit on and a
Communion rail. However, after our move to the actual rail
laying force, there were no more chapels built. Frank spent his
time going out with the work force initially, until the number of
sick in the camp took up his full time. He ministered to the sick
and he buried the dead.

One task he took upon himself to do was the erection of crosses on the graves. These were made of quite solid wood, to try and make sure they would not rot away. He carved the names on the crosses when possible and when time permitted.

Whenever possible he gave communion to small groups. I recall in the 131 Kilo camp there was a thicket. Frank waited in the thicket with a small silver chalice which he carried, and we went in one at a time, to avoid suspicion. My memory does not recall the wine! But the bread was pieces of burnt rice. The wine was probably a mixture of burnt rice and hot water, which produced something we called coffee. Naturally, Frank's chalice held cold coffee.

Frank was very direct, and could never be described as a 'Holy Joe'! He had volunteered to go with the Japan Parties, but in view of the horrible loss of life to those parties [from torpedoes], his group was still in Saigon when the war ended. After the war Frank served as the chaplain at the Heidelberg Repatriation Hospital.

Frank baptised both our children; he also performed the marriage ceremony for my brother Alan's wedding. [He] never missed a reunion until near the end of his life, when he became very crippled. He died around 1982.

It has given me much pleasure to write about him . . .[2]

Driver Thomas Fagan, who did not survive captivity, kept a detailed diary, which was saved by his friends and given to his family after liberation. On 2 October 1943, he wrote:

I must pay homage to our respective Padres. It is not only what they say and how they say it, but what they do. They give as much physical help as they do spiritual. They are universally appreciated. They hold services in the various huts and it matters little whether one is a Church of England, a Catholic or Methodist, or whatever. The denomination is of little concern. We all join in and pray not only for ourselves, mainly for our loved ones waiting back home.[3]

Earlier that same year, on 10 June 1943, Fagan wrote: 'Many exist, I am sure, purely on the power of prayer and a determination to make it, no matter what they may have to suffer to be alive when this war is over. I, for one, have my faith and my religion.'[4]

One of the most memorable settings for being reminded of the strength which one's faith provides was described to Benjamin Dunn by another American ex-POW, Gene Stevens, a survivor from the

USS *Houston*. Stevens told of an incident which happened in the jungle of Thailand:

> It was on one of those forced marches at night, during the rainy season, and most of the men were sick, hungry, tired and almost without hope. As the men were being prodded by the Japs after a rest period to continue with their march, the place was as quiet as a tomb, when a Scotsman began singing a hymn, 'The Old Rugged Cross', in a beautiful voice. Everyone stood perfectly still, and the only sound we could hear was the hymn. Tears ran down my cheeks, and the men near me were crying. I have never heard anyone sing 'The Old Rugged Cross' like that Scotsman did. I'll never forget that as long as I live.[5]

Although not labelled as such, it was the ministry of one man to another which created the most enduring memories. Gordon Hamilton remembered the special ministries of Cecil Dickson and fellow Pioneers: 'Without the companionship and encouragement of Cec, together with Pearse McCarthy and Wally Summons, who visited me in the "Death House" at the 30 Kilo camp, I do not think I would have survived those very dark days of 1943. One or the other of them visited every day, and I cannot say how sustaining they were.'[6]

Ernest Gordon wrote of lying in a similar 'Death House', and being ministered to by fellow POWs—some of whom he had not known before—whose caring and coaxing gave him a renewed will to live, when he had all but lost it.[7]

And Ronald Searle credits 'A bunch of cheerful Australians and two Dutch officers, all of whom were still in rather a mess themselves' with nursing him back to health in the hospital hut at Kanchanaburi. 'They nursed me, spent their money on eggs and extras from the natives for me, washed me and, of all unlikely things, procured some sulphur drugs from somewhere for me. Anything was possible for the Australians—even the impossible. They saved my life and got me back on my bare feet again.'[8]

Whether they were conscious of it or not, these men were practising the one new commandment of their faith: '. . . That you love one another as I have loved you'.[9] In so doing, they gave the Japanese an example that some would never forget. Henry Shigeru Yagake, the former Japanese Air Force officer who finally asked POWs about their cheerful outlook (see Chapter 12), reflected further on how much he admired their spirit: 'They displayed not a scintilla of bitterness nor poor spirit,' he wrote. 'They encouraged each other to act happy even when they faced difficulties, were sad, mortified, or felt down and out. I noticed all that. They had splendid character. They did not acquire that trait from some others, but had learned [it] personally from trying to stay alive . . .'[10]

That so many succeeded is a tribute to all.

16

We're Well on the Way!

24 OCTOBER 1945: It was 11.00 a.m. on a beautiful Sunday morning aboard the troopship *Circassia*, 1200 miles from the Equator, and steaming for home at last. Apparently the *Circassia* waited for Dickson and his party of 75 to reach Singapore; this was the last ship out, laden with recovered POWs, combat troops and civilians. Only a hospital ship arrived in Australia later than this one.

Possibly unbeknown to one another, Dickson and his good friends Ron Winning and Gordon Hamilton, along with 514 other recovered POWs, were on the same ship. No doubt Winning and Hamilton were billeted with other officers; Dickson good-naturedly points out in his letter that he and other sergeants were 'bumped' from their quarters by civilians, so they were crowded in with the troops.

Dickson used real ink, and tissue-thin airmail stationery emblazoned with the Salvation Army shield, the six-sided Australian Comforts Fund star, and the inverted triangle of the YMCA. In the upper right-hand corner he sketched a map, showing how the ship had rounded the northern tip of Sumatra and crossed the Equator, headed first (he believed) for Fremantle, then Melbourne, and finally Sydney. He expected to post this letter at the first stop (which turned out to be Perth), and did so; the carefully preserved envelope shows that it passed through the Melbourne post office on 31 October at 9.30 p.m.

Not only did he have to re-open the envelope to postscript the very important estimated date of arrival in Melbourne, but he completely forgot to mention the name of the ship (causing much microfilm searching by a certain researcher several decades later).

Dear old Binks,

That's where we are at 11 a.m. Sunday, 24 Oct. So we're well on the way. Expect to berth at Fremantle sometime in the dark of Tuesday night, & there I shall put this on the airmail—if they have such modern innovations in this new country we're rapidly approaching. Well—not so very rapidly, but not bad—15 knots, or 400 miles (approx.) a day. I don't expect to feel really excited about it until I actually sight you on the wharf at Port Melbourne, or Victoria dock, or wherever it will be. We embarked about 10 a.m. on Monday, 15th, and, contrary to expectations, sailed the same day about 3.30 p.m. Turned north-west up Malacca Strait (between Java and Sumatra), where at Oosthaven, on 15 Feb. 1942, we nearly landed to defend Palambay aerodrome, but were too late and returned to the ship. On Wednesday morning we rounded the top of Sumatra and headed for home. The weather has been very good—fair breeze and easy swell—and as the result of a good run we are actually some hours ahead of schedule. We are carrying a number of civilians, who are occupying the space that would otherwise have been allotted to the sergeants, who therefore are living & eating on the troop decks with the men. I am in a small mess of 7, a good crew, including a fellow sgt. of the 2/2 Famous Famous, (Arthur Gordon), a sailor (ex-'Perth') and the rest Malay volunteers. Quite uneventful.

Very much love to you old darling.

Pop

P.S.   After sealing down the envelope it occurred to me that I had omitted one of the most important items. We are due to arrive in Melbourne about Wednesday, 31st Oct. Won't it be fun!

Ron Winning remembered some shipboard details before the *Circassia* reached Melbourne:

It was a very relaxing trip to Perth; weather good, and the knowledge that we would soon be home was wonderful. We reached Perth, and were able to phone our families. After a day in Perth we sailed again. However, there was a tragedy. One of the men [see below] phoned home and was told his wife had formed a liaison with another man. After we sailed, he slipped over the side. He wasn't missed for awhile. The ship hove to, but [the] search was hopeless. After all he had been through![1]

In a front-page article in its Monday, 5 November 1945 edition, the Melbourne *Sun* referred to the incident mentioned by Winning, but apparently the ex-POW's friends were not quite so forthcoming with newspaper reporters at the time. The story says: 'When only two days from home after being a prisoner of war for more than four years, Private F.B. Coughlin, married, of Kew, was missing

Ex-POWs on deck of Highland Brigade *bound for Australia, October 1945. Mitchell brothers Cal* (hatless, balding head, arrow, right) *and Alan* (arrow, near centre background) *are coming home together at last.* (COURTESY OF C.J. MITCHELL)

from the *Circassia*. The ship stopped and a vain search carried out for more than an hour in the dusk. Friends of Pte Coughlin said he had been suffering from malaria and the effects of ill-treatment by the Japanese.'[2]

Possibly because of the delay in searching for the missing man, the *Circassia* sat in Port Melbourne Harbour during the night of 2 November, and did not dock until the following morning. Tom O'Brien recalled how 'We sat up all night, looking at the lights of home. No one slept.'[3]

The next morning, Ron Winning said, 'We sailed through the Heads into Port Phillip Bay and were welcomed by an escort of small ships and yachts.'

Cal Mitchell, who arrived on 23 October on the *Highland Brigade*, noted the universal welcome troopships received in Australia: 'As the ship came up Port Phillip Bay, we saw the words "Welcome Home" printed in huge letters on the roof of the sheds of the wharf.'

The *Sun*'s account added this detail: 'As the *Circassia* berthed in front of the [British battleship] *King George V*, two banners were seen on the rail. One bore the inscription: "Salute to [General H. Gordon]

Bennett"; and alongside it, one showing a bowler hat with the words: "A Soldier's Reward". Sailors on the battleship turned out on deck to welcome the returning prisoners.'

Each shipload was met on the wharf by a fleet of buses and driven through Melbourne. According to the *Sun*, the route took them via Bay Street, City Road, Swanston, Queensberry and Elizabeth Streets, Flemington Road and Racecourse Road, to the Agricultural Hall Showgrounds, where relatives had been assembled to greet them. The itinerary was announced because citizens were encouraged to greet each shipload of troops as they returned.

And indeed they did. Mitchell remembered one incident: 'As we were being driven through the city, through crowds of cheering people, our bus stopped outside of Town Hall and I vividly recall a very well dressed lady wearing quite magnificent silver earrings running from the crowd and with tears streaming down her face, [she] gave me a beautiful kiss. Perhaps she had lost someone. I was leaning out the window at the time . . . I found my people and it was a wonderful moment. Cars or taxis were provided to take us home.'[4]

Possibly Cal Mitchell's face, with his jaunty smile and thin moustache, reminded the woman in the crowd of a loved one who had not returned, and when she spotted Mitchell, she determined to give out the welcome-home kiss she had saved for so long.

Eileen Mitchell's reunion with her fiancé, Cal's brother Alan, reads as well as any romance novel:

> Of course, the day of home-coming, was perhaps the most wonderful day of my life—though we were married six days after. We had planned in our letters from Bangkok the way we would meet. He hoped we would be all alone. I pictured he would get off a train and walk towards me, and I would hurry to him.
>
> What actually happened was that hundreds of soldiers were unloaded from buses at the Showgrounds in Flemington and we all milled about in confusion till we bumped into the one we were seeking. The first moment was his huge dark eyes and gaunt face.
>
> We had such a frantic six days before our wedding that the memory of what he felt is a blur. He must have felt strange and unreal, but seemed his own delightful, thoughtful self that I took everything for granted.
>
> I know I failed to grasp what he had suffered and the horrors he had been through. Jim was born in August '46 and the two little girls quickly, so that our life was a rush.

There was a school of thought that the men should not be reminded of their experiences. I am glad that I understood things better as the years went by.[5]

The stages of Kevin Nolan's journey home could not be outdone by Hollywood:

When I finally got to Singapore, I was given a cake of soap, a big fluffy towel and directed to a battery of hot showers. Whilst luxuriating under the hot water, my delight turned to ecstasy when over the Public Address system came the voice of a prewar favourite of mine, John Charles Thomas, singing 'the Lord's Prayer'. My reaction was to think to myself: 'This has *got* to be heaven.'

Later that day, after much searching, I located four letters from my beloved. She had waited all those years. The war was over and life was about to begin!

I embarked from Singapore on the *Moreton Bay*, headed for Fremantle, where one of the joys of leave was the allowance of a direct phone link to Victoria. I got through to Marj, and we spoke to each other for the first time in four and a half years— and all we could manage to exchange were banalities such as: 'How are you, Darling? Yes, I'm fine thanks. You are well? That's good. No really, I'm in good shape. See you soon.' Couldn't think of anything intelligent to say! A few days later, we were reunited on the 31st of October, 1945, and had no trouble carrying on from where we had left off, so long ago . . . We married and settled on a mixed farm in western Victoria and raised, among other things, four very nice children.[6]

As mentioned earlier, Dickson did not recognise his wife for several minutes after she first approached him. For Tom O'Brien, the memory of reunion with his loved ones was still an overwhelming reminder of all the family years he lost: 'I had been away five years [including the time in Syria]—and this lovely young woman came up and threw her arms around me. I didn't know who she was. It was my younger sister. She had been a child when I left, just about 13 years old. While I was gone, she had grown into a young woman. I recognised my older sister, of course—but I didn't even recognise my own sister . . .' He turned away, unable to finish the sentence.[7]

As for Dickson, all his hints, requests and reminders in letters home during the previous two months paid off. Freda came to meet him unaccompanied by other relatives, and the quiet cottage in

Queenscliff she had booked for an extended stay was not the scene of family reunions for several weeks.

Time enough to again hear English spoken all day in complete sentences, and in a recognised accent; to slip into a familiar jacket and select a favourite necktie; to sit outdoors in comfortable shade with a minimum of winged pests; to savour favourite brands each day, from toothpaste to tea; to gaze at the stars each night, without longing; to share silence with a beloved; to make your own plans, and know that tomorrow will come.

17

Lost and Found

Could anything have been done to ease the suffering of POWs on the Railway? Whether the International Red Cross could have been more persistent in periodically requesting to visit POW camps, or to otherwise check on conditions in various locations, will probably continue to be a source of debate. Certainly it is possible to wonder why that agency, once equipped with hard proof that its parcels were *not* being distributed to POWs, did not find more vigorous ways to pursue this particular subject. Such an opportunity was repeatedly presented all during 1943–44, after many pre-printed postcards had been received in Australia, for example, with no mention whatsoever of Red Cross parcels. Surely it would have been reasonable for the International Red Cross to once again request a reinstatement of the original arrangement (receipts signed by POWs), or some other proof, which might have pressured local camp commandants to release the desperately needed packages they were hoarding.

An even stronger protest might have been mounted once the handful of torpedoed Japan-bound POWs were rescued and brought to Brisbane, because they confirmed that Red Cross supplies were not being made available to prisoners. Some complaint was made to the Japanese following these disclosures, but in view of the forceful public statements made by heads of government in Australia, the United Kingdom and the United States, it is puzzling why relief agencies did not take more effective advantage of this occasion to insist upon verifiable, more humane conditions in the camps.

Later in this chapter, we will see how Australian ex-POWs found the International Red Cross to be a continuing source of frustration for several years following their release.

As to whether anything might have been done to ease the suffering caused by the day-to-day treatment of prisoners on the Railway by the Japanese and their Korean conscripts, the sad answer is: probably not, given the mind-set and training of camp staff.

At the very end of his book, *Crosses and Tigers*, Japanese military police interpreter Nagase says: 'No Japanese soldiers were taught about the treatment of prisoners.'[1] He goes on to quote Japanese camp staff personnel who were convicted of war crimes as grumbling about this lack of instruction from their superiors.

A documentary shown on American television in the summer of 1992 suggests that the attitude within Japan, regarding prisoners, has not changed much in the last 50 years. On the ABC program, '20/20', viewers were shocked to see scenes of Japanese civilian prisoners being routinely subjected to terrific beatings while in gaol awaiting trial. The reason given was that just being suspected of criminal behaviour in Japan is taken very, very seriously, and is cause for punishment, regardless of the disposition of the case.

Similarly, TV and newspaper accounts of stories about rigorous enforcement of rules in Japanese schools are a disturbing echo of prison camp life, where the punishment far exceeded the degree of infraction. Shock waves reverberated throughout Japan and the world in July 1990, when a high school girl was crushed by an iron gate being slammed shut by a teacher as the final 8.30 a.m. bell was sounding.[2]

And the following year, debate was renewed in Japan over (as the *New York Times* phrased it) 'The near-obsession of some school authorities in enforcing rules', in an article describing how two teenagers, at a private institution for troubled children, were put to death after being caught smoking in violation of school rules. The youngsters, a 14-year-old boy and a 16-year-old girl, were placed in a windowless shed, similar to the 'hot box' used for discipline in some prison camps. After 45 hours in temperatures as high as 122°, the children died. The school's principal was arrested, but no mention was made in the article, or in a subsequent CBS News story on the incident, of what action, if any, the children's parents planned to take.[3]

Such incidents tend to reinforce the belief echoed by several of Cecil Dickson's friends, who spoke or wrote the same sentiment: 'I just don't trust them.'

Sitting in Margaret Dickson's living room at the War Veteran's Village in Narrabeen, New South Wales, Harry Whelan reflected softly: 'They'd do the same thing again, if they had the chance.' Gazing out the window, he added: 'Let's hope they don't get the chance.' Then, with a laugh which may come easily to someone in his ninth decade, Whelan slapped his knee and exclaimed: 'At least not in our lifetime, eh, Margaret?'

Whelan and his fellow ex-POWs might be surprised to learn that many Japanese agree with them. Intense pressure was put on Japan by the United Nations, led by the United States, to contribute not only more money, but troops as well, to the peacekeeping forces in the Persian Gulf War during 1990–91. But the Japanese government, in keeping with its Constitution, steadfastly refused to deploy troops overseas at that time, while heated public debate took place.

Continuing diplomatic and political pressure by other world powers resulted in a reluctant 1992 agreement by the Japanese parliament to allow military personnel to serve under United Nations command, with a special vote necessary for each deployment. But a member of the Japanese parliament, Masao Kunihiro, may have spoken for many Japanese, other Asian nations, and ex-POWs as well, when he told some Americans: 'I know the day will come when you will regret it.'[4]

Jay N. Woodworth, a New York banker who has made over 60 business trips to Japan and other Asian countries in recent years, stated that many Japanese have stressed to him their belief that the continued presence of United States troops on their soil provides them with security against a resurgence of military power in their nation. Moreover, he agrees with Nagase that the Yasukuni Shrine, where Imperial War Minister Hideki Tojo is buried along with many other military leaders, is a disturbing reminder of the militarism which is still just below the surface in Japan.[5]

Can the Japanese move toward a national understanding of their full role in World War II? And will remorse ever be part of the national psyche, as it has been in Germany?

The Reverend Yuri Ando, pastor of the United Japanese Church of Westchester, an interdenominational Christian congregation which meets in Scarsdale, just north of New York City, summed up what she saw as the prevailing current sentiment among her countrymen: 'When you have a victim mentality, you have no room in your heart to see the sorrows of those who suffered at the hands of the Japanese.'[6]

Pastor Ando commented: 'My parents lost their childhood,' and says her mother still has nightmares about walking to work and crouching against a wall during air raids. Her father, who volunteered to be a language teacher in the Philippines rather than serve in the Japanese army, was nevertheless terrified to surrender to United States troops when ordered to do so in August 1945. He had seen how the Japanese treated civilian prisoners, and he was sure American soldiers would do the same, so he fled into the hills. After living on snakes and lizards, and contracting malaria (a familiar scenario to

Railway POWs), he finally turned himself in, and was astounded to be given chocolate and cigarettes, as well as spiritual comfort, by a United States Army chaplain who became a lifelong friend.

Pastor Ando, who was born in 1954, said that in Japan history classes are taught as a chronology, without comment. In fact, 'It is not considered polite to interrupt the teacher,' added Reiko Sasso, who was educated in Japan a generation earlier than Pastor Ando, and who now heads the library at the Japan Society in New York City. Even today, if children ask too many questions in class, this is often reason for censure and a parental conference.

Pastor Ando remembered history textbook stories about how the Japanese people suffered during the war, but students were not told about prisoners, civilian or military, being taken by the Japanese. Her recollections were substantiated by Ryushi Hara and his mother, Yasuko. Ryushi was born in Melbourne in 1972, and started school there. He completed elementary and junior high school in Japan (where he was strongly chastised for speaking English), before moving with his family to Scarsdale, New York, completing high school there, and continuing his education at a United States university. Yasuko Hara recalled learning 'a little' about World War II, but 'It was only a few paragraphs at the end of the textbook.' The subject would not be discussed unless the teacher found time to bring it up. By the time Ryushi was in junior high school, he said, the students learned a little more about the war, primarily the important military engagements such as the naval battles of the Coral Sea and Midway. But, Ryushi confirmed, there was no mention of Bataan, Corregidor, the Burma Railway or civilian internees.[7]

Pastor Ando summarised what had until recently been the view of the Japanese Ministry of Education: 'If we show that shameful part of our history, then our children will not respect our country.' She observed that 'Japanese take many things personally, so they would feel personally shamed to learn of the atrocities committed by their troops during World War II.'

But it looks as if, finally, the efforts of Michiko Asano of the College Women's Association of Japan, and others concerned with education in that country, have begun to pay off. Until 1992, a typical textbook in Japan read: 'We must not forget that Japan caused inconvenience to neighboring Asian countries in the past.' After strong urgings by the Ministry of Education, publishers distributed new textbooks beginning in April 1993 which have altered that same passage to read: 'We must not forget that Japan caused unbearable suffering to neighboring nations in the past.'[8]

With the publication of this book, close-up photographs taken secretly, showing emaciated Allied POWs in Japanese camps, are being generally circulated for the first time, and have become part of the permanent POW exhibit at the Australian War Memorial in Canberra. Although some photos like the ones in these pages were shown as evidence in War Crimes Trials in Tokyo, Singapore and other tribunals immediately after World War II, they were not widely distributed. Most have remained in military archives, or in the hands of private collectors, or former POWs like Cal Mitchell. For many years it may not have seemed appropriate to release these photos for general viewing; after all, most are taken at quite close range, so that many faces are recognisable. Some POWs shown here did not return. Only those who survived can easily say to children or grandchildren: 'Look how skinny I was then!' But for a parent, wife or sweetheart whose loved one is buried in Burma or Thailand, these pictures will never be easy to look at. So Cal Mitchell waited a long time to pass them along; no doubt he hesitated for many of the same reasons Sir Edward 'Weary' Dunlop expressed in the preface to his *War Diaries* (published in 1986): 'I have shrunk from publishing these diaries for over 40 years. It seemed that they might add further suffering to those bereaved, and add to controversy and hatred . . .'[9]

But eventually the need for an accurate record of history takes precedence over other considerations, and to his credit, Mitchell recognised this. Since nearly all those pictured are Australians, and since a book was being written centring on members of his battalion, he decided to hand them to the author as soon as her plane landed at the airport in Melbourne, in October 1991.

None of the photos in these pages have been retouched or altered in any way. What you see is what was there, in the jungles of Burma and Thailand during those awful years of internment, under what Cecil Dickson frequently referred to as 'unspeakable' conditions. These photos speak of camp conditions as no words can. Some others, such as those Colonel Williams described taking of himself and other officers after 30 days of non-stop torture, might have spoken even louder. But those additional prints did not survive, being in what the Battalion Commanding officer called 'unexpected places', so the very worst situations are not depicted here—only day-to-day life is glimpsed.

There is little question that without the constant reminders afforded by oft-printed photos of Nazi concentration camp inmates, the German public might never have built up the sense of collective shame they have been made to feel about what went on under their very noses, in some cases—or what they turned away from seeing. As a result, a 'never again!' determination still pervades the German conscience, despite increasingly bold neo-Nazi activity in recent times.

But apparently until now, the Japanese have had few, if any, pictorial reminders of POW internment, in their own country or at other locations. So the textbook alterations mentioned above represent what for many schoolchildren will be a first step in developing a collective awareness of and sensitivity to the reasons many Westerners and other Asians still feel such hostility and bitterness towards them.

Perhaps by the time Japanese elementary-school children of the 1990s are old enough to travel as tourists to the Australian War Memorial, they will actually visit the POW exhibit there—in contrast to the two busloads of young Japanese seen by this writer arriving at the War Memorial just fifteen minutes before closing time, and emerging just twelve minutes later to re-board their buses. It is partly this kind of insensitivity on the part of his countrymen who travel abroad which prompts Takashi Nagase to warn that 'Hatred and resentment towards the Japanese are more fierce than the Japanese imagine.'[10]

To his family, Cecil Dickson did not display a lingering resentment of the Japanese. When he did mention some aspect of camp conditions, he was likely to add that in the worst locations, 'The Japanese had no better.' But few of his friends were so sanguine; perhaps in private conversations with them, Dickson acknowledged feelings he was otherwise reluctant to express.

Ron Winning wrote: 'I share with Col. Williams and Cec Dickson an abiding hatred of the Japs';[11] and Leo Cornelius added: 'I do not share or understand forgiveness for wanton cruelty and in fact bestiality.'[12]

'I do find thinking or talking of our experiences at hands of the Japanese quite distressing' Gordon Hamilton admitted;[13] while Harry Bishop decided that 'When you get into the eighties, it's time to relax a bit.'[14]

Cal Mitchell picked up on the theme struck by Takashi Nagasi when he observed: 'The Japanese are not only buying up [US] assets; they are busy doing the same thing here, although they seem to be very surprised at the ex-servicemen's reaction.'[15]

Increasingly, when old World War II wounds are re-opened, the Japanese government is responding with acknowledgement of the pain its policies caused, and attempting to make some sort of compensation. For example, when Japanese officials visited Seoul in 1990 and were confronted by Korean women who had been forced to be 'comfort girls' for Japanese troops during the 1940s, they is-sued an apology and arranged for some payment to the victims.[16]

Similarly, the United States government, by an act of Congress in 1988, apologised for the internment of 120 000 Japanese in the United States during World War II, and authorised a payment of $20 000 to each survivor. After Pearl Harbor was attacked, the American public was led to believe that Japanese families were uprooted from their homes and gathered into common barracks at 'relocation camps' (primarily in remote desert locations of Arizona, Texas and California) because they posed a 'security risk' on the Pacific Coast. This ex-planation was plausible, especially to many Americans living along the Atlantic Coast, because German agents had been infiltrating the civilian population there all during the 1930s and early 1940s, with considerable success: numerous U-boat (submarine) sightings had been reported, and some landings had even occurred. So a large Japanese population, concentrated near so many military bases and shipyards in California, was a sudden cause for alarm. By mid-February 1942, President Franklin D. Roosevelt had signed an Ex-ecutive Order to remove 'all persons' from the vicinity of military zones. Although many people were in such zones, only those of Japanese descent were moved—despite the fact that over two thirds were United States citizens by birth. (No one of Japanese descent was allowed to apply for United States citizenship until 1952.)

The official explanation of 'national security' for these forced relocations has been perpetuated for over half a century, although the *New York Times*, in a 1992 editorial, belatedly recognised that the policy was based on a 'mistaken belief'.[17]

However, in her meticulously researched book, *Years of Infamy: The Untold Story of America's Concentration Camps*, published in 1976, Michi Nishiura Weglyn details a different and bizarre reason for the internment of herself, her family and so many others. It was done, she documents, in order to amass hostages to exchange for sick and wounded United States military prisoners, as well as the many American civilians who were being held in Japanese-occupied ter-ritories. As of June 1942, Ms Weglyn discovered, the United States had precisely one Japanese POW in custody: an airman captured in Pearl Harbor when his plane ditched in shallow water.

So the roundup began, and even third-generation Japanese nationals from as far away as Peru were brought to detention centres in the south-western United States. Over the next 20 months, nearly 3000 Japanese were exchanged for a comparable number of Americans. But in late 1943, a demonstration over poor living conditions took place at the Tule Lake detention centre in California, and it was put down with force. Two Japanese died, and several more were wounded. In protest, Tokyo abruptly halted the exchange of prisoners—ironically, in November 1943, just after the Burma–Thailand Railway had been completed under far worse living conditions, and with such an appalling loss of American and other POW lives—but these details were unknown to the world at that time.

Despite its act of atonement, the United States government underfunded this compensation program, and by 1992 many Japanese-Americans were still awaiting their cheques.

But four years represents lightning speed, compared with the runaround Australian ex-POWs got from their government following World War II. Citing War Financial Regulations entitling them to a subsistence allowance when the military could not provide meals for them, ex-POWs requested that they be paid three shillings a day for all the meals they literally missed while prisoners of the Japanese. However, a 26 September 1950 government report contains the astounding conclusions that, among other findings, conditions to which Australians were subjected while prisoners was beyond the government's control; and besides, the government had lost the services of its soldiers during their captivity!

Worse still, the Australian government ultimately decided that, rather than pay direct compensation to its ex-POWs, as the United States had done, payments should be distributed through the International Red Cross, lest the government appear to be setting a 'monetary premium' for soldiers remaining prisoner during future wars![18]

To add insult to injury, the government rejected the requests for subsistence pay or additional compensation for those interned by the Japanese, while acknowledging that conditions for these men had been notably more harsh than those encountered by prisoners in Europe and the Middle East. Payment would be made, the government determined, from three sources: reparation funds from the Japanese government, turned over to the International Red Cross; the cash value of Japanese assets frozen in foreign countries; and, finally, proceeds from the sale of the Railway by the Thai government.

Eventually, the IRC amassed over £4.5M from these sources, and the sum gathered interest during nearly seven years of delay, while the IRC ponderously attempted to get accurate figures from each nation as to how many of its citizens were interned during the war, and to determine the value of frozen Japanese assets, etc. During much of this time, Colonel Williams just happened to be serving as

Above, Pioneers assembling for their first postwar Anzac Day parade, Melbourne, April 1946. Nearly all are ex-POWs. Below left Pioneers marching, Anzac Day, Melbourne, April 1990. Below centre Colonel J. M. Williams ready to lead the march, Anzac Day, April 1989. (PHOTOS COURTESY 2/2 AUSTRALIAN PIONEER BATTALION ASSOCIATION)

President of the New South Wales branch of the Ex-POW Association of Australia, and he relentlessly pressed to have the matter resolved.

Finally, in early 1958, it was announced that each former prisoner of the Japanese would receive a grand total of 86 pounds (a little over US $100 equivalent), and the government of Australia stated: 'It is not expected that further funds will become available to enable additional payments to be made.'[19]

It would be the understatement of the century to say that no payment could begin to compensate prisoners of any nationality for their suffering; for prisoners of the Railway, their best compensation is the triumph which each day since 16 August 1945 has represented. Although every man had ample entitlement to feel otherwise, most recognised that, in order to have a future, one must let go of the past. For many, their first act of power was choosing *not* to seek revenge. The moment that each ex-prisoner was able to turn his back on his former tormentors, to dismiss them from his sight, he took back the power over his own life—which had been denied to him for so long. And each time that a flashback from captivity fills his mind, he is a prisoner again, if only for a few minutes.

Cecil Dickson took great pride in telling members of his family how he had greeted a Japanese businessman at the London office of J.B. Were & Co. in the mid-1960s, only to discover that he was looking into the face of an especially unpleasant former commandant of one POW camp. Dickson was able to be civil to the Japanese, and conclude business with the man in a highly professional manner, to his own everlasting satisfaction and, perhaps, relief.

Not all ex-POWs have had the opportunity to confront their past so directly; and some found, to their dismay, that even a lifetime later they could not do so with Dickson's aplomb. One former prisoner of the Japanese, a physician who became a prominent throat specialist in New York City, confided to a friend that he had always avoided Japanese patients. One day in the late 1980s, he decided that 40 years was surely long enough to get over his feelings, and he agreed to see a Japanese businessman who had been referred by a colleague. As he began to examine the patient, the physician suddenly realised that he was choking the Japanese who, incidentally, was a total stranger. Chagrined, the physician released his hold on the patient's throat, turned away, and asked the man to please put on his shirt and leave the office.

Reflecting on Cecil Dickson's bearing, former United States Navy Chaplain Peter MacLean remarked: 'I knew that I was in the presence of someone who had been to Hell, but Cecil lived very much in the present. By the time I met him, in the late 1970s, whatever hatred there was in him, had been left somewhere.'[20]

What remained, like gold purified by fire, was a joy in, and reverence for, life—and the brotherhood shared with his closest friends, most of whom were fellow Pioneers. Because theirs was mostly a home-town unit, drawing recruits primarily from the environs of either Melbourne or Sydney, many Pioneers already shared a familiarity which the crucibles of combat and captivity strengthened into lifelong friendships. The 2/2 Pioneer Battalion Association is one of the most active in Australia, and includes men from the reconstituted unit as well as ex-POWs.

The Battalion's Commanding Officer, by constantly challenging the treatment of his men by the Japanese, earned the title of 'No. 1 bad man, Australian' from his captors, and by all accounts he paid dearly for that distinction. Colonel Williams is acknowledged to have been more harshly treated, and with greater frequency, than any other prisoner. Often, after arguing unsuccessfully with Japanese camp officials over the conditions imposed upon the men under his command, Colonel Williams would enforce his own rigorous sanitation measures, driving his exhausted troops to scrub, burn and dig when they arrived at some filthy campsite just vacated by coolie labourers. Some men in his unit deeply resented him for this, until they discovered, after the war, that the Pioneers had just about the lowest death rate on the Railway: of 865 who became POWs, 607 managed to survive.

It would be hard to measure how many lives were sustained with fellowship, or how many final moments were comforted by it, when there was nothing else to give. I had an opportunity to see this spirit at work on one of the final days of my visit to Australia in October 1991, a little over three years after Cecil Dickson died. His brother John lay gravely ill in a Melbourne hospital after two emergency surgeries. Sadly, I realised my long-anticipated meeting with the younger Dickson would not take place after all, and I reluctantly gathered my things together to leave for Sydney and New York.

Cal Mitchell stopped by my hotel for a few minutes; we sat in the sunlit breakfast room while he identified when and where each captivity photograph had been taken. Typically, Mitchell balanced the grim reality of each scene with a few light anecdotes of camp life, as if the see-saw in his mind could remain level, and not ever quite crash to the ground. He looked at his watch, and as I carefully replaced each photo in the manila envelope, he stood, picked up his hat, and said quietly: 'I'm on my way to visit John this morning. You see, in the camps, no one ever died alone.'

And then he was off, stepping briskly into the fine spring morning, making sure the tradition would continue.

2/2 Australian Pioneer Battalion Prisoners of War

Listed below are the names of 2/2 Australian Pioneer Battalion members who were ordered to surrender to the Japanese, beginning 8 March 1942, or who were subsequently captured.

Each asterisk indicates a man who died in captivity while trying so hard to live, often knowing his friends were nearby—always knowing he would not be forgotten.

All deserve our remembrance and our gratitude for the example they set.

Abbott, Pte E.*	Baade, Pte S.A.	Belchambers, Pte P.G.
Acheson, Pte A.A.	Bacon, Pte F.J.	Bell, Pte C.J.
Adams, Pte D.K.	Bailey, Cpl L.W.	Benfield, Pte J.M.
Adolphson, Pte F.A.*	Bailey, Pte M.*	Bennett, Pte W.H.
Adolphson, Pte R.G.	Baines, Pte W.T.	Bergin, Pte E.F.
Aggett, Pte T.A.	Baker, Pte A.E.	Beverly, Pte C.W.S.
Aiken, Pte F.C.	Baker, Pte S.R.	Biesse, Pte R.C.*
Alexander, Pte J.W.	Banfield, Pte A.G.*	Birkitt-Vipont, Pte S.A.
Allardice, L/Cpl M.D.	Barber, Pte B.*	Bishop, Capt A.H.
Allchin, L/Cpl C.E.*	Barden, Pte W.J.E.	Bishop, Pte H.C.S.
Allen, Pte E.	Barker, Pte C.R.	Bishop, Pte H.R.
Allen, Pte F.A.	Barlow, Pte J.J.J.	Bishop, Pte W.T.
Allen, Pte K.E.*	Barnes, Pte A.J.	Black, Sgt H.
Allen, Lieut R.W.	Barnes, Pte F.G.*	Blake, Pte A.E.*
Allingham, Pte J.F.C.	Barnes, Pte J.C.	Blake, Pte W.
Altman, Pte J.F.C.	Barnett, Pte E.N.	Bland, Pte B.G.
Amoore, Pte J.	Barnstable, Pte F.J.	Blyton, Pte H.W.
Anderson, L/Cpl A.	Barrett, L/Cpl K.T.	Bock, Pte E.W.*
Anderson, Pte A.W.J.	Barrett, L/Cpl W.J.	Bond, Cpl J.C.*
Anderson, Cpl D.R.	Barry, Pte S.R.*	Boreham, Pte H.E.*
Anderson, Pte W.	Bateson, L/Cpl N.*	Bould, Pte K.A.*
Anning, Pte C.C.	Batten, Pte L.E.*	Bourke, Pte L.J.
Archibald, Pte G.S.	Batten, Pte W.J.	Bourne, Pte W.E.*
Armstrong, Pte E.B.	Battye, Cpl D.H.	Bover, Cpl C.F.
Armstrong, Pte W.*	Baylis, Pte J.W.	Box, Pte R.J.*
Ashford, Cpl H.*	Beadle, Pte A.J.*	Boyd, Pte W.
Atkin, Pte H.	Beaumont, Pte A.C.	Boyd, Pte H.W.
Atkinson, Pte N.H.*	Beecham, Pte C.E.	Boyes, Pte H.C.*

Brackley, Pte W.E.A.
Bradley, Pte J.J.
Brady, Pte C.*
Bramfitt, Pte A.E.
Bredin, Pte G.H.
Britt, L/Sgt C.W.
Broadhurst, Pte T.B.
Brodribb, Pte J.E.E.*
Broes, Pte J.
Broome, Pte A.L.*
Brown, Pte A.M.*
Brown, Pte L.C.*
Brown, Pte L.D.
Brown, Pte L.G.
Bruce, Cpl J.H.
Buchanan, Pte E.A.D.
Buckland, Pte A.B.
Budge, Pte W.G.*
Buerckner, Pte E.F.
Bulmer, Pte C.F.
Burke, Pte F.J.
Burkitt, Pte A.J.E.
Burns, Pte A.*
Butler, Pte A.F.*
Butler, Pte L.V.*
Cain, Pte K.K.
Cameron, Pte A.
Cameron, Pte I.D.*
Cameron, Pte J.J.*
Camm, L/Cpl A.S.
Camm, Pte R.*
Campbell, Pte D.
Campbell, Capt E.
Campbell, Capt I.A.
Carne, Pte W.*
Carpenter, Pte C.A.
Carroll, Pte F.J.
Carroll, Pte G.P.
Carroll, Pte P.J.
Carter, Sgt S.G.
Casey, Pte F.
Cassidy, Pte S.N.
Cavanagh, Pte C.*
Cattanach, Pte S.J.
Chandler, Pte S.P.
Cheeseman, Pte W.H.
Chick, Pte A.V.*

Childs, Pte R.W.
Chivers, Sgt F.A.*
Chivers, Pte H.C.
Christie, Pte C.J.
Christie, Pte D.E.*
Clark, Pte F.
Clark, Pte F.D.
Clark, Pte W.M.*
Clarkson, Pte F.
Cleary, Pte R.
Clement, Pte J.T.L.
Clements, Pte E.G.*
Clifford, Pte V.
Close, Pte V.T.*
Coatsworth, L/Cpl G.E.
Coe, Pte J.C.G.
Collins, Pte H.
Comptom, Pte S.A.W.
Connan, S/Sgt A.D.*
Connell, Pte D.W.*
Connell, Pte W.E.
Connelly, Pte N.A.
Connors, Pte F.
Connors, Pte S.J.*
Cook, Pte P.C.
Cook, Pte W.R.*
Cookson, Pte W.R.
Coombe, Pte J.
Cooper, Pte C.W.*
Cooper, Pte G.J.*
Conder, Pte E.G.C.
Condon, Pte D.A.J.
Cornelius, L/Sgt L.G.
Corrie, Sgt E.C.W.
Cosson, Pte E.G.
Coughlin, Pte F.B.
Coulsell, L/Cpl C.B.
Coulson, Pte G.C.
Courtney, Cpl E.R.
Cousins, Pte A.H.
Cowden, Cpl M.B.
Cowley, Pte H.
Craig, Pte W.J.
Cramsie, Pte B.
Craven, Pte D.F.
Cream, Pte G.T.J.
Croft, Sgt T.M.

Cross, Pte R.C.
Crozier, Pte T.J.
Cunningham, Pte W.F.
Curry, Pte M.J.
Cutter, Sgt A.R.
Dale, Pte J.S.
Daly, Maj E.A.
D'Argaville, Pte J.
Dart, Pte S.W.
David, Pte H.
Davidson, Pte A.L.*
Davidson, Pte N.A.
Davis, Pte H.H.
Dawson, Pte A.W.
Dean, Cpl W.*
Delaney, Pte R.
Dellaca, Pte J.T.*
Denholm, Pte D.G.
Dewsbury, Pte A. deF.*
Dibb, Pte H.L.*
Dickinson, Pte R.W.*
Dickson, Pte D.H.
Dickson, Cpl J.B.
Dickson, S/Sgt T.C.
Dixon, Pte J.
Dixon, Pte J.H.
Dobson, Cpl G.K.*
Doherty, Pte A.
Doig, Pte A.C.*
Donald, Pte J.
Donnelly, Pte R.A.
Donovan, Pte N.R.*
Dosser, Pte H.
Douglass, Pte N.*
Dowie, Pte J.W.*
Down, Pte R.V.*
Downes, WO W.
Drew, Pte C.E.*
Drury, Cpl A.L.
Duggan, Cpl. J.C.
Dunn, Cpl B.
Durkin, Pte J.E.*
Dyer, Pte L.J.
Dyson, Pte F.A.*
East, Pte W.*
Easton, Pte H.W.
Eather, Pte A.

Edmondson, Pte F.E.
Edward, Pte A.H.*
Edwards, Pte F.G.
Eley, Pte I.S.*
Ellis, Pte S.
Enever, Pte K.J.
English, Pte D.W.*
Eva, Sgt C.S.*
Evans Pte A.L.
Evans, Pte G.P.
Evans, Pte J.R.
Fallon, Pte H.V.*
Fallows, Pte W.J.*
Farlow, Pte F.L.
Farnell, Pte J.C.
Fearn, Pte D.A.
Feehily, Pte A.A.
Fell, Cpl K.V.*
Fenwick, Pte H.G.
Field, Pte A.F.E.
Finch, Cpl W.
Firth, Pte J.F.
Fisher, Pte A.
Fisher, Pte L.K.
Fitches, Cpl A.J.
Fitzclarenee, Pte J.
Fitzgerald, Cpl E.T.
Fitzgerald, Pte J.
Foote, Pte M.
Forbes, Pte W.
Foreman, Pte B.H.
Forrest, Pte G.
Foster, Cpl F.F.
Fowler, Pte G.W.
Fraser, Pte F.V.*
Fraser, Pte S.
Free, Pte H.S.
Freebody, Pte I.
French, Pte J. StG.
French, Pte R.J.*
Fuller, Pte B.A.*
Gannaway, Pte W.D.*
Gapes, Pte L.C.*
Garvie, Pte W.L.
Garvin, Cpl J.S.*
Gathercole, Pte M.V.
Gaut, Cpl T.G.

Gay, Cpl M.V.*
Gazzard, Pte B.W.
Gee, Pte G.A.*
George, Pte T.
Gill, Pte R.
Girdlestone, Pte R.H.
Gist, Pte H.E.
Gladstone, Pte D.S.*
Glazner, Pte R.W.
Glover, Pte J.F.
Glynn, Pte F.W.
Goding, Capt J.R.
Goodman, Pte R.G.
Goodman, Cpl G.J.P.*
Goon, Pte E.
Gooney, Sgt P.J.
Gordon, Sgt A.W.
Gordon, Pte J.V.
Gordon, Cpl P.J.
Gore, Pte W.T.
Goss, Pte L.T.*
Gottschutzke, Cpl A.V.*
Graham, Cpl A.*
Grandland, Pte L.J.*
Grant, Pte A.A.
Grant, Pte B.R.
Grant, Pte E.*
Gratten, Pte G.A.
Gray, Pte N.A.
Green, Pte L.J.
Greenham, Sgt R.A.
Greenhatch, Pte M.W.
Greening, Pte R.J.
Gregson, Pte H. McD.
Griffith, Pte J.
Griffith, Pte A.
Grigg, WO E.C.
Grumley, Pte E.T.
Grundy, Pte H.A.*
Gunning, L/Cpl G.W.
Guy, L/Sgt J.
Haig, Pte A.J.
Haines, Pte L.L.
Haines, Pte C.W.*
Haldane, Pte S.E.
Hall, Pte F.J.
Hall, Pte G.R.*

Hamilton, Lieut C.G.
Hamilton, Pte K.H.
Hamilton, Pte T.A.V.
Hamley, Pte C.
Hamley, Cpl D.J.*
Hamling, Pte L.C.*
Hammond, Pte G.
Hampton, Pte R.J.*
Handasyde, Capt S.J.
Hands, Pte R.*
Hanrahan, Pte M.J.*
Hansen, Pte E.J.
Harbridge, Pte G.
Hardstaff, Pte T.J.*
Harper, Pte R.J.J.
Harrington, Pte J.J.
Harris, Pte C.H.*
Harrison, Pte E.W.
Harrison, Pte H.
Harvey, Pte R.H.
Hattley, Pte W.A.R.
Hay, Pte C.E.*
Haydon, Sgt J.P.
Hayes, Pte V.A.
Hayhoe, Pte S.H.
Hayles, Pte W.T.
Haynes, Pte H.G.
Head, Cpl F.E.*
Heard, Pte S.
Hellier, Pte J.L.
Henderson, Pte E.*
Henderson, L/Sgt J.S.
Hendy, Pte G.E.
Herbert, Pte T.J.
Herbert, Pte O.A.
Heron, Pte O.
Hicks, Pte J.A.*
Hill, Pte R.R.
Hillas, L/Cpl G.L.*
Hills, Pte H.R.*
Hindrickson, Pte C.H.*
Hoban, Pte D.*
Hock, Pte L.J.
Hocking, Cpl J.R.
Hocking, Pte P.A.
Holden, Pte H.J.
Holdsworth, Pte K.W.

Holmes, Pte S.J.
Holt, Pte A.F.
Hook, Pte A.H.
Hooper, Pte E.E.
Hooper, Pte G.M.
Hooper, Pte G.R.*
Hopkins, Pte J.G.
Hopkins, Sgt R.C.
Horsburgh, Pte A.C.*
Horskins, Pte A.C.
Horton, Pte C.
Hose, Pte D.C.
Hough, L/Sgt E.A.B.
Houston, Lieut R.G.
Hovenden, Sgt J.B.
Hovenden, Pte R.S.*
Howard, Pte C.N.*
Howarth, Pte R.T.
Hoyle, Sgt P.A.
Hughes, Pte J.*
Hughes, L/Cpl L.G.
Hughes, Pte R.E.*
Hunt, Pte F.
Hunt, Pte H.B.
Hunt, Pte R.S.
Hunter, Pte M.C.
Hutchinson, Pte A.
Hutchinson, Pte R.
Hutchinson, Pte V.S.
Hutton, Pte L.G.
Iles, Pte R.J.
Ilsley, Cpl A.C.W.
Irwin, Pte J.R.*
Jackman, Pte G.C.
Jackman, Pte J.H.
Jackson, Pte D.
Jackson, Pte G.S.
Jackson, Pte P.F.
Jean, Pte H.C.
Jeffery, Pte L.
Jellett, Pte J.S.
Jenkins, Sgt C.L.
Jenkins, Pte C.S.
Jensen, Pte C.*
Jewell, Pte C.H.*
Johnson, Pte L.H.*
Johnston, Pte H.E.*

Johnston, Pte P.J.
Johnstone, Cpl G.L.
Johnstone, Pte H.M.
Johnstone, Pte J.J.*
Jones, Pte A.A.L.
Jones, Pte G.S.*
Jones, Sgt L.
Jones, Pte R.J.
Juers, Pte H.M.
Junek, Pte B.
Kellow, Chaplain F.
Kelly, Pte G.A.
Kennedy, Pte P.J.
Kimber, Pte J.*
King, Pte A.E.
King, Pte B.J.
King, Pte G.H.
King, Pte H.G.E.
King, Pte J.L.
Kinnear, L/Sgt L. McD.*
Kirby, Cpl J.
Klicke, Pte A.R.*
Knape, Pte A.S.
Knape, Pte J.E.G.
Knight, Pte A.
Knight, Pte H.W.
Knudsen, Pte H.S.N.
Krygger, Pte R.G.
Kuno, Pte R.A.
Lamb, Lieut G.H.*
Lambert, Pte C.*
Langer, Pte F.B.
Lawley, Pte J.A.
Lawrence, Pte F.H.*
Lay, Pte F.W.
Leach, Pte A.W.*
Leahy, Pte A.H.
Lebas, Pte K.A.*
Lechmere, Pte A.R.*
Ledwidge, Pte L.A.J.*
Lee, Pte C.J.
Leigh, Pte A.G.
Lennard, Pte R.*
Letchford, Pte J.T.*
Lewis, L/Cpl W.A.
Limbrick, Pte L.G.*
Lindrea, Pte R.T.

Linklater, Pte S.R.
Linnane, Pte V.P.P.*
Litchfield, Pte E.V.
Lloyd, Pte W.E.*
Lock, Pte W.E.
Long, Pte F.M.*
Lorimer, Pte G. McL.
Lott, Pte C.R.
Lowe, L/Cpl G.H.
Lowe, Pte H.E.*
Lowe, Pte W.H.
Lupton, Pte L.*
Lynch, Pte R.T.*
Lynn, Cpl K.H.*
Lyon, Pte E.
Magnuson, Pte C.H.
Magrath, Pte R.H.
Maher, Pte W.R.
Mailes, Cpl C.V.
Malady, Pte L.
Malone, Pte T.L.
Manning, Pte C.J.*
Mansfield, Pte J.
Mansfield, Pte J.F.*
Marks, Pte R.E.*
Marquis, Pte A.
Marquis, L/Cpl G.F.
Marr, Pte C.D.
Marr, Pte W.
Marsh, Pte A.D.
Marshall, Pte J.*
Marshall, Lieut J.H.
Marson, Pte E.
Marston, Pte R.N.*
Martin, Pte A.
Martin, L/Cpl A.E.
Martin, Pte A.W.
Masterman-Smith, Sgt B.
Matheson, Pte M.D.
Mathews, Pte E.W.
Mathewson, Pte J.W.*
Matthews, Pte C.H.
Matthews, Pte H.L.
Matthews, Pte N. McK.*
Mawby, Pte R.H.
May, Pte H.
Mayne, Pte W.E.J.

Maynard, Pte T.P.
Meagher, Maj E.R.
Medcraft, Pte A.
Meddings, Cpl F.R.
Meers, Pte J.
Melbourne, Pte L.
Melhuish, Pte R.L.
Menzel, Cpl J.C.
Mermod, Pte J.W.*
Merritt, Pte R.*
Merton, Cpl L.F.
Miley, Pte L.T.
Millar, Pte E.S.C.
Miller, Pte C.J.
Miller, S/Sgt F.C.
Miller, L/Cpl J.M.*
Miller, Pte N.L.
Milliken, Pte D.*
Minns, Pte E.K.
Mitchell, Lieut A.A.
Mitchell, Pte A.W.*
Mitchell, Lieut C.J.
Mitchell, Pte J.S.
Moore, Pte A.
Moore, L/Cpl T.A.*
Morgan, Pte E.C.
Morris, Pte A.J.*
Morris, Pte C.L.
Morton, L/Cpl E.
Moss, Pte J.C.*
Mucklow, Sgt C.W.*
Mulholland, Pte P.J.
Mumford, Pte W.*
Munro, Pte C.
Munro, Pte J.H.
Munro, Pte W.S.
Murnane, Pte J.A.
Murphy, Pte J.C.*
Murphy, Pte T.R.*
Murphy, L/Cpl W.P.
Murray, Pte R.M.
Murray, Pte T.L.
Murrihy, Pte M.J.
MacGregor, Pte J.M.
MacMillan, Pte W.*
MacPherson, Pte N.O.
McArdle, Pte J.P.

McCann, Pte K.
McCarthy, Pte H.C.
McCarthy, Pte J.*
McCarthy, Pte T.W.*
McCarthy, WO W.R.P.
McClelland, Pte D.
McConnell, Pte A.E.
McCrae, Pte V.L.J.
McDermott, Pte J.D.*
McDiarmid, Pte N.F.
McDonald, Pte J.*
McDonald, Cpl N.L.
McDonough, Pte V.G.
McGillien, Pte E.G.
McGovern, Pte J.R.*
McGrath, Pte A.T.
McGrath, Cpl F.X.*
McGuigan, Cpl J.K.
McInnes, Pte F.
McIntosh, Pte H.T.A.
McIntosh, L/Sgt P.
McIntyre, Pte L.S.
McKay, L/Cpl L.W.
McKenzie, Pte D.
McKenzie, Cpl K.V.
McKinnis, Cpl R.*
McLean, WO A.
McLean, Pte W.J.
McLennan, Pte K.W.*
McLennan, Pte W.J.
McLeod, Pte R.M.
McNally, Pte L.R.
McNeil, Pte A.
McPhee, Pte A.J.
McPherson, Pte H.T.
Nankivell, Pte H.R.
Nason, Capt C.H.T.
Nelson, Pte C.R.
Nicholls, Pte A.S.
Nicholls, Pte J.
Nicolson, Capt I.D.
Nightingale, Pte J.K.*
Noble, Pte A.W.J.*
Noble, Pte C.J.*
Nolan, Sgt K.
Nolan, Pte L.R.
Noonan, L/Cpl H.W.

Norton, Pte M.
Nugent, Pte J.D.S.*
Nutt, Cpl W.G.
Nybo, Pte P.W.
Oats, Pte C.H.
O'Brien, S/Sgt T.
O'Brien, Pte T.R.
O'Connor, Pte J.H.*
O'Donnell, Pte B.A.*
O'Keeffe, Pte E.V.*
Oldham, Pte G.F.*
Oldham, Pte H.J.
Oliphant, Pte T.
O'Loughlin, Pte T.
O'Loughlin, Pte V.
O'Neil, Pte T.E.
O'Rourke, Pte P.J.
Osbourne, Pte B.S.*
Osmond, Pte A.W.
O'Sullivan, Pte J.J.*
Page, Pte E.C.*
Paine, Pte F.
Pallss, S/Sgt J.E.
Pannowitz, Pte N.O.
Parker, Pte J.H.*
Parker, Pte J.R.*
Parrett, Pte R.
Pattison, Pte F.C.
Payne, Pte A.C.*
Peady, Pte S.
Pearce, Pte L.T.
Pearson, Pte F.C.
Peck, Pte H.J.T.
Peck, Pte M.E.
Peeler, WO W.
Pell, Pte L.*
Pemberton, Lieut J.M.
Penaluna, Pte J.S.*
Peter, Pte C.T.*
Peters, Pte V.*
Peterson, Pte C.W.*
Phillips, Pte C.W.
Phillips, WO F.V.
Phillips, Pte R.J.*
Plain, Cpl T.W.*
Pople, Pte W.R.*
Poulton, Cpl C.H.

Powell, Pte L.
Power, Pte K.L.
Prescott, Pte H.J.
Prior, Pte A.N.*
Pritchard, L/Cpl G.
Prydderch, Pte S.*
Pugh, L/Cpl H.B.A.
Pugh, Pte A.*
Pugsley, Pte H.C.
Quinn, Cpl A.J.
Quinn, Pte J.W.
Radcliffe, Pte K.E.*
Rampling, Pte R.W.*
Ramsey, Pte H.G.
Ransome, Pte E.G.
Rayment, Pte K.C.*
Rea, Pte E.A.
Rees, Pte L.W.
Reese, Pte L.R.*
Reilly, Sgt W.J.
Renton, Pte K.C.
Reshke, Pte B.
Rex, WO R.
Reynolds, Pte G.H.
Rhook, Pte W.D.
Rice, Pte R.C.
Richards, Cpl A.J.
Richards, Pte E.
Richards, Cpl F.A.
Richards, Lieut G.W.
Richards, Pte J.T.*
Richardson, Pte W.H.*
Richter, Pte W.A.*
Ridley, Pte T.A.
Rielly, Pte J.
Rielly, Pte W.G.
Ritchie, L/Sgt J.G.
Rivett, Pte L.
Rixon, Pte S.K.
Roberts, Pte D.*
Roberts, Pte H.G.
Roberts, Cpl J. McA.
Robertson, Cpl H.S.*
Robertson, Sgt J.H.
Robertson, Pte K.C.
Robertson, Pte T.*
Robinson, Pte F.R.*

Robinson, Pte J.C.*
Robinson, L/Cpl T.*
Rodd, Pte S.J.J.*
Rodie, Lieut A.F.D.
Rohead, Pte N.
Rolston, Pte J.*
Rose, Pte V.
Ross, Capt A.H.J.
Ross, Pte G.
Rossiter, Lieut F.M.
Rowe, Pte A.W.
Rowe, Pte E.A.
Ruddle, Cpl J.W.
Rumble, Pte A.J.
Rumble, Pte J.
Ryan, Pte J.
Ryan, Pte J.J.
Ryan, Sgt W.A.G.*
Sadler, Sgt H.R.K.
Sargent, Pte F.J.
Sarkies, Pte R.G.
Saw, Pte G.E.R.*
Schultz, Pte A.J.*
Schannahan, L/Sgt E.*
Scott, Pte T.*
Shannon, Cpl T.A.*
Sharman, Pte L.V.
Sharock, Pte W.J.
Shepherd, Pte W.J.
Sheridan, Pte J.A.*
Sherritt, Pte D.
Shrader, Pte A.C.*
Simpkins, L/Cpl W.A.
Sinclair, Pte C.H.
Sipthorpe, Pte A.
Skipper, Pte J.C.
Smith, Pte A.C.
Smith, Pte C.W.
Smith, Pte G.
Smith, Pte H.J.*
   (VX40057)
Smith, Pte H.J.
Smith, Pte J.W.P.*
Smith, L/Sgt L.J.*
Smith, Sgt N.L.
Smith, Pte P.C.*
Smith, Pte P.H.

Smith, Pte R.*
Smith, Pte T.G.*
Smith, Pte W.T.
Smythe, Pte E.J.
Somers, S/Sgt R.P.
Somerville, Pte A.C.*
Sorley, Pte H.
Spence, Pte A.T.*
Spence, Cpl W.L.*
Spiken, Pte T.*
Sprague, Pte C.G.
Spriggs, Cpl W.
Spriggs, Pte J.J.
Stafford, Cpl T.J.
Stammers, Pte W.G.*
Staples, Pte W.C.
Steel, Sgt J.H.*
Stephenson, Pte J.
Stevenson, Pte F.
Stewart, Pte E.D.
Stewart, Sgt H.K.
Stilley, Pte G.*
Stockton, Pte F.
Stockton, Pte T.H.
Stokes, Sgt A.
Stokes, Pte F.E.
Stokes, Pte S.F.
Strahan, Pte L.J.
Stratton, Pte G.F.
Stuart, Pte A.*
Sunderland, Pte N.
Sullivan, Pte W.B.*
Sullivan, Pte T.A.
Summons, Lieut W.I.
Sutherland, Pte J.
Swanson, Pte K.J.
Tait, Pte A.J.
Taylor, Pte A.
Taylor, Pte D.E.
Taylor, Pte D.G.
Taylor, Pte H.
Taylor, Sgt L.F.
Templeman, Lieut J.H.
Thomas, Pte H.I.
Thomas, Pte H.R.
Thomas, L/Cpl T.C.
Thompson, Pte C.G.

Thompson, Pte H.W.*
Thompson, Pte R.A.*
Thompson, Pte R.E.
Thompson, Pte F.S.
Thomson, Pte W.J.
Thorn, Cpl C.
Thorn, Pte L.*
Thornton, Pte D.J.S.*
Tilney, Lieut W.W.
Timms, Pte B.J.
Timms, Pte D.W.
Todd, Cpl G.B.*
Tolliday, Pte L.R.
Tomison, Pte A.G.
Tomlin, Pte G.B.
Toogood, Pte R.W.*
Toomey, Pte J.J.H.
Topfer, Lieut G.H.G.
Tottenham, Pte N.C.
Towers, Pte A.W.
Tranter, Lieut N.G.H.
Tregea, Pte P.J.
Trewin, Cpl R.L.
Tubb, Lieut F.H.
Tuck, Pte W.G.
Tully, Pte A.J.*
Tully, Pte F.W.*
Turner, Pte G.H.
Tyrrell, Cpl A.*
Upton, Pte H.P.
Vale, Pte F.P.
Vandervord, Pte A.S.
Vardy, L/Sgt M.*
Veal, Pte E.S.

Veitch, Pte A.E.
Verrall, Pte F.C.
Vickery, Pte C.
Vincent, Pte R.W.
Waddell, Pte H.A.*
Waddell, Pte R.F.
Waite, Pte W.J.*
Walker, Cpl H.E.
Walker, Pte W.D.
Wallis, Pte F.J.
Walters, Lieut J.H.
Warren, Cpl F.E.*
Watkins, Pte W.R.
Watson, Pte J.*
Watson, Pte K.B.
Waugh, Pte A.L.*
Waugh, Pte J.T.
Webb, Pte P.J.
Webster, Lieut G.N.
Webster, Pte T.H.
Weir, Pte J.A.*
Westbrook, Pte H.
Westgarth, Sgt A.T.
White, Sgt C.N.
White, L/Cpl F.S.
White, Pte J.J.
Whitfeld, L/Sgt L.E.*
Whitmore, Pte R.
Whytcross, Pte L.W.
Wild, Sgt L.J.
Wilkie, Pte S.R.
Wilkinson, Pte M.W.
Wilkinson, Pte R.W.

Willard, Cpl J.A.*
Willey, Pte H.A.*
Williams, Pte B.
Williams, Pte J.
Williams, Lieut Col J.M.
Williams, Pte L.J.
Williams, Pte M.A.
Williams, Pte P.H.
Williams, Pte R.N.
Williams, Pte R.T.
Williamson, Pte K.M.*
Willoughby, Pte M.
Wills, Pte A.
Wilson, L/Cpl A.W.
Wilson, Pte K.V.
Wind, Pte K.K.
Windebank, Pte N.S.
Winning, Capt R.F.H.
Wood, Pte P.J.
Wood, Pte W.A.*
Woodhead, Pte J.A.*
Woods, Pte P.J.G.*
Wornes, Pte R.S.
Worrall, Pte E.W.*
Worrall, Pte N.E.
Wrathall, Pte D.*
Wright, Pte G.
Wright, Pte V.J.
Wust, Pte V.G.*
Wyatt, Pte A.A.
Yorston, Cpl J.W.
Youens, Pte H.L.
Young, Sgt K.L.

Notes

Chapter 2

1   Benjamin Dunn, *The Bamboo Express*, privately printed, 1979, p. 170.
2   Conversation with the author, Melbourne, October 1991.
3   E.E. Dunlop, *The War Diaries of Weary Dunlop*, Penguin Books, Ringwood, p. xxviii.
4   D.M. Horner, *High Command*, Allen & Unwin, Sydney, 1982, p. 443.
5   *The New York Times*, 28 February 1992, p. 1.
6   *Australian National Dictionary*, Oxford University Press, Melbourne, 1988, p. 492.
7   Dunn, *The Bamboo Express*, p. 171.
8   Walter Summons, *Twice Their Prisoner*, Oxford University Press, Melbourne, 1946, p. 63.
9   E.F. Aitken and T.C. Dickson, *Story of the 2/2 Australian Pioneer Battalion*, privately printed, Melbourne, 1953, p. 136.
10 Australian War Memorial Research Centre, Document #AWM 52, item 8/6/2.
11 Summons, *Twice Their Prisoner*, p. 13.
12 A.H. Bishop, letter to the author, 30 April 1992.
13 *Battalion History*, p. 139.
14 ibid.
15 Ruth Benedict, *The Chrysanthemum and the Sword: Patterns of Japanese Culture*, Meridian Books, New York, 1967, p. 241.
16 Conversation with the author, 16 February 1992.
17 Benedict, *The Chrysanthemum and the Sword*, pp. 190ff.
18 *Holy Bible*, the Book of Genesis, Chapter 45.
19 Dunlop, *The War Diaries of Weary Dunlop*, p. xxiii.
20 *New York Times*, 1 April 1992, p. 1.
21 *Battalion History*, p. 143.
22 Leslie Hall, The Queen of Hearts, unpublished manuscript, p. 259.
23 *Battalion History*, p. 145.
24 Leslie G. Hall, *The Blue Haze*, privately printed, 1985, p. 62.
25 Letter to the author, 2 December 1992.
26 *Battalion History*, p. 145.
27 Dunn, *The Bamboo Express*, p. 31.
28 Letter to the author, 2 December 1992.
29 From a letter to the author, 10 November 1992.

30 Letter to the author, 24 January 1992.
31 Letter to the author, 8 October 1992.
32 Conversation with the author, Melbourne, 29 October 1991.
33 Conversation with the author, Jell's Park, Melbourne, 27 October 1991.
34 *Battalion History*, p. 146.
35 A.H. Bishop, A Voyage With the Jap in South East Asia, unpublished article, pp. 14–17.
36 *Battalion History*, p. 155.
37 United States Government, Department of State File # 740.0015, Pacific War/290, RG 59, National Archives. First researched by Michi Weglyn for her book, *Years of Infamy* (see Bibliography).

Chapter 3

1 Kevin Nolan, letter to the author, 21 August 1992.
2 Hall, *The Blue Haze*, pp. 296–97.
3 Ernest Gordon, conversation with the author, 19 August 1991.
4 Ronald Searle, *To the Kwai—and Back*, The Atlantic Monthly Press, New York, 1986, p. 104.
5 Hall, *The Blue Haze*, p. 208.
6 Joan and Clay Blair, *Return From The River Kwai*, Vanguard Press, New York, 1954, p. 15.
7 Hall, *The Blue Haze*, p. 129.
8 Lavinia Warner and John Sandilands, *Women Beyond the Wire*, F.A. Thorpe Publishing, Leicester, 1982, p. 358.
9 Hall, *The Blue Haze*, p. 208.
10 Nagase, Takashi, *Crosses and Tigers*, The Post Publishing Co., Bangkok, 1990, p. 13.
11 Hall, *The Blue Haze*, p. 191.
12 Searle, *To The Kwai—and Back*, p. 10.
13 Hall, *The Blue Haze*, p. 146.
14 Holy Bible, King James version, Second Epistle of Paul the Apostle to the Thessalonians, Chapter 10, verse 3.
15 Benedict, *The Chrysanthemum and the Sword*, p. 37.
16 Sir Edward Dunlop, letter to the author, 9 November 1992.
17 L. Hall, *Blue Haze*, p. 300.
18 Hank Nelson, *Prisoners of War: Australians Under Nippon*, Sydney, Australian Broadcasting Company, 1985.
19 Conversations with the author, Melbourne, October 1991.

Chapter 4

1 *Battalion History*, p. 166.
2 From an interview with the author at Dr Gordon's summer home, Amagansett, NY, USA, 29 August 1991.
3 Letter to the author, 8 January 1993.

4 From an interview with the author, Melbourne, 29 October 1991.
5 From a conversation at Narrabeen, NSW, 23 October 1991.
6 From a letter to the author, 9 November 1992.
7 Nagase, *Crosses and Tigers*, p. 18.
8 Ernest Gordon, *Miracle on the River Kwai*, William Collins & Co., Glasgow, 1963, p. 169.
9 Letter to the author, 30 April 1991.

Chapter 5

1 Hall, The Queen of Hearts, unpublished manuscript, 1991.
2 Hall, *Blue Haze*, p. 300.
3 ibid., p. 141.
4 Nagase, *Crosses and Tigers*, p. 30.
5 ibid., pp. 30–31.
6 From a letter to the author, 26 January 1992.
7 Hall, The Queen of Hearts, p. 269.
8 Dunn, *The Bamboo Express*, pp. 167–68.
9 From a letter to the author, 21 August 1992.
10 From letters to the author, February, April, July 1992.
11 From a letter to the author, 12 June 1992.

Chapter 6

1 G. Hamilton, letter to his family, 8 September 1945.
2 H. Whelan, letter to the author, 26 January 1992.
3 From a letter to the author, 3 August 1992.

Chapter 7

1 From a letter to the author, 16 February 1991.
2 Dunn, *The Bamboo Express*, p. 27.
3 Hall, *The Blue Haze*, excerpt from diary of Lt. Col. Williams, p. 315.
4 ibid.
5 Dunn, *The Bamboo Express*, p. 180.
6 ibid., p. 125.
7 Hall, *The Blue Haze*, p. 310.

Chapter 8

1 Peter N. Davies, *The Man Behind The Bridge: Colonel Toosey and the River Kwai*, Athlone, London/Atlantic Highlands, NJ, 1991, p. 177.
2 From a conversation with the author, Melbourne, 27 October 1991.
3 From a conversation with the author, Narrabeen, NSW, 25 October 1991.
4 Hall, *The Blue Haze*, pp. 133–34.
5 ibid., p. 286.
6 Warner and Sandilands, *Women Beyond the Wire*, p. 171.

7 Blair, *Return from the River Kwai*, p. 16.
8 From a conversation with the author, Shelter Island, NY, 26 May 1992.
9 Letter to the author, 10 September 1992.
10 Warner and Sandilands, *Women Beyond the Wire*, p. 146.

Chapter 9

1 Letter to the author, 6 June 1992.
2 Warner and Sandilands, *Women Beyond the Wire*, p. 23.
3 Letter to the author, 23 October 1992.
4 Letter to the author, 12 June 1992.
5 Letter to the author, 23 October 1992.
6 Dunn, *The Bamboo Express*, p. 187; and conference with the author, 10 November 1992.
7 H. Nelson, 'Prisoners of War', Australian Broadcasting Company, 1985, p. 45.
8 Hall, *The Blue Haze*, p. 135.
9 Benedict, *The Chrysanthemum and the Sword*, p. 159.
10 ibid., p. 210.
11 Colonel Harold Doud, 'How the Japanese Army fights', *Infantry Journal*, 1942, pp. 54–55. First quoted by Ruth Benedict in her book, *The Chrysanthemum and the Sword*, p. 181.
12 From a letter to the author, 7 October 1992.
13 From a conversation with the author, Melbourne, 28 October 1991.
14 From a letter to the author, 3 October 1992.

Chapter 10

1 Hall, *The Blue Haze*, diary excerpt, p. 307.
2 ibid., p. 255; Fagan diary entry for 2 October 1943.
3 Searle, *To the Kwai—and Back*, p. 114; Imperial War Museum # P91.

Chapter 11

1 Hall, *The Blue Haze*, p. 294; Williams Diary entry, 6 October 1943.
2 From a letter to the author, 16 February 1991.
3 From a letter to the author, 30 April 1991.
4 Conversation at a Pioneer Battalion Association gathering, Jell's Park, Melbourne, 27 October 1991.
5 Dunn, *The Bamboo Express*, pp. 164–65.
6 From a letter to the author, 30 April 1991.
7 From letters to the author, 25 August and 12 November 1992.
8 From a letter to the author, 19 March 1992.

Chapter 12

1 Conversation with the author, Jell's Park, Melbourne, 27 October 1991.

2 Summons, *Twice Their Prisoner*, p. 174.
3 From a letter to Dickson's widow after his death, 8 August 1988.
4 Letter to the author, 8 January 1993.
5 From a letter to the author, 16 July 1992.
6 From a letter to the author, 11 July 1992.
7 From a letter to the author, 16 July 1992.
8 ibid.
9 Essay from the *Rafu Shimpo*, January 1992 edition. Quoted with permission of the essayist, Henry Shigeru Yagake. Translated from the Japanese by Reiko Uyeshima.
10 From a letter to the author, 6 July 1992.
11 From a conversation with the author, Narrabeen, NSW, 19 October 1991.
12 From a recollection by Ralph Gross, 12 September 1992.

Chapter 13

1 From a conversation with the author, Melbourne, 28 October 1991.
2 From a letter to the author, 16 July 1992.
3 G. Hamilton, letter to his family, 8 September 1945.
4 Nagase, *Crosses and Tigers*, p. 15.
5 From a letter to the author, 21 August 1992
6 From a letter to the author, 16 July 1992.
7 From letters to his family, 1 and 8 September 1945.
8 From a letter to the author, 25 August 1992.
9 From a conversation with the author, Amagansett, NY, 27 August 1990.
10 From a letter to the author, 3 April 1992.

Chapter 14

1 Nagase, *Crosses and Tigers*, p. 17.
2 Letter to the author, 12 July 1992.
3 Nagase, *Crosses and Tigers*, pp. 39–41.
4 ibid., p. 42.
5 Nelson, *Prisoners of War*, p. 147.
6 Article in the Melbourne *Herald*, 22 May 1946, p. 1.
7 Dunn, *Bamboo Express*, p. 188.
8 Captain James Norwood and Captain Emily Shek, 'Prisoner of War Camps in Areas Other Than the Four Principal Islands of Japan', Liaison & Research Branch, American Prisoner of War Information Bureau, 1943. Declassified 31 July 1946. Document courtesy of Otto Schwarz, President, USS *Houston* Survivors Association.
9 *Battalion History*, p. 172.
10 Benedict, *The Chrysanthemum and the Sword*, p. 182.
11 Peter N. Davies, *The Man Behind The Bridge*, Athlone, London, 1991, p. 58.

12 Nagase, *Crosses and Tigers*, p. 46.
13 Letter to the author, 29 July 1992.
14 Letter to the author, 6 July 1992.
15 Gordon, *Miracle on the River Kwai*, pp. 162–63.
16 Letter to the author, 26 January 1992.
17 Letter to the author, 21 August 1992.
18 From a conversation with the author, Shelter Island, NY, May 1979.

Chapter 15

1 Letter to the author, 4 December 1992.
2 Letters to the author, 29 October and 4 December 1992.
3 Hall, *The Blue Haze*, p. 257. Extract from diary of Thomas Fagan.
4 ibid., p. 221.
5 Dunn, *The Bamboo Express*, pp. 181–82.
6 Letter to the author, 17 March 1992.
7 Gordon, *Miracle on the River Kwai*, pp. 73ff.
8 Searle, *To the Kwai—and Back*, p. 128.
9 Holy Bible, Gospel according to John, Chapter 13, verse 35.
10 From a letter to the author, 20 June 1992, commenting on his essay in the *Rafu Shimpo*, 1 January 1992.

Chapter 16

1 Letter to the author, 3 April 1992.
2 Melbourne *Sun*, 5 November 1945, p. 1.
3 Conversation with the author, Jell's Park, Melbourne, 27 October 1991.
4 Letter to the author, 16 February 1991.
5 Letter to the author, 25 August 1992.
6 Letter to the author, 16 July 1992.
7 Conversation with the author, Jell's Park, Melbourne, 27 October 1991.

Chapter 17

1 Nagase, *Crosses and Tigers*, p. 75.
2 The *Washington Post*, 15 July 1990, p. 22.
3 *New York Times*, 4 August 1991, p. 1.
4 The *New York Times*, 16 June 1992, p. 15.
5 Jay Woodworth, conversation with the author, 19 October 1992; T. Nagase, *Crosses and Tigers*, p. 76.
6 Conversation with the author, 13 October 1992.
7 Conversation with the author, Scarsdale, New York, 8 January 1992.
8 The *New York Times*, 22 November 1992. 'The Week in Review', p. 5.
9 Dunlop, *War Diaries*, preface, p. xxi.
10 Nagase, *Crosses and Tigers*, p. 61.
11 Letter to the author, 6 July 1992.

12   Letter to the author, 8 January 1993.
13   Letter to the author, 17 March 1992
14   Letter to the author, 30 April 1992.
15   Letter to the author, 30 April 1991.
16   *New York Times*, 7 July 1992, p. 1.
17   *New York Times*, editorial, 5 August 1992.
18   Excerpts from *Barbed Wire and Bamboo*, official organ of the New South Wales Ex-Prisoners of War Association, December 1950 issue, pp. 4ff.
19   *Barbed Wire and Bamboo*, February 1958 issue, p. 11.
20   Conversation with the author, 18 November 1992.

Bibliography

Books

Aitken, E.F. and Dickson, T.C., *The Story of the 2/2nd Australian Pioneer Battalion*, privately printed, Melbourne, 1953.

Arneil, Stan, *One Man's Battle*, Sun Books Pty Ltd, South Melbourne, 1983.

Australian National Dictionary, Oxford University Press, Melbourne, 1988.

Benedict, Ruth, *The Chrysanthemum and the Sword: Patterns of Japanese Culture*, Meridian Books, New York, 1967.

Blair, Joan and Clay Jr., *Return From The River Kwai*, Vanguard Press, New York, 1954.

Boulle, Pierre, *The Bridge Over The River Kwai*, The Vanguard Press, New York, 1954.

Bowden, Tim, *The Photographer of Changi: George Aspinall's Record of Captivity*, William Collins Pty Ltd, Sydney, 1984.

Boyle, James, *Railroad To Burma*, Allen & Unwin, Sydney, 1990.

Braddon, Russell, *The Naked Island*, Werner Laurie, London, 1952.

Clarke, Hugh V., *A Life For Every Sleeper*, Allen & Unwin, Sydney, 1986.

Davies, Peter N., *The Man Behind The Bridge: Col. Toosey and the River Kwai*, Athlone Press, London, 1991.

Dunlop, E.E., *The War Diaries of Weary Dunlop*, Penguin Books, Ringwood, 1990.

Dunn, Benjamin, *The Bamboo Express*, privately printed, 1979.

Gordon, Ernest, *Miracle on the River Kwai*, William Collins Sons & Co., Glasgow, 1963.

Hall, Leslie G., *The Blue Haze*, privately printed, 1985.

Horner, D.M., *High Command*, Allen & Unwin, Sydney, 1982.

LaForte, Robert and Marcello, Ronald, *Building the Death Railway: The Ordeal of American POWs in Burma 1942–45*, Scholarly Resources, Inc., Wilmington, Delaware, 1992.

Lord Russell of Liverpool, *The Knights of Bushido: A Short History of Japanese War Crimes*, Cassell & Co. Ltd, London, 1958.

Nagase, Takashi, *Crosses and Tigers*, The Post Publishing Co., Bangkok, 1990.

Nelson, Hank, *Prisoners of War: Australians Under Nippon*, Australian Broadcasting Company, 1985.

Rivett, Rohan, *Behind Bamboo*, Angus & Robertson, Melbourne, 1946.

Searle, Ronald, *To the Kwai—and Back: War Drawings, 1939–1945*, The Atlantic Monthly Press, New York, 1986.

Summons, Walter, *Twice Their Prisoner*, Oxford University Press, Melbourne, 1946.
Wall, Don, *Heroes at Sea*, privately printed, 1991.
Warner, Lavinia and Sandilands, J., *Women Beyond the Wire*, F.A. Thorpe Publishing Ltd, Leicester, 1982.
Weglyn, Michi N., *Years of Infamy: The Untold Story of American Concentration Camps*, William Morrow & Co., New York, 1976.

Newspapers and periodicals

Barbed Wire and Bamboo, Ex-Prisoners of War Assn, official publication, various editions.
The *Argus*, Melbourne, various 1945 editions.
The *Sun*, Melbourne, various 1945 editions.
Yagake, H. Shigeru, essay in the *Rafu Shimpo*, Los Angeles, CA, January 1992 edition.
Bhimaya, K.M., 'Leadership in Captivity: A Case Study of Kwai Prison Camp', article in *Journal of the United Services Institution of India*, January–March 1986 edition.
The *New York Times*, various editions.

Archives

Australian War Memorial Research Centre, Canberra
Boy Scouts of America, International Division, Irvine, TX
The Herald and Weekly Times Archives, Melbourne
US Army Military Institute, Carlisle, Pennsylvania
US Library of Congress Archives, Washington, DC

Unpublished manuscripts

Bishop, A.H., A Voyage With The Jap in South East Asia, 1991.
Hall, Leslie G., The Queen of Hearts, 1991.

Index